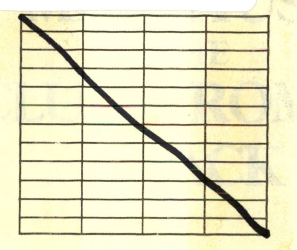

IE

COLUMBIA UNIVERSITY SEMINAR SERIES

The University Seminars at Columbia University welcomes this study of *From Malthus to the Club of Rome and Back: Problems of Limits to Growth, Population Control, and Migrations* by Paul Neurath to the Columbia University Seminars Series. The study has benefited from Seminar discussions and reflects the advantages of scholarly exchange provided by the Seminar Movement.

Aaron W. Warner
Director, University Seminars
Columbia University

THE FUTURE OF AMERICAN BANKING
*James R. Barth, R. Dan Brumbaugh, Jr., and
Robert E. Litan*

THE EVOLUTION OF U.S. FINANCE, VOLUME I
FEDERAL RESERVE MONETARY POLICY: 1915–1935
Jane W. D'Arista

THE EVOLUTION OF U.S. FINANCE, VOLUME II
RESTRUCTURING INSTITUTIONS AND MARKETS
Jane W. D'Arista

HOW CREDIT-MONEY SHAPES THE ECONOMY
THE UNITED STATES IN A GLOBAL SYSTEM
Robert Guttmann

THE ANTITRUST IMPULSE, VOLUME I AND II
AN ECONOMIC, HISTORICAL, AND LEGAL ANALYSIS
Theodore P. Kovaleff

FROM MALTHUS TO THE CLUB OF ROME AND BACK
PROBLEMS OF LIMITS TO GROWTH, POPULATION
CONTROL, AND MIGRATIONS
Paul Neurath

FROM
MALTHUS
TO THE
CLUB OF ROME
AND BACK

**Problems of Limits to Growth,
Population Control,
and Migrations**

Paul Neurath

M.E. Sharpe
Armonk, New York
London, England

Library of Congress Cataloging-in Publication Data

Neurath, Paul.
From Malthus to the Club of Rome and back :
problems of limits to growth, population control,
and migrations / by Paul Neurath.
p. cm.
Includes index.
ISBN 1–56324–407–1.—ISBN 1–56324–408–X
1. Population policy. 2. Demography. 3. Malthusianism.
I. Title.
HB883.5.N48 1994
363.9—dc20
94-8979
CIP

Printed in the United States of America.
The paper used in this publication meets the minimum
requirements of American National Standard for
Information Sciences—Permanence of Paper for
Printed Library Materials, ANSI Z 39.48-1984.

∞

MV 10 9 8 7 6 5 4 3 2 1
MV 10 9 8 7 6 5 4 3 2 1

*To the members of the Columbia University Seminar
on Content and Methods of the Social Sciences
and
to my colleagues at the Institut fuer Soziologie at the
University of Vienna*

Contents

of as yet unused propaganda slogans, waiting to be raised by future alarmists. Robert Malthus's claim that man, if not checked from time to time by famine, war, or pestilence, had a tendency to multiply his own numbers faster than he could increase his food supply was, if taught at all, presented as an oddity in the history of classical economics, easily inveighed against by first attacking his database—he had primarily used figures from the former British colonies in North America and thereby presumably neglected the increase of population through immigration—and then the mathematical formulation: if it was true, as Malthus claimed, that man tends to multiply his own numbers at a geometrical ratio, but could increase his food supply only at an arithmetical one, then we would have all died of starvation long ago instead of still being here in ever growing numbers, having a good laugh at silly old Malthus.

It was by sheer good luck that, while attending Commercial Academy in Vienna in 1931–32—parallel to my first year studying law at the university—I had a quite remarkable teacher of economics, Dr. Michael Kroell, who presented Malthus to us in a way that left an indelible impression. I can still hear Dr. Kroell's sonorous voice now, over sixty years later, as he quoted to us Malthus's most famous passage:

> A man who is born into a world already possessed, if he cannot get sustenance from his parents, upon whom he has a just demand . . . has no business to be where he is. At nature's mighty feast there is no vacant cover for him. She tells him to be gone.

I think it was Dr. Kroell's impressive presentation that, in connection with social and political interests acquired elsewhere in political movements, created in me an abiding interest in everything having to do with "population" and its ramifications in other fields. Thus, when a dozen years later, in 1943, I had to make my choice of subfields for the oral examinations on my way to the Ph.D. in sociology at Columbia University, I took demography as one of them. Then, in 1946, when I joined the Department of Sociology at Queens College in New York, I selected "Population Problems" as one of the courses I would teach. And I have been teaching it ever since, both in New York and, since my retirement from Queens College in 1977, through the 1980s and into the 1990s at the University of Vienna, where I am still at it.

Thus, when the great debate began after World War II about the "Great Population Explosion," particularly in the countries of the Third World, I followed it with great interest. In particular, I followed the lively argumentation of, on the one hand, those who saw in this "population explosion" a serious threat, and, on the other hand, those who saw it only as a challenge that would spur mankind to greater efforts, with both sides presenting data and arguments to fortify their own and to weaken the opposing position. The arguments sounded all too familiar to me, having studied the same kind of raging debate for and against Malthus of the late eighteenth and early nineteenth century—debate that eventually led, as I intimate in the first chapter of this volume, to the development of demography as a modern science.

When the first of the "Club of Rome Reports," *The Limits to Growth* by Meadows et al., burst on the world in 1972, for a few years turning "population explosion" and "world models" into household words with which to conjure or start an argument, I assiduously collected articles pro and contra—first by the dozen, then by the hundred, trying to gain as balanced a view as possible for myself and for my students.

As I now present here a collection of papers given in the course of more than a decade and a half spent dealing with "population" in many different aspects—some more specifically connected with the "limits to growth" debate, others more with problems of "population control," with migration, and so forth—then, in spite of some disjointedness (and also some unavoidable repetitions, because these papers were given on rather different occasions and to rather different audiences), I have one main purpose: to create a better understanding of some of the problems of population and their implications, including the orders of magnitude—when they come in thousands, when in tens of thousands, when in hundreds of thousands, and when in millions—and, where suitable, also to indicate how they grew historically out of the exigencies of various social and political situations.

The chapters of this book include papers ranging in time from one given at the Columbia University Seminar on "Content and Methods in the Social Sciences" in 1975 at the height of the debate about the "Club of Rome models" to one about "The Great Migrations of the Nineteenth and Twentieth Century," given at the same Columbia University Seminar in 1991. They are presented, however, not chronologically, but grouped around some main themes.

The book opens with a historical overview of the early development of the thought on "population" up to the time when, with Malthus's *Essay on the Principle of Population* (1798), the "prehistory" of demography ends and its history as a modern science begins. This is followed in chapter 2 by another historical overview of the discussion during the latter part of the nineteenth and through the twentieth century about the potential maximum number of people who could possibly live on this earth. The most characteristic aspect of this discussion is that, regardless of exactly what various authors considered the maximum, most, considering the then contemporary annual increase of world population, always predicted it would take some 150 to 300 years to reach that maximum—always with the assumption that agricultural technology and the development of new lands would improve so much during that time that the maximum could yet be much greater than had been estimated before. This was so until, with the recent rapid growth of world population, the estimated maximum would be reached so fast that there would not be enough time left for the development of new agricultural technology. At this point the argument suddenly shifts into what were once considered nonconventional sources of food and energy: food grown from algae, energy gained directly from the sun, and the like.

Then follows a group of four chapters dealing directly with the debate about global models, beginning with *The Limits to Growth* by Meadows et al. in 1972 and *Mankind at the Turning Point* by Mesarovic and Pestel in 1974, through the "MOIRA" model by Linneman et al. in Amsterdam in 1979, and finally, from the opposite side of the ideological divide, the "Bariloche model" by Herrera et al. in Buenos Aires in 1976. Two of these chapters present the main ideas of these books, chapter 3 in more general terms, chapter 4 concentrating on some more technical (although not specifically mathematical) aspects of the models. Chapter 5, though rather brief, is actually remarks from the closing session of a 1978 IIASA (International Institute of Applied Systems Analysis) symposium on global modeling in Laxenburg-Vienna, and discusses global modeling briefly (and in a lighter vein) as a new branch of science and the (then) still somewhat insecure position of its practitioners within the general realm of science. Chapter 6 deals specifically and in detail with what appears to me to be so serious a contradiction within the Bariloche model—specifically, its basic conceptual treatment of population size generated endtogenously within the model itself as part of the mathematical equations of the model itself—that it in fact leads to doubts about the very meaningfulness of the whole model.

Of the next two chapters, one was originally presented in 1984 at the Columbia Seminar, and the other was given in the same year at an international conference in Alpbach, Tirol. Chapter 8 deals specifically with the development and various changes of population policy in China from the Communist takeover in 1949, when Chairman Mao most optimistically declared that "the more population, the more production, the faster the development of socialism," to the utterly anti-natalist policy of "only one child per family" established in 1979. Chapter 9 compares population problems and population policies in Japan, China, and India, more or less expressing the impression that "in Japan it works without force, in China it works with force, while in India it does not work at all—or at least almost not at all."

Finally, chapters 7 and 10 address two more specific topics. One is on the role that oil, more specifically the price of oil, plays in the overall food situation of developing countries, where the dramatic rises in oil prices through OPEC led to difficulties with payments for imported oil-industry by-products that are the basis for artificial fertilizer—followed more or less automatically with a rise of other raw materials for artificial fertilizer (especially phosphate from Morocco). This chapter is an excerpt from a more general paper on "Population Problems of the Third World and the World Models" given at the University of Munich in 1986.

The last chapter, originally a paper given in 1991 again at the Columbia University Seminar, deals with the great migrations of the nineteenth and twentieth century, essentially from the time of the migration of the "Potato Irish" to North America in the 1840s up to the late 1980s, before the fall of the Berlin Wall, as well as before the war in the former Yugoslavia and the dissolution of the Soviet Union. In the earlier parts the chapter concentrates heavily on the first great transatlantic migrations before World War I, then the population shifts (nowadays called "ethnic cleansing") after the Balkan wars of 1912 and 1913 and their aftermath, followed by the Turkish expulsion of the Greeks from Asia Minor in 1923, plus subsequent "population exchanges" between Greece and Turkey, the population shifts in the aftermath of the two world wars, including the shifts (mutual expulsions) between India and Pakistan, and finally considering the newer developments of "guest workers"—the semipermanent and in part nevertheless permanent migration of millions of workers, with or without their families, in part from southern and southeastern Europe (Spain, Portugal, Yugoslavia, Turkey) into central and northern Europe, in part from North Africa into southern Europe, in part from Arab countries (especially from Egypt) and from India and Pakistan into the oil countries on the Persian Gulf and into Saudi Arabia, and other movements, including those from Mexico into the United States.

This last chapter treats as a separate topic the whole problem of refugees all over the world, including those who are officially designated as such under the Geneva Convention of 1951 and others who are not so designated but are in fact in a very similar position, including those who are refugees within their own countries, especially in countries with civil wars in Africa and in Central America and elsewhere. If one adds to these those who are currently being driven about or in flight within or from the former Yugoslavia and within or from some parts of the former Soviet Union, refugees add up to about 50 million, possibly even more. This means that currently about one in every 110 human beings on this earth—man, women, or child—is some kind of a refugee, expellee, or escapee. Just giving a picture of the magnitude of these numbers, mostly quite unknown to all but experts or persons specifically interested in these problems, is one of the objectives of this discussion.

Since several of these chapters were originally presented as papers at the Columbia University Seminar on "Content and Methods of the Social Sciences," it seems appropriate to explain briefly this particular setting: these "Columbia University Seminars" are not the usual one- or two-semester courses for which one registers as a student. They are actually permanent seminars in which college and university professors from throughout the New York area are members, usually for many years at a time. This particular one, that is, on "Content and Methods," was founded in 1947. I myself have been a member of it for well over twenty years.

These "University Seminars," of which there are currently some sixty to seventy, form a separate organization within Columbia University, with a separate secretariat and a university-appointed director, currently Professor Aaron Warner. The seminars cover an incredible variety of fields both in the natural and the social sciences and in the humanities. Each seminar elects its own chairperson and secretary. The

seminars meet regularly once a month during the academic year, usually for a one-hour presentation by one of its own members or by an
invited guest, with subsequent discussion, usually also for about one
hour. The secretary, in addition to the ordinary organizational chores,
takes notes during presentation and discussion, which are afterwards
distributed to the members. The whole institution owes its existence to
an initiative by the late Professor Frank Tannenbaum, a political scientist and a specialist on Latin America, who founded the first such
seminars in the 1940s as a place where scholars could present their
own ideas to a group of fellow scientists from their own field—not
within just narrow specialities, but from wider fields—and could have
them discussed by their own peers.* I for one have over the decades
found this one of the most congenial and at the same time most stimulating groups I have ever participated in.

Thus, I take this occasion first of all to thank my colleagues at the
seminar for "Content and Methods" for the years of stimulating discussion and exchange of ideas, then to thank its chairman of many years,
Professor Joseph Maier, formerly of Rutgers University, who actually
initiated the present publication by originally suggesting to the director
of the seminars, Aaron Warner, that the various papers I had presented
over the years at the seminar on "population" and related subjects
should be published together. Then thanks are due to Professor Warner
for not only taking up this suggestion at once, but also adding his own
suggestion that some other papers I had given on these and related
subjects should be included. Further thanks are due, of course, to Dr.
Richard Bartel, the editor of M. E. Sharpe publications, for having
acted positively on this suggestion.

Thanks are also due to my colleagues at the Institut fuer Soziologie
at the University of Vienna, Professors Leopold Rosenmayr, Robert
Reichardt, Wolfgang Schulz, Anton Amann, and Doz. Dr. Georg
Wieser, who, beginning in the 1960s, has invited me again and again
first to shorter guest professorships, and then, after my retirement from
Queens College, to by now already five two-year appointments as
guest professor, thus giving me an opportunity to present and discuss
these (and other) subjects with graduate students, and providing me

---

*Frank Tannenbaum, "Origin, Growth and Theory of the University Seminar
Movement." In Frank Tannenbaum (ed.), *A Community of Scholars. The University Seminars at Columbia University.* New York: Praeger, 1965, pp. 3–45.

with study and working facilities and a generally stimulating environment that enabled me to keep up my work as though I had never heard
of retirement.

Last but not least I have to thank two of my former assistants at the
Vienna Institute, by now long since scholars in their own right: First,
Professor Roland Girtler, who hunted up for me some old out-of-the-
way historical materials, including in particular a pamphlet by
Suessmilch, published in 1756, in which he defended his *Goettliche
Ordnung* against criticism by Johannes von Justi (1717–1771), one of
the German cameralists, as well as getting me a photocopy of all three
volumes of the fourth edition of Suessmilch's *Goettliche Ordnung*,
published posthumously in 1775 by Suessmilch's son-in-law.

Second, to Mrs. Margarete Nagel-Mahidi, now with Oesterreichisches
Statistisches Zentralamt, who way back in 1974 assembled for me
within a matter of weeks some 200 articles on the "Limits to Growth,
debate" in newspapers, magazines, and scientific journals in German,
English, and French, enabling me to produce within the few weeks
then at my disposal an extensive presentation of the pros and cons in
that debate when the discussion was at its highest.

FROM
MALTHUS
TO THE
CLUB OF ROME
AND BACK

Chapter 1

The Early History of Demography before Malthus

Introduction

The would-be author of an "Early History of Demography" soon finds himself pondering which author of what period to take as the decisive turning point at which "population" changed from a subject of occasional (albeit at times quite extensive) general discussion among philosophers, economists, politicians, statesmen, and others into a distinct, separate modern science. Not even the specialists in the field can quite agree among themselves on this point. Some see the beginnings with early "Political Arithmetics" in England, with men like John Graunt (1620–1674), William Petty (1623–1687), and Edmund Halley (1656–

Paper presented to the Columbia University Seminar on "Content and Methods of the Social Sciences," March 13, 1985, augmented with materials from a similar paper given at the University of Munich, January 1989, meanwhile published as "Die Fruehgeschichte der Demographie vor Malthus," in *Jahrbuecher fuer Nationaloekonomie und Statistik* (Stuttgart: 1991), Vol. 208/5, pp. 505–24.

Of the many sources that will be cited or simply listed in the references, this chapter is particularly indebted to Spengler (1942), Hutchinson (1967), and Stangeland (1904). While the first two of these are still well known (Spengler's in a 1965 reprint), Stangeland's book, which appeared as a Columbia University doctoral dissertation, seems—quite undeservedly—more or less to have fallen into oblivion. (It is still quoted, though, in the United Nations publication, *Determinants and Consequences of Population Trends* [1973].)

1742). Others see it with the beginnings of "German University Statistics" in the late eighteenth century, with Gottfried Achenwall (1719–1772) and August Schloezer (1735–1809), or perhaps with their earliest forerunner, Hermann Conring (1608–1681). Yet others see it with Suessmilch's (1707–1767) *Die Goettliche Ordnung in den Veraenderungen des Menschlichen Geschlechts* (The Divine Order in the Changes of Mankind), first published in 1741, or perhaps with Pehr Wargentin (1717–1783), who as chairman of the Swedish Academy of Science arranged the first modern census of population in 1776 (although this census was still in an indirect manner, based on church and other official registers).

But, looking through the literature up and down, the most popular contender of all for the honorary title of founder of demography as a modern science is apparently still Robert Thomas Malthus (1766–1834), whose claim to the title is most lapidarily presented by the American demographer Ralph Thomlinson, who states:

> The history of population theory can be summarized in three words: pre-Malthusian, Malthusian and post-Malthusian. [1932, p. 30]

With this, Thomlinson means to say that, even though many of Malthus's ideas had been expressed by others—some of them decades, others even centuries before—it was Malthus who, with his *Essay on the Principle of Population* (first published as an anonymous pamphlet in 1798), was the first one to bring all the ideas together in some kind of coherent theoretical system. True enough, Malthus's main idea—that man's innate biological urge to procreate is stronger than his ability to provide the necessary food for the ever increasing numbers of his offspring, so that Mother Nature must from time to time interfere with her "positive checks" (as he called them) of famine, war, or pestilence in order to restore the balance between man and food supply—had been voiced as far back as the second century by Tertullian (A.D. 160–220), one of the early "Fathers of the Church." And Malthus's detailed claim that, if unchecked in this manner, mankind has a tendency to double its numbers at intervals of about twenty-five years, in the manner of a geometric progression of the type 1, 2, 4, 8, 16, 32, . . . (and he pointed out that such had indeed been the case in the British colonies in North America during the preceding 150 years) had already been made some 130 years earlier by Mathew Hale (1609–1676), and as recently as some twenty years before Malthus by Gianmaria Ortes (1713–1790) and by Adam Smith (1725–1790). In *The Wealth of Nations* (1776) Adam Smith had pointed at the same North American figures Malthus cited twenty years later.

Still, Malthus was the first to make a coherent theoretical system out of it. And perhaps it may be claimed with some justification that it was out of the immediately following discussion pro and contra Malthus, in which each side found it necessary to present more and more data and arguments in support of its own and in refutation of the opposite point of view, that at long last "demography" as a modern science developed. (Its name, however, it received only much later. It seems that the term first occurred in Achille Guillard's (1799–1876) *Elements de statistique humaine, ou démographie comparée* (1855), by which, however, Guillard originally meant to designate more or less the natural and social history of human society (Lorimer, 1959, p. 159).

Malthus's *Essay* itself, of course did not spring from his head suddenly and in perfect shape like Pallas Athena from the head of Zeus. It was actually his contribution to a discussion that had then already been raging for many years about the true causes of poverty and human misery he and his contemporaries saw developing before their very eyes in quite shocking forms during the beginning of the Industrial Revolution. Some of them, especially the forerunners of the later socialists, blamed everything primarily on the rapaciousness of the new factory owners, and in general on the existing social order that they wanted to replace with a more just and better one. It was in the context of this discussion that Malthus's first *Essay* (in 1798) was specifically directed against men such as William Godwin (1756–1836) in England and M.J. Condorcet (1743–1794) in France, who spoke of man's infinite perfectibility—a conviction that Malthus's father shared—while the younger Malthus was convinced that man's innate urge to procreate faster than he could feed his offspring condemned him to permanent poverty and misery. The first *Essay* was in fact written as the younger Malthus's counterargument to his father's optimistic belief concerning man and his future. The argument of the younger Malthus, that the poor were the cause of their own poverty because they produced more children than they could properly feed, created a storm of criticism. Even years after his death (in 1834), Malthus was still denounced by Marx and Engels as a "lackey of bourgeoisie."

The topic here, however, is not the social and political ramifications within which this debate took place, but rather a brief historical over-view of earlier and later forerunners who from various points of view and out of various historical situations either more cursorily touched upon, or dealt more extensively with problems of population, that eventually led to the more systematic treatment of the subject at the time of Malthus.

Early Thought on "Population"

In the sixth century B.C., Confucius (551–478 B.C.) cautioned, along with other Chinese writers at that time, that "excessive growth may reduce output per worker, repress levels of living for the masses and engender strife," and that "mortality increases when food supply is insufficient; that premature marriage makes for high infantile mortality rates, that war checks population growth, etc." (*Determinants*, 1973, p. 33).

Plato (427–347 B.C.) and Aristotle (384–322 B.C.), in discussing the best population size for the Greek cities of their time, pointed out that cities should be small enough for efficient administration and direct participation of the citizens in public affairs, but at the same time large enough to be able, if need be, to ward off attacks by hostile neighbors, who were of course also small city-states. For Plato the best size was 5,040 families (which, together with the appropriate number of slaves, meant a city of perhaps some 40,000 population). That number, he pointed out, is divisible by all numbers up to 12 (except by 11), which presented certain advantages in arranging administrative divisions and subdivisions. (In modern times, E.P. Hutchinson [1967, pp. 11–12] cites this passage verbatim from Plato and adds somewhat skeptically that the same would be just as true for half and of course also for twice that number.)

More relevant than what they may have decided was the desired optimum number is what Plato and Aristotle advise for maintaining that number: encouraging procreation and, if need be, immigration, should the number become too small, or discouraging procreation or sending people off to colonies should the number become too big—essentially the same methods that recur in the utopias of the sixteenth century (Hardin, 1969, p. 18).

Aristotle in particular pointed out—as had Confucius some 150 years earlier—that too much increase of population would bring "certain poverty on the citizenry, and poverty is the cause of sedition and evil." Should population increase too fast, then Aristotle recommends abortion and the exposing of newborns (Hutchinson, 1967, p. 13).

Around 300 B.C. in India, Kautilya also pondered the question of population in his *Artashastra*. According to Keyfitz (1972, p. 42), he considered population

> as a source of political, economic, and military strength. The necessary complement of land and mines. Though a given territory can hold too many or too few people, the latter is the greater evil. Kautilya restricted asceticism to the aged, favored the remarriage of widows [which in India was traditionally forbidden—P.N.], opposed taxes so high as to provoke emigration. The optimum village consisted of 100 to 300 agricultural families on a square mile or two.

The Romans, especially during the time of Augustus (63 B.C.–A.D. 14), in need of manpower for amassing and administering their huge empire, instituted a series of laws to encourage people to marry early and to beget offspring often, with great advantages for those who complied and disadvantages for those who did not. The best known of these laws, the Lex Julia (18 B.C.) and the Lex Papia Poppaea (A.D. 9), provided relief from taxation and preferential treatment when applying for public office, among other benefits for those who complied, but imposed severe limitations on the rights of inheritance, for example, on those who did not. People unmarried or still childless past their early twenties could only accept half of what others bequeathed to them— the other half was confiscated by the state. Of childless couples, the surviving spouse could only inherit one-tenth of the fortune of the deceased, all else went to the state.

Among their more curious provisions, these laws decreed that women above the age of twenty-four, if unmarried or if married but without children, were not permitted to wear jewelry or to use a sedan chair (Stangeland, 1904, p. 12).

In the long run, resistance on the part of the population at large allowed first the strictest and later also other provisions of these laws to fall into disuse and eventually led to their abolition as obsolete and unenforceable.

The Roman experience, together with the most modern example of a similarly strict government population policy in the opposite direction— the "only one child per family" law in the People's Republic of China, promulgated in 1979, where the government has also been forced, through the resistance especially of the rural population, to grant quite a number of exceptions, seem a clear indication that governmental policies in regard to population, be they pro- or antinatalist, need to be introduced but gradually in such a manner that at least the great majority of the population can willingly go along with them.

An early voice interpreting "pestilence, famine, and wars" as preventives against overpopulation, as was done much later by Malthus, was Tertullian (ca. A.D. 160–220), one of the early "Fathers of the Church":

> The strongest witness is the vast population of the earth to which we are a burden and she scarcely can provide for our needs; as our demands grow greater, our complaints against Nature's inadequacy are heard by all. The scourges of pestilence, famine, wars, and earthquakes have come to be regarded as a blessing to overcrowded nations, since they serve to prune away the luxuriant growth of the human race. (Hardin, 1969, p. 18; Cromm, 1988, pp. 34–35)

Through the Middle Ages, "population" was hardly ever discussed as a separate subject. The attitude was generally pronatalist. This, however, was not out of any considerations concerning the possible advantages of a growing population, but rather in line with the biblical command, "Be ye fruitful and multiply," and out of more general ideas of the meaning of procreation and morality. The celibacy of priests was occasionally criticized as a contradiction to that command of Holy Writ, but without any serious consequences.

Another early attempt at looking at "population" as part of a total process comes from Ibn Khaldoun (1332–1406), who looked on population increase and decrease as stages of development like that of a human being: from high fertility in youth to declining and finally totally disappearing fertility in old age. But these stages were connected with economic developments: high birth and low death rates occurred in times of economic upswing and the reverse in times of downswing. Khaldoun emphasized (as did William Petty some 300 years later in England [1623–1687], and others) that high population density rather than high population numbers were desirable for more efficient division of labor and for cheaper administration (*Determinants,* 1973, p. 35).

"Population" as a Topic in the Sixteenth Century

As one of the first, Niccolo Machiavelli (1469–1527) took up the topic of population again:

> When every province of the world so teems with inhabitants that they can neither subsist where they are nor remove themselves elsewhere, every region being equally crowded and over-peopled, . . . it must needs come about that the world will purge itself in one or another of these three ways [floods, plagues, or famines]. [Hutchinson, 1967, p. 17]

Machiavelli's somewhat younger contemporary Martin Luther (1483–1546) was much more sanguine about the problem:

> God makes children. He is also going to feed them. [Stangeland, 1904, p. 93; Hardin, 1969, p. 19]

Jean Bodin (1530–1596), in "Six livres de la republique" (1576), anticipated by a hundred years the notion of the mercantilists, that a bigger population would mean more production and, with that, more export which would increase the influx of silver and gold and thus make the country richer. Bodin remarked (contrary to the earlier warnings of Confucius or Aristotle) that "there is nothing that does keep a city more free from mutinies and factions than the multitude of citizens" (Hutchinson, 1967, p. 18)—certainly a strange thought, considering the many rebellions and revolutions that started in cities, unless he had in mind the peasant wars and revolutions of the late fifteenth and early sixteenth centuries which, of course, usually started in the country.

Bodin's contemporary, Giovanni Botero (1540–1617), was much more ambivalent about the growth of population. On the one hand, in *Delle Cause della Grandezza Citá* (1588), he emphasized that "the Greatness of a city rests on the multitude of its inhabitants and their power," while on the other hand he pondered, as did Malthus two hundred years later, that a population cannot increase beyond its food supply. As these limits were being approached, late marriage and emigration would serve to restore the balance. And so would war (Hutchinson, 1967, p. 19).

Still somewhat ambivalent, but already more outspoken concerning the possible negative consequences of population growth, was a younger, English contemporary of Bodin and Botero, Richard Hakluyt (1527–1616). On the one hand, Hakluyt quoted, as did others in those days, King Solomon—

> The power and strength of a prince consists in the multitude of the people. [Proverbs 14:28]

He even added that the realm could be much more populous and still provide enough food for its people if they were industrious enough. On the other hand, he advocated at the same time in *A Discourse on Western Planting* (1584) the emigration of surplus population; his argument is almost like that of Malthus a good two hundred years later:

> Throughe our longe peace and seldome sickness . . . wee are growen more populous than ever heretofore; . . . so many, that they can hardly lyve one by another; yea, many thousandes of idle persons are within this realme, which, havinge no way to be sett on worke, be either mutinous and seeke alteration in the state, or at leaste very burdensome to the commonwealthe. [Hutchinson, 1967, pp. 24–25]

Which, Hakluyt continues, leads to crime and fills the jails. This agrees, almost verbatim, with what Aristotle said on this point.

As the cities grew more rapidly than before, during the sixteenth and early seventeenth century, discussions of advantages and disadvantages of a growing population became more frequent. For example, Walter Raleigh (1552–1618), in his *History of the World*, wrote that:

> if by wars or pestilence they were not sometimes taken off by many thousands, the earth with all the industry of men could not give them food. [Hutchinson, 1967, p. 34]

Similarly, an anonymous propaganda tract for the colonies, *The Planter's Plea* (1630), averred that

> Warres, Pestilences and Famines, which unless they had wasted the people of these parts of the world, we would ere this have devoured one another. [Hutchinson, 1967, p. 39]

This, however, was written at the beginning of the Thirty Years

War, and in the face of that war's huge devastation and mass dying—more of hunger and disease than in battle—the concern began returning toward worries about depopulation.

But, of course, there were also, then as now, those who argued that the very fact that the cities grew, stimulated agricultural production and thus was a good thing.

Typical for the proponents of this point of view was James Harrington (1611–1677), who wrote the utopic *The Commonwealth of Oceania* (1656), where he claimed that

> The more mouths there be in a City, the more must of necessity be vented by the Country, and so there will be more Corn, more Cattel, and better Markets; [and this will produce] more Laborers, more Husbandmen, and richer Farmers. . . .
> The Country then growing more populous, and better stock'd with Cattel, which also increases Manure for the Land, must proportionally increase in fruitfulness. [Hutchinson, 1967, p. 42]

This anticipates practically line for line one of the most popular arguments in the debate against Malthus, some 140 years before Malthus made his famous statement. It also anticipates the same argument against Malthus that is presented in our own time by Colin Clark or by Esther Boserup and others.

"Political Arithmetics" in England

Modern authors such as Hauser and Duncan in their *The Study of Population* (1959) often divide "demography" into two parts: "demographic analysis" and "population studies." The former deals with the more formal and the mathematical-analytical, while the latter comprises the social and economic aspects and consequences of changes in the size and distribution, age structure, and so on, of populations.

This division parallels to some extent the historical development of "Political Arithmetics" in England in the latter part of the seventeenth century, and of the so-called German University Statistics during the seventeenth and eighteenth century. This discussion is confined to the main representatives of both schools: of "Political Arithmetics" in England, to John Graunt (1620–1674), William Petty (1623–1687), and Edmund Halley (1656–1742); and of "German University Statistics," to its first forerunner, Harmann Conring (1608–1681), and then to its main representatives, Gottfried Achenwall (1719–1772) and August Schloezer (1735–1809).

John Graunt (1620–1674)

John Graunt was a merchant with comparatively little formal education, and thus he was but little prepared with the routine knowledge and approach, particularly in mathematics, that would have facilitated his analysis of the data before him. He took, as he himself states in the "Dedicator's Epistle" to his famous book *Natural and Political Observations . . . upon the Bills of Mortality* (1657), "I do not know by what accident" an interest in the "Bills of Mortality" (Graunt, 1975, p. 3). These were weekly published lists of who and how many people had died, and of what causes, in the City of London and the surrounding parishes outside its walls, with an annual summary published around Christmas time. The Bills of Mortality had originally been instituted during the Big Plague of 1592, but had fallen in disuse when the plague was over. Revived again at the next plague in 1602, they again fell into disuse when that one was over. Only after the Great Plague of 1625 were they finally made permanent in 1629.

At that time a number of elderly women were appointed as "searchers" whose task was to examine the recently deceased and to record their sex and the cause of their death, and in particular, which ones had died of the plague. These records were always kept in a somewhat chaotic fashion, particularly concerning the cause of death, since the women and often the doctors themselves were hardly in a position to know what people really had died of.

What, for example, could one make of a record of 9,535 deaths in London and environs in 1632, 1,108 of whom had died of "fever," 1,797 of "consumption" (which Graunt suspects must have included many who had actually died of "French Pox"—that is, syphilis—because only twelve were listed under that latter cause; 2,268 were "Chrisomes and infants," meaning children newly born, baptized, and died very early; 628 died as "aged," and so on through a number of causes, some with today strange sounding names. Eighteen had been "executed and prest to death," while seven had been "murdered" (a surprisingly low number)—not to speak of eleven who died of "Grief," and one who had been "affrighted." That eight were listed as having died of the plague sounds particularly suspicious, because 1632 was not a plague year (Graunt, 1975, p. 24).

Nevertheless, Graunt's interest fastened on these Bills of Mortality, noting that most of those who read them

> made little or no use of them, than to look at the foot, how the burials increased or decreased . . . and with all in the Plague time, how the sickness increased and decreased, so that the rich might judge of the necessity of their removal [to the country] and Trades men might conjecture what doings they were likely to have in their respective dealings. [p. 17]

As he examined these Bills of Mortality, and made his "natural and political observations" on them, Graunt came up with a great number of heretofore unexpected results.

Perhaps of greatest importance for the later development of demography was his distinction between two kinds of events: those that, although in their individual occurrence always highly unusual, such as accidents and suicides, occurred nevertheless with fairly constant regularity (today we would say with fairly constant probability); and those that occurred without any visible regularity, such as major epidemics and here in particular the plague. (We may note that this was 230 years before Emile Durkheim used the stability or the change of the suicide rate as an indicator of the stability or instability of certain social institutions.)

Graunt found that of all those born alive, about one-third died before reaching the age of five; and that 36 percent died before the age of six. (These observations appear plausible in the light of later studies.) Then he showed how many died within each successive decade of life until the age of seventy-six, establishing in effect the first, albeit somewhat crude, mortality table.

Later historians pointed out that the Bills of Mortality and the funeral lists were deficient because they excluded Catholics and Dissenters as not having been properly baptized or properly buried according to the rites of the Church of England (Cullen, 1975, p. 8). Although certainly true and certainly a defect, this deficiency does not diminish Graunt's pioneering status in the early development of demography. Nor is it really relevant that he made several incorrect assumptions while making his computations: for example, he assumed that the sex and age distributions remained constant over long periods of time while actually they changed considerably through natural increase of the population and through migration from country to city. He also assumed the death rate to be constant from decade to decade after the sixth year of age, which certainly also was incorrect. These defects were subsequently improved upon by people like Halley, thirty-six years his junior, who knew more mathematics and had access to better data. But it was Graunt who started this new way of looking at birth and death data.

Comparing birth and death rates in the city and in the country, Graunt concluded that life in the country was healthier and that "London now is more unhealthful than heretofore, partly for that it is more populous but chiefly, . . . sixty years ago few Sea-Coales were burnt in London, which now are universally used. For I have heard that Newcastle is more unhealthful than other places . . . and many people cannot at all endure the smoke of London" (Graunt, 1975, p. 76). This certainly seems like a remarkable anticipation of today's discussion about air pollution through coal-burning factories and the potential deleterious consequences for general health! It is all the more remarkable because this was apparently the very first time that references in birth and death rates in polluted and not polluted areas were used to make that claim.

Graunt was also the first to show that generally the annual number of male births slightly exceeds the number of female births, to which he adds

> That Christian Religion, prohibiting Polygamy, is more agreeable to the Law of Nature, that is, the Law of God, then Mahumetism, and others, that allow it. [p. 57]

This was a first indication of what later developed into the kind of theologically based demography of people such as Derham and later Suessmilch. In particular, it was this observation that led fifty years later to John Arbuthnot's main argument in "An Argument for Divine Providence, Taken from the Constant Regularity Observ'd in the Births of Both Sexes" (1710).

Graunt can perhaps also be credited with another remarkable "first." After he had—on the basis of the appropriate birth and death rates— divided a period of seventy years into "healthy" and "sickly" years, he showed that this does abundantly counterpoint the opinion of those who think great Plagues come in with kings reigns, because it happened so twice, viz. Anno 1603 and 1625, whereas as well the year 1648, wherein the present King commenced his right to reign, as also the year 1660, wherein he commenced the exercise of the same, were both eminently healthful, which clears both Monarchie and the present King's family from what seditious men have surmised against them. [Graunt, 1975, p. 51]

For better or for worse, this may have been the first time in history when long-term statistical—and in this case demographic—analysis was used to support one side in a political argument (in this case the English monarchy) against a widely held popular belief of the other side. Sadly, it remains unknown whether or not this newfangled kind of argumentation managed to convince many on the other side.

William Petty (1623–1687)

William Petty came from the same social background as Graunt; in fact, the two were close friends. Petty's father was a textile merchant. (Incidentally, the third of the great pioneers of "Political Arithmetics," Edmund Halley, also came from this background.)

Petty attended university, studied medicine, and became professor of anatomy, physics, and chemistry—and, by the way, also Lector of Musics at Gresham College in London, a position which he turned over to his friend Graunt after he himself had changed over to an entirely different career.

At the age of twenty-nine he became the head physician of the British army in Ireland, which was then putting down an uprising of the Irish. Eventually Petty became administrator for the distribution of confiscated Irish land to British soldiers, which position, it seems, he also exploited to increase his own wealth through successful land speculations.

One by-product of Petty's administrative activity became the *Political Anatomy of Ireland* (1672), which offered many useful suggestions for better administration and better collection of statistical data concerning administration and industry.

As distinct from Graunt, who made the most important original contributions, Petty was more engaged in the spreading of the new method of analyzing data, especially through numerous publications such as *Observations upon the Dublin Bills of Mortality* (1681) and a book called *Political Arithmetick* (1690) which, when it became widely known, gave the new field its name. Frank Lorimer, in our own time, therefore, calls Graunt its father, but Petty its godfather.

Actually, Petty, who was so much better trained in mathematics, helped Graunt with it so much that eventually in the literature a lengthy discussion arose as to which of the two was the "real" author of the *Observations upon the Bills of Mortality* (Cullen, 1975, pp. 152–53). Petty's own important contributions lay more in the field of administration. In addition to the above-mentioned *Political Anatomy of Ireland*, he wrote *A Treatise of Taxes and Contributions* (1662).

Petty, like the mercantilists later, was in favor of an increase of population under the overall point of view of "more people, more production," but without the additional notion of the latter that "more production means more export and thus more silver and gold into the country." In a letter to his friend Southwell in 1685, he wrote:

> (1) . . . about this matter of Multiplication of Mankind, I must rebuke you . . . that you say the speedy peopling of the Earth is an Evil Designe—whereas I say it tends greatly to the honor of God and the benefit of all mankind.
>
> (2). I am of the opinion, that the urge to replenish the Earth may decrease when there will be only 3 acres of land per one person to till and to enjoy—which will not happen in a 1000 years. [Petty-Southwell, 1967, p. 153]

Little could he foresee that only 270 years later (around 1950), there would already be quite a hefty discussion about whether Frederic Osborn's claim in *Our Plundered Planet* (1948) that one acre of arable land was necessary on the average per capita was not set much too high. In fact, China today has less than 0.6 acre per capita—only one-fifth of what Petty thought would "not happen in a 1000 years."

He did, however, like Ibn Khaldoun some 250 years before him and Emile Durkheim some two hundred thirty years after him, emphasize that it was not simply the greater size of population that was important, but above all its greater density that made possible a more efficient division of labor as well as cheaper administration per capita.

On the political side, he used *Political Arithmetick* to prove that England was then the strongest country of Europe in economic terms, and that London was greater than Paris—both issues at that time much discussed as matters of political prestige.

But the one who made the greatest contributions toward turning these new methods of analysis into a real science was Edmund Halley (1656–1742). By the time he came into contact with political arithmetics, he was already an accomplished astronomer who, in 1681, at the age of twenty-five had discovered the comet that has since been named after him.

Into Political Arithmetics he came by a rather circuitous and accidental route.

Kaspar Neumann (1648–1715)

It all began in far away Silesia, where a Protestant cleric, Kaspar Neumann (1648–1715), had under his jurisdiction the supervision of schools and churches in the city of Breslau. Like Graunt in England before him, Neumann developed an amateur's interest in the detailed study of church registers—although not, like Graunt, "by I know not what accident." Rather, it was because he, together with his friend, the physician Gottfried Schulz, wanted to contradict with birth and death data a widespread belief that in a person's life, the years divisible by 7 and 9 were especially dangerous (particularly the $7 \times 7 = 49$th and the $7 \times 9 = 63$d years), and that the weeks in the first year of a newborn that were similarly divisible (the so-called septenarii and nonarii) were particularly dangerous to the infant's life. It was also commonly believed hat sickness had something to do with the phases of the moon.

While Neumann and Schulz were indeed able to demonstrate with the help of those church registers that this was superstitious nonsense, they felt that a real mathematician could probably get much more out of these data than they, the amateurs, could. Thus, they decided to send their data and computations to Wilhelm Leibniz (1646–1716), the best-known polyhistor of his time, who in turn passed them on to the then already well-known Royal Society of London (founded in 1660). The Royal Society in turn handed these data to its member Edmund Halley, who was well versed in things mathematical.

Edmund Halley (1656–1742)

This whole circuitous route by which Halley eventually became the one to make a permanent science out of Political Arithmetics was less unusual in those days than it might sound today. Paul Lazarsfeld

(1961, p. 101), in a paper "Notes on the History of Quantification in Sociology," wrote:

> I have the impression that something like a community of aficionados developed: all over Western Europe, empirical data were traded for mathematical advice.

On the basis of these data from Breslau for the years 1687–91, which were more detailed and more accurate than the political arithmeticians in England had ever seen, Halley published his report in the *Transactions of the Royal Society* for the year 1693 in two papers: "An Estimate of the Degree of Mortality of Mankind, Drawn from Curious Tables of the Births and Funerals of the City of Breslaw," and "Some Further Considerations of the Breslaw Bills of Mortality."

With these publications, Halley made history in two ways: first, he presented the first modern mortality table, which has, with some small improvements here and there, remained in use in English life insurance for some 150 years. Second, with these mortality tables, the monetary value of a particular kind of insurance that was then becoming popular could be determined: the client gave the insurance company a sizable sum of money in return for a lifelong annual payment of fixed amount. While this kind of insurance had existed before— usually taking the form of one person giving to another person a house or a piece of land against such a permanent annual payment for the length of his life—the value had essentially rested on the personal estimates the two sides to the bargain made of how long the "giver" of the house or land might still live.

The great improvement, which made this kind of insurance commercially possible, was Halley's introduction of the concept of "average life expectancy" for certain categories of people defined by a kind of common risk or death probability.

True enough, Halley, like Graunt before him, made the assumption that the sex and age structure remained constant over long periods of time, but he was lucky in that this was actually true to a much higher degree in Breslau than it had been in Graunt's time in London, so that the error implied in this assumption was less disturbing with his than it had been with Graunt's computations.

The great importance of Halley's contribution, however, beyond its immediate usefulness for the insurance industry, was that this kind of analysis of data could be applied to all sorts of data that later on played an important role in the development of demography as a science.

Gregory King (1648–1712)

In passing, it should be mentioned that Gregory King (1648–1712)—about thirty years younger than Graunt and Petty, eight years older than Halley—used the methods of Political Arithmetics for a first fairly reliable estimate of the population of England (about 5.5 million). He was probably also the first to attempt a serious account of the social structure of the population of England. In *Natural and Political Observations and Conclusions on the State and Conditions of England* (written in 1696, published later—the title certainly indicates the strong influence of Graunt's work), he divided the population of England into twenty-four social categories in a hierarchy from the high clerical and worldly lords down to the lowest level of vagabonds. For each of these twenty-four social status groups, he estimated the number of families and their average income; this certainly can be considered the beginning of our modern ways of analyzing social structure (Lecuyer and Oberschall, 1968).

In conclusion, it may be useful to place the development of Political Arithmetics into a greater sociohistorical context. The seventeenth century saw much growth of the cities, and the first beginnings of what was to become modern industry; with all this came the development of a new rationality that was favorable to the development of new branches of science, of which the new "Political Arithmetics," with its interest in the growth and structure of populations, was one.

Part of this development also entailed the rise of the new middle class in political and social importance, especially for those of its sons who went to universities. The life histories of these three protagonists of this newly developed science, Graunt, Petty, and Halley, may serve as a good example:

Graunt, son of a merchant, with little formal education, remained a merchant, although he became in the end a member of the prestigious Royal Society. Petty and Halley both came from the same middle-class merchant background as Graunt, but attended universities and became famous professors and scientists and, in Petty's case, a very high level administrator.

The case of Graunt is, in one particular incident, perhaps even more dramatically symptomatic of the rise of the middle class: unlike the others, Graunt did not first become a professor or other academic, but became a member of the highly prestigious Royal Society in full awareness of his (seen from the generally high social level of the Society's members) rather lowly social status as a "tradesman." Robert Merton relates the story: When Petty became a founding member of the Royal Society, this was obviously in view of his position as a highly respected university professor, so that his middle-class origins were apparently deliberately overlooked. But when Graunt was suggested for membership, the Society at first demurred because of his lowly social standing as "only a tradesman." It was only, so Merton relates, when King Charles II, to whose Lord Privy Seal Graunt had dedicated his book, "severely reproved" them and announced that "if they found any more such tradesmen, they should be sure to admit them all without any more ado," that Graunt was admitted to membership (Merton, 1938).

German University Statistics

"German University Statistics" is the designation for a system of teaching about various European states that originated in the mid-seventeenth century in Germany as an early form of political science. It has nothing in common with today's usage of the word "statistics" beyond its etymological origin.

The subject matter that was later designated as German University Statistics began with the first lectures of Hermann Conring (1606–1681) at the University of Helmstaedt in the duchy of Saxony as a comprehensive description of various European states, their rulers, the genealogies of the ruling families, overall forms of government, some information about land and people, and their habits and mores, economics, business, culture, and so forth.

Conring was not the first ever to teach or write about this subject in this general manner. There were forerunners particularly in Italy, such as Francesco Sansovino (1521–1586), with his *Del Governo e Administrazione dei Diversi Regni e Republiche cosi Antiche e Moderne* (About the Government and Administration of Various Kingdoms and Republics in Antiquity and in Modern Times) (1562), or Giovanni Botero (1564–1617), whose *Della Ragione di Stato* (Of the Cause—or of the Foundations—of the State) (1589)

Conring translated in 1666 into Latin (in which language he gave his own lectures on the subject).

Those who, like Sansovino and Botero, dealt in detail with matters of states (in Italian, *lo stato*) were called "statista." It was from this meaning of the word that much later, in 1749, Gottfried Achenwall coined the German noun "Statistik," which then for well over a hundred years was used with this particular meaning of dealing with matters of the state. It was only toward the middle of the nineteenth century that its meaning changed over into today's usage of the word, particularly under the influence of Karl Knies's *Die Statistik als Selbstaendige Wissenschaft* (1850).

Hermann Conring (1608–1681)

Hermann Conring began, as did William Petty, with the study of medicine at various universities, including Leyden. And, just like Petty, he became professor of various somewhat disparate subjects, including medicine, philosophy, and comparative politics. He was also personal physician to Queen Christine of Sweden and other European royalty and was considered, together with the somewhat younger Leibniz, the greatest polyhistor of his time.

In 1660, Conring began at the University of Helmstaedt lectures about "notitiae rerum politicarum" (notes about matters of the state), which Achenwall was later to translate as "Lehre von den Staatsmerkwuerdigkeiten" or "science of that which is noteworthy [or remarkable] about various states."

Following Aristotle, Conring spoke of the four main "causes" or basics of the state: the "Causa finalis" (meaning and purpose), the "causa materialis" (land and people), the "causa formalis" (constitution and law), and the "causa efficiens" (administration) (Westergaard, 1932).

In 1675, much to Conring's chagrin, according to Westergaard (1932, pp. 6–7), one of his students published his notes taken during the professor's lectures. But since all of this took place in Latin, the subject did not get widely known.

Gottfried Achenwall (1719–1772)

It was only eighty years later, when Gottfried Achenwall (1719–1772) as professor in Goettingen began to lecture on the subject in German, that it gained wider popularity both in Germany and in neighboring countries. (Achenwall himself was a student of August Schmeitzel [1679–1747] who was born in Kronstadt, in today's Romania, but lectured as professor in Halle.)

It was in the opening sentence of Achenwall's later famous book *Abriss der neuesten Staatswissenschaft der vornehmsten Europaeischen Reiche und Republicken zum Gebrauch in seinen akademischen Vorlesungen* (An Outline of the Newest Political Science of the Most Important European Empires and Republics) (1749) that the noun "Statistiks" occurred for the first time in German (it had been used as an adjective before). Because of this, Achenwall's former student and later successor August Schloezer (1735–1809) called him the "Father of Statistics"—a designation that still occasionally causes confusion among authors trying to trace the early history of the subject that is today known under that name but with an entirely different content and meaning. (Achenwall himself modestly averred that the title of "Father of Statistics" properly should belong to his predecessor, Hermann Conring.)

This, then, is Achenwall's opening sentence:

> The meaning of so-called Statistics, that is the Science of the Politics of the various states, gets interpreted in various ways.

Apparently still uncertain about the proper content and also the limits of this new "science," Achenwall states quite early, in the tenth paragraph of his book:

> The first sight of the many remarkable observations to be made about an empire ["Merkwuerdigkeiten eines Reiches"] when taken by itself impresses me like a maze. . . . it is easy to get in; but how does one find one's way out again? One must divide everything into two categories: an empire consists of land and people. Under these two categories everything can be brought.

He proceeds indeed to "bring everything" under them:

> From its beauty and its steadiness one appreciates the beauty of the human body. How different from each other are the various peoples in color, length, and strength! There are even certain illnesses that are characteristic for certain peoples. [Achenwall, 1749, ¶ 21]

Or:

> One also depicts the various nations by their prevailing mood: There is
> no denying, that temperaments are different, that one nation has more
> sense of humor but is also more pensive, and is faster or slower in
> thinking, talking and acting. Nor are the various emotions all the same
> everywhere. [¶ 22]

Or:

> Of the four main religions the Heathen one has been extirpated in Europe,
> the Mohammedanic survives only at the very borders, the Jewish creeps
> about in the dark, the Christian alone occupies the throne. [¶ 44]

As time went on, the content and form of this new subject of "Statistics" began to change: voluminous verbiage was slowly replaced by
a kind of semitabular form that—at the same time including more
numerical material than before—facilitated comparison among countries, in that more or less the same kinds of data about population,
economy, trade, industry, and the like appeared for each country in
about the same place of this semitabular arrangement.

Those, especially at the University of Goettingen, who still upheld
the older form of presentation, prided themselves on giving readers a
genuine picture of the true spirit of the various nations, while others
tried to compress it in soulless figures and tables, for which they were
contemptuously called "Tabellenknechte" (slaves of their own tables).
As Harald Westergaard in his *Contributions to the History of Statistics*
(1932) summarizes their contempt for those "others":

> slaves of the tables, that bring only the dry bones of Statistics, without
> clothing them with the flesh of descriptive reality; they have no feeling
> for the spirit of a nation, its love of Liberty, its genius. [Westergaard,
> 1932, p. 14]

The Goettingen school, on the other hand, proudly made clear that they
themselves were engaged in a "noble" science.

Anton Friedrich Buesching (1724–1793)

One of the best-known representatives of this newer version, Anton
Friedrich Buesching (1724–1793), was for some time Professor of Phi-

losophy in Goettingen, afterward director of a Gymnasium in Berlin. Buesching wrote a *Neue Erdbeschreibung* (New Geography) in 1754, and in 1758, with a rather lengthy title, a new description of the various European states—for all of which Meitzel in the 1924 (fourth) edition of the *Handwoerterbuch der Staatswissenschaften* bestowed on him the title of "father of comparative statistics of states."

Friedrich Wilhelm Crome (1753–1833)

It was then Friedrich Wilhelm Crome (1753–1833) who, again with a rather comprehensive description of "The Size and Importance of the Various States of Europe" in 1785 (about thirty years after Buesching), made the definitive transition to this newer form of presentation, which from then on centered very much on numerical data.

In the end, the field belonged to the Tabellenknechte, the "slaves of their own tables," whose writings, with ever more figures and tables and fewer and fewer verbal descriptions, eventually became the forerunners of today's "Statistical Yearbooks."

Nonetheless, the historical contribution of Conring, Achenwall, Schloezer, and all the others, continues to be that they were the ones who developed the conceptual framework, without which Buesching and Crome and others could not have made the transition that eventually led to the development of today's descriptive branch of demography—especially as it appears in those "Statistical Yearbooks" in which governments or special governmental agencies give annual accounts of the "state of the nation" (and usually of the world as well).

In particular, it is unlikely that "Political Arithmetics" alone would in the end have also developed this second—and today so necessary—branch of demography.

Population Discussion and Policy in France
during the Seventeenth and Eighteenth Centuries

Whereas in England and Germany during the seventeenth and eighteenth centuries, "population" was largely a topic for interested amateurs and university professors, in France, with its well-established, strong central government, it was a topic primarily for statesmen and high-level administrators. There was first of all the tenet of the mercantilists, that the wealth of a country consisted in its hoard of gold and silver, and that more people meant more production and with that more export of goods which brought more gold and silver into the country. This was a sentiment shared to some extent by the German cameralists at the time, such as J.J. Becher (ca. 1625–1685), L. v. Seckendorf (1626–1692), and J. H. v. Justi (1717–1771).

One may recall that in 1949, when the Communists took power in China, Mao Tse Tung, in a famous speech that for many years was to guide the population policy of the new state, voiced almost the same sentiments as those French bourgeois some 250 years before: that a country as rich in land and minerals and other resources as China need not fear any increase in population. On the contrary: more population means more hands for production and more production means a faster achievement of socialism. Yet, what may have sounded plausible and even convincing in the first flash of victory, when China had about 540 million people, sounds strangely unrealistic in retrospect: the population of China had grown to over 1,000 million by the mid-1980s, and with agricultural production in spite of numerous improvements unable to keep pace, China has been forced to institute the most restrictive population policy ever: only one child per family.

But back to seventeenth- and eighteenth-century France: A second main reason for favoring a growing population was the ever growing need for soldiers in France's many wars, especially under Louis XIV and his immediate successors. Thus, both mercantilist and pre-mercantilist considerations of increased production and export, and military needs for more soldiers made "population," so to speak, an "object" of administration that had to be cared for and increased by the king's statesmen and administrators. (This may bring back memories of the strong pronatalist measures in fascist and nationalist countries in our own time, such as in Germany, Italy, and Japan.)

One of the earlier French writers on the subject, Antoine de Montchretien (1575–1611), however, was not a servant of the state, but a dramatist. He wrote somewhat ambivalently about population and its increase, speaking on the one hand of its dangers:

> Since we enjoy peace, the people have multiplied infinitely in this Kingdom. They suffocate one another. . . . how many are there of men, burdened with large families, living in extreme poverty. [Spengler, 1965, p. 18]

On the other hand, he believed that population is a source of national power and that France's greatest wealth consisted in the "inexhaustible abundance of her men," and that France could support an unlimited number of them (Spengler, 1965, p. 16).

Montchretien did, however, take into consideration that increased population and its concomitant increased production and export also would bring about increased import of food, should the country's own agriculture no longer suffice to support the increased number of people. This obviously is not different from the situation of many an industrialized country today (e.g., Belgium) that could not possibly feed its own people with its own agricultural production but does so by using payments for its exports to import food and other necessities.

Unlike many others of his time, Montchretien looked upon the colonies not simply as places where criminals and other undesirables could be unloaded, but as an integral part of the motherland whose inhabitants would help to increase its wealth. This sounds modern enough when we recall that before Algeria and Morocco became independent, they were treated legally not as colonies but as integral parts of the French motherland.

Sebastien Vauban (1633–1707) was a military engineer whom Suessmilch (in 1741) mentions as a former marshal of France. Vauban headed the construction of the harbor of Dunkirk and of the citadel of Strassbourg. He maintained that it is not enough to have a large population—the people must also be able to live with a reasonable standard of living, which certainly was not the case for the vast majority of the people of France. (As will be discussed later, Vauban's contemporary Bossuet held the same opinion, although he based his on Christian-religious arguments.)

In his main work, of 1707, the *Dixme royal* . . . (the complete title of the book covers several lines in print), Vauban makes numerous suggestions for the improvement of the miserable conditions of most of the people. He went so far in the drastic description of these conditions that he incurred the ill will of the king and parliament. The book was condemned in a regular trial and then solemnly burned in public by the executor (Westergaard, 1932, p. 38).

Vauban's slightly younger contemporary Pierre le Pesant Boisguillebert (1646–1714) also argued that the people would have to have a certain minimum standard of living, so that not as many as half the newborns died in infancy and many adults were cut down by death before life had run half its course (Spengler, 1965, p. 34).

Perhaps the greatest practitioner of mercantilist population policy was Jean Colbert (1619–1683), minister of finance from 1661 to 1683 under Louis XIV. Spengler (1965, p. 21) calls him the "archpopulationist of the mercantilist era." From French sources, Spengler relates that "Colbert's program, in fact, appears to have been based on the principle, then generally accepted, that the masses (whom kindness, well-being, and wealth tended to corrupt) made satisfactory beasts of burden only so long as wages were kept at a subsistence level and conditions of work were made onerous and unfavorable" (Spengler, 1965, p. 21). (This is not dissimilar to Malthus's argument 120 years later against any kind of legal support for the poor, because if given money they would only procreate even more and yet continue to live in poverty.)

Colbert (according to Spengler) furthered the immigration of foreign, especially of skilled labor. He even sent recruiters abroad to bring such to France, while at the same time forbidding emigration, except into French colonies. Even Huguenots, among the most persecuted people in France, were forbidden to emigrate and were threatened with the death penalty if they tried. Premiums were paid to informers who reported on those intending to emigrate. Had we not seen the same thing taking place in our own time, for example, in Germany under Hitler and Russia under the Communists, to name just two twentieth-century instances, Colbert's policy might sound more paradoxical.

Industriousness had to be furthered and idleness prevented by all means, especially through keeping wages so low that people simply had to work, or else they would starve to death. This sentiment was widely held well into the time of the Industrial Revolution, not only by Malthus, but, for example, by Arthur Young, who wrote in 1771, some one hundred years after Colbert:

> Everyone but an idiot knows that the lower classes must be kept poor or they will never be industrious. . . . they must (like all mankind) be in poverty, or they will not work. [Overbeek, 1974, p. 7]

In order to bring as many people as possible into useful agricultural and industrial production, Colbert also severely limited access to such "unproductive" occupations as jurisprudence, finance, and service within the church. Laws, not unlike those under the emperor Augustus in Rome, provided tax relief and monetary rewards for those who married early and had children soon, and disadvantages and fines for those who did not. Young French girls, especially from houses of correction and from rural districts, were sent by the boatload to the colonies, where the soldiers were forced under threat of punishment to marry them and to produce offspring. In the French colonies in Canada, "fines were made imposable upon fathers of unmarried sons (20 and over) and daughters (16 and over)" (Spengler, 1965, pp. 23–26).

In the end, as in Rome of antiquity, these harsh laws fell into disuse over the resistance of the people, but they wrought unmeasured suffering and humiliation for those affected by them as long as the laws could still be enforced.

As a kind of positive bequest of the era, Colbert left to modern demography the lists of taxes, production, and trade, as well as of births, baptisms, and funerals, which the chiefs of administration in the various provinces had instituted at his request. Many of those records were preserved and serve today's demographers in reconstructing population developments, sex, and age distributions, and so on, of that time.

Throughout the eighteenth century, pronatalist sentiment remained strong in France, among both authors and administrators; the measures suggested, however, were for the most part less grim; some were really quite mild. Ange Goudar (1720–1791), for example, presented a whole catalog of measures for increasing the population: the unmarried were to pay higher taxes, to have no access to public office, to face limitations on the right to inherit and to bequeath, and to be excluded from academies and from professorships. On the other side of the ledger, those who married early and had many children would be offered relief of taxation, preferential treatment when applying for public office, and all sorts of honors. For example, Goudar recommended that the fathers of eight or more living children should receive a letter of thanks from the king or his minister, designating them as outstanding citizens. He also suggested that citizens with ten or more living children be given membership in a special honors society, that each citizen with eight or more children would have the right to wear a sabre, and so on. These provisions are reminiscent of the "mother cross" (Mutterkreuz) and other measures under Hitler—different only in that in the eighteenth century it was the father, not the mother, who was to be given the honor (Spengler, 1965, pp. 57, 62).

M. Moheau (1733–1820), whom Spengler considers the most competent of the authors on population in eighteenth-century France, presented careful statistics about the excess of births over deaths in France. He dealt especially with the "cultural and non-biological character of many of the principal determinants of population growth, the moeurs [mores] on which depended both the frequency of marriage and fertility within marriage" (Spengler, 1965, pp. 101, 102).

In that context, Moheau saw Catholicism as favorable to population growth "because of its insistence that cohabitation was a duty whose end was generation" (Spengler, 1965, p. 103). (Similarly, his contemporary, Poncet de la Grave, criticized Mohammedanism as "unfavorable to population growth because it sanctioned polygamy, which deprived many males of mates and many females of sufficiently frequent sexual relations" [Spengler, 1965, p. 106]). Similarly, de la Grave criticized Christianity for its approval of celibacy and its essentially negative attitude toward sexual relations (Spengler, 1965, p. 106).

Moheau recommended that the minimum age at marriage be raised for males from fourteen to eighteen and for females from twelve to sixteen years. Similarly, for pronatalist reasons, he took the unusual stance of describing war as "a check to population growth as great as famine and pestilence" and "urged the adoption of a policy of peace . . . [and that] soldiers be allowed to marry and that, for eugenic reasons, the physically less able be used for military purposes in so far as possible" (*Recherches et considerations sur la population de la France*, Paris 1801, cited in Spengler, 1965, p. 103). Moheau's *Recherches* contains many other unusual suggestions. For example, because vice in big cities was "destructive to population," he suggested special taxation to check urban growth and to use the money so obtained to support the rural areas (Spengler, 1965, p. 103).

Ponce de la Grave recommended, as had Goudar before, that parents of many children be given preference when applying for public service and be given special honors—which, so he emphasized, would further the increase of population without costing anything.

Richard Cantillon (?–1734) was born in England but lived for a long time in Paris and was one of the first who tried to assess the influence of foreign trade and the distribution of income and wealth on the growth of population. As a forerunner of the physiocrats, he saw the wealth of a country primarily in the productivity of its soil and—like others at that time—considered luxury detrimental to population growth. This view led occasionally to slightly grotesque forms of argument. Spengler cites one example: the waste of the product of French labor and French soil to pay for the importation of Brussels lace, then fashionable with the rich ladies in France: lace, made from flax grown on a single acre of land in Belgium, was paid for by the price of wine grown on sixteen thousand acres in France (Spengler, 1965, p. 118). Aside from the grotesqueness of this particular example, this was, for that time, quite a novel analysis of the intertwined relations of production, expenditure, and population growth which has become characteristic only of the computer-based world models in our own time.

Essentially the same kind of argumentation, if in more theoretical (and less grotesque) form, was presented by Etienne de Condillac (1715–1780), who also saw land as the main source of wealth, but who dealt more directly with the relation between population and food supply. According to Condillac:

> There is in a country always only the quantity of inhabitants that it is able to nourish. There will be fewer, other things being equal, if each of them consumes more; there will be fewer still, if a part of the land is consecrated to productions which do not nourish them. [Spengler, 1965, p. 137]

More detailed discussions by Condillac about how, if all the land is being used up, producing more of one thing must mean cutting down on production of another—for example, producing more forage cuts down the acreage available for grain—anticipate today's discussions about the pernicious consequences of replacing the production of food for people with the production of monocultures for export and profit.

Condillac actually already represents the transition to the physiocrats who, because they belong more in the field of economics, are not discussed here.

I should note, however, that the physiocrats, especially Quesnay (1694–1774), did not, like Malthus and his adherents, consider war a necessary part of human history—specifically, as a corrective that Nature applies when populations grow faster than their food supply. On the contrary, they saw peace as the normal condition of mankind that could best be maintained through furthering agricultural production (rather than industrial production and the production of arms).

It may be interesting to add that the widespread pronatalist attitude in France at that time was based not only on the overall theories and argumentation of the mercantilists but also on a widely held belief, repeated by many authors, that the population of France was shrinking and was considerably less than it had been in antiquity.

Demography on a Theological Basis

At about the same time that the pioneering work of John Graunt led to the development in England of the new science of "Political Arithmetics," there developed, also in England and in part based on the very same work of John Graunt, a new kind of more or less theology-based demography that interpreted the very same regularities in birth and death rates and in the growth of human populations that had attracted the attention of Graunt, Petty, and Halley, as proof of the all-pervading workings of divine providence, which thereby regulated the fate and destiny of mankind.

Actually, much earlier writers had referred to the biblical command, "be ye fruitful and multiply," and it had been quite customary in discussions of the growth of populations in favorable terms to quote from King Solomon's proverbs, "The strength of the King lies in the multitude of his people" (Proverbs 14:28). But they had done so more as a general religious justification for an overall pronatalist attitude, rather than as a kind of theoretical basis for explaining the growth of populations in theological terms.

Indeed, in France, J.B. Bossuet (1627–1704) had already gone one step further in proclaiming, not only that it was the king's obligation to follow God's command and see to it that his people multiplied, but that he was also obliged to create the necessary living conditions so that people really could multiply. And this meant furthering trade and imposing less oppressive taxes, to facilitate people marrying young, and so on through a whole catalog of pronatalist measures, many of which paralleled those of his contemporary Jean Colbert, discussed above (Spengler, 1965, p. 22).

But it was John Derham (1675–1735), a contemporary of Edmund Halley, who made some kind of a science of theology-based demography. Derham, like Malthus after him, was an Anglican cleric interested in problems of population. He was familiar with the work of Graunt and others in Political Arithmetics but gave it this new, theological orientation. The title of his main work, "Physiotheology or a Demonstration of Being and Attributes of God from His Work of Creation" (1713), announced at the same time its content and its program.

In it, Derham makes it quite clear that the regularities in the development of population pointed out by the authors on Political Arithmetics were by no means something that more or less grew by itself, but were, rather, a proof that divine order permeates the whole universe. He did not overlook the necessity of a balance between the number of people and their resources. At least as far as the world of animals is concerned, he wrote in a chapter titled "The Balance of Animals, and the Due Proportion in which the World Is Stocked by Them":

> The whole surface of our globe can afford room and support only to such a number of all sorts of creatures. And if by their doubling, trebling, or any other multiplication of their kind, they should increase to double or treble that number, they must starve or devour one another. [Hutchinson, 1967, p. 126]

A similar theological interpretation of demographic data was presented in John Arbuthnot's (1667–1735) "Argument for Divine Providence" (1710): that the fact that year after year the number of male births exceeds but slightly that of female births was proof positive that polygamy is a contravention against the divine order of things:

> Among innumerable footsteps of Divine Providence to be found in the Works of Nature, there is a very remarkable one to be observed in the exact Ballance that is maintained, between the numbers of Men and Women; for by this means it is provided, that the Species may never fail, nor perish, since every Male may have its Female, and of a proportionable age. This Equality of Males and Females is not the Effect of Chance but Divine Providence, working for a good End. [Arbuthnot, 1710, p. 186]

He also explains that there are always slightly more male than female births because later on in life the males incur greater risks of death while providing food (Arbuthnot, 1710, p. 188).

The height of this theological kind of demography was reached with Johann Peter Suessmilch's (1707–1767) *Die Goettliche Ordnung des Menschlichen Geschlechts aus der Geburt, dem Tode und der Fortpflanzung desselben erwiesen* (The Divine Order of Mankind, Proven from the Birth, the Death, and the Propagation of Same) (1741). Suessmilch also was a Protestant cleric, originally in the army of Frederick the Great of Prussia, then in Coelln (a small town near

Berlin), and finally member of the Prussian Academy of Science. In the preface to his book, he emphasizes his great debt to the works of Graunt and Petty, and in particular to Derham, whom he repeatedly cites as one of his sources.

But whereas Derham still showed some concern about the necessary balance between population size and food supply, Suessmilch—quite in the spirit of French mercantilism and the similarly oriented camera-lism in Germany—was quite optimistic in that respect: on the basis of detailed information he had collected from all kinds of sources about many countries, he concluded that the population of the world was then about 1,000 million (today it is assumed that this was somewhat too high; the figure probably stood closer to 750 million) and then declared:

> 13,942,000,000 or almost 14 thousand million people could live upon this earth.
>
> And if anybody thinks that this is too much, well, he can always assume only 10 thousand million, or even only half of that. For my intent and proof that is quite superfluous, because further on I shall prove that currently not more than one thousand million people can be computed to live upon this earth; from which it follows that the earth has by far not reached as yet the full measure of its population and that therefore it does not require any pestilence, war or famine to keep the balance [between man and food supply—P.N.]. [Suessmilch, 1775, vol. 2, p. 177]

The last sentence sounds strangely like a verbatim refutation of what Malthus was to utter only almost sixty years later, in 1798—that fam-ine, war, and pestilence were Nature's "positive checks" whenever the relation between man and his food supply threatened to get out of balance.

For a better understanding of Suessmilch's view of his own figures, one should keep in mind that populations even in the then industrializ-ing nations of Western Europe grew presumably at a rate of only 0.3 percent, and at even less, perhaps 0.2 percent or so, in the rest of the world. Thus, in his mind, it would take an unbelievably long time for the world's population to increase from his estimate of 1,000 million to the 14 thousand millions that he thought the earth could feed.

As a kind of later historical footnote, it might be added that the Population Division of the United Nations presented an estimate at the

World Population Conference in Bucharest in 1974 that the world's population might stabilize at about 13,000 million toward the middle of the twenty-second century—that is, some 1,000 million below Suessmilch's estimate of the maximum the earth could feed (United Nations, 1975, vol. 1, pp. 204, 205).

Suessmilch also noted that, while God bade man, "Be ye fruitful and multiply and replenish the Earth," He bade the animals only to be fruitful, without adding "to replenish the Earth." According to Suessmilch, this was because in that case the animals might have eaten up all the fruit there was and in the end devoured all men as well, so that the most beautiful regions of the Earth would remain un-populated—which obviously would be contrary to the Lord's plans.

Suessmilch's most important contribution toward the future development of demography was that, in his book, he assembled abut everything known about the topic at his time, so that this became, as it were, the first real "Handbook of the Science of Population." It is primarily for this reason that German demographer Juergen Cromm gives to Suessmilch the palm:

> Even if today some things in Suessmilch's work may sound quaint to some readers, we nevertheless see in him not only the beginning of scientific population statistics but "the very beginning of Demography." [Cromm, 1988, p. 143]

It is interesting to note in what systematic (and for his time quite novel) manner Suessmilch arrived at his estimates. Influenced by the work of Graunt and Petty, he first persuaded a great number of Protestant ministers, to begin with in Prussia, then in Holland, England, Denmark, and Belgium, to send him excerpts from their church registers concerning births, deaths, weddings, and so on. In addition, he collected reports from travelers about the size of populations and related problems in many countries, including Russia.

He then computed the potential agricultural fertility of each land by comparing it with that of Prussia, and, based on this, estimated how much grain could be grown there, then how much flour could be ground out of that, and how much bread could be baked from it. And finally, he calculated how many people could be fed with it, based on the daily bread ration of a Prussian soldier. Giving gave due consideration to the differences in the daily requirements of a grown man, a woman, and a child—he anticipated in fact the concept of "unit of consumption," the full development of which by economists and empirical sociologists had to wait until the nineteenth and twentieth century.

Later Developments and Conclusion

Although for good reasons this chapter concentrated specifically on the development of demography toward a modern science, which left no room for dealing with the writers on economics, this too was in the process of developing into a modern science at about the same time. And as this happened, the writers on economics, who began more and more to take center stage in what was to be the future social sciences, "population" as a separate topic began to recede into the background, becoming for quite some time no more than a side issue in this rapidly developing other field.

James Steuart (1712–1780), in *An Inquiry into the Principles of Economics* (1767), emphasized that increase of population was not so much a consequence as a cause of improvements in agricultural technology and production—anticipating what is today one of the most widely used arguments of anti-Malthusians. And Adam Smith (1727–1790) pointed out in *The Wealth of Nations*, twenty-two years before Malthus, that the population of the British colonies in North America had been doubling about every twenty-five years during the preceding 150 years. But this was not a central topic for Smith.

If today "demography" appears again as a separate "science," then this is no longer, as was true in the time of Malthus, because its practitioners or even other scientists treat it as a topic in isolation but more as part of the division of labor within the social sciences, which are all interconnected in many ways, but which require a certain amount of specialization in terms of both the special history of the subject and its particular methods of analysis, especially a certain amount of mathematics.

It would be an illusion, however, to think that because today's demographers have at their disposal so much better data and also better methods of analysis than their predecessors some 200 years ago, with which they may analyze the numerical and the structural ups and downs of populations, they are also in a better position to decide who is right and who is wrong in the eternal discussions about the implications and expected future developments of population, especially in terms of population increase.

Is it the pessimists, who see in the "population explosion" of the last few decades (we have grown from a world population of about 2,500 million in 1950 to over 5,200 million in 1985 and presumably will reach some 6,200 million by the year 2000 and perhaps 8,000 million only twenty years later) a great danger with impeding catastrophic shortages of food and other materials?

Or is it the optimists, to whom the very fact that in spite of numerous pessimistic predictions during the last one hundred, two hundred, even three hundred years, mankind has always been able to overcome all of its difficulties, to develop new methods of agriculture, to discover new deposits of necessary minerals, new sources of energy, new materials, and to replace exhausted ones, and so on?

Pessimists, however, like to come back with the story of the man who, having fallen off the 106th floor of the Empire State Building, while passing by the 26th floor, mumbles to himself: "so far, so good!"

Demography can only deliver better figures for this debate. But whether the recipients of the data then give them a more pessimistic or a more optimistic interpretation is a matter outside of science, even if the scientists themselves keep entering the debate on one or on the other side.

My own task I saw only in showing how, primarily out of the debate between optimists and pessimists and their need to produce ever more data and arguments to support their own and to contradict the other side, especially during the last two or three centuries, and particularly in the debate pro and contra Malthus, eventually demography became a modern science in its own right—albeit not in splendid isolation, but heavily interwoven with all the other social sciences.

References

Achenwall, Gottfried. *Abriss der neuesten Staatswissenschaft der vornehmsten Europaeischen Reiche und Republicken zum Gebrauch in seinen akademischen Vorlesungen* (An Outline of the Newest Political Science of the Most Important European Empires and Republics, for the Use in His Academic Lectures). Goettingen: Schmidt, 1749.

Arbuthnot, John. "An Argument for Divine Providence, Taken from the Constant Regularity Observ'd in the Births of Both Sexes." *Phil. Transactions 27* (1710): 186–90. (Reprinted in Maurice Kendall and R.L. Plackett [eds.], *Studies in the History of Statistics and Probability*, vol. 2. London: Griffin, 1977.)

Cromm, Juergen. *Bevoelkerung, Individuum, Gesellschaft. Theorien und soziale Dimensionen der Fortpflanzung* (Population, Individual, Society. Theories and Social Dimensions of Procreation). Opladen: Westdeutscher Verlag, 1988.

Cullen, Michael J. *The Statistical Movement in Early Victorian Britain. The Foundations of Empirical Social Research.* Hassocks, Sussex: Harvester Press, 1975; New York: Harper and Row, Barnes and Noble, 1975.

The Determinants and Consequences of Population Trends. New Summary of Findings on Interaction of Demographic, Economic and Social Factors. New York: United Nations, 1973 [first ed. 1953].

Graunt, John. *Natural and Political Observations Mentioned in a Following Index and Made upon the Bills of Mortality.* London: 1662. Rept. New York: Arno Press, 1975.

Hardin, Garrett. *Population, Evolution and Birth Control: A Collage of Controversial Ideas,* 2d ed. San Francisco: Freeman, 1969.

Hutchinson, E.P. *The Population Debate: The Development of Conflicting Theories up to 1900.* Boston: Houghton Mifflin, 1967.

Keyfitz, Nathan. "Population Theory and Doctrine: A Historical Survey." In William Peterson (ed.), *Readings in Population.* New York: Macmillan, 1972.

Knies, Karl Gustav Adolph. *Die Statistik als selbstaendige Wissenschaft. Zur Loesung des Wirrsals in der Theorie und Praxis dieser Wissenschaft.* Kassel: 1850.

Lazarsfeld, Paul F. "Notes on the History of Quantification in Sociology—Trends, Sources and Problems." *Isis 52* (1961): 277–333. (Reprinted in Patricia L. Kendall [ed.], *The Varied Sociology of Paul F. Lazarsfeld.* New York: Columbia University Press, 1982.)

Lecuyer, Bernard, and Oberschall, Anthony R. "The Early History of Social Research." In *New Encyclopedia of the Social Sciences.* New York: Macmillan and Free Press, 1968.

Lorimer, Frank. 1959. "The Development of Demography." In Philip M. Hauser and Otis Dudley Duncan (eds.), *The Study of Population.* Chicago: University of Chicago Press, 1959.

Meitzel. "Buesching, Georg Friedrich." In *Handwoerterbuch der Staatswissenschaften.* 4. Aufl., 1924.

Merton, Robert K. "Science, Technology and Society in 17th Century England." New York. (Originally published in Georg Sarton, [ed.], *OSIRIS, Studies in the History and Philosophy of Science.* Belgium: Bruges, 1938, pp. 362–632.)

Overbeek, J. *History of Population Theories.* Rotterdam: Rotterdam University Press, 1974.

Petty-Southwell correspondence 1676–1687. Marquis of Lansdowne, ed. Reprints of Economic Classics. New York: Augustus M. Kelley, 1967.

Population Reference Bureau. Washington, DC: World Population Data Sheet, 1975.

Spengler, Joseph J. *French Predecessors of Malthus.* Chapel Hill: University of North Carolina Press, 1942. [Reprinted: New York: Octagon Press, 1965.]

Stangeland, Charles Emil. *Pre-Malthusian Doctrines of Population: A Study in the History of Economic Theory.* Doctoral dissertation, Columbia University, 1904.

Suessmilch, Johann Peter. *Die Goettliche Ordnung in des Menschlichen Geschlechts, aus der Geburt, dem Tode und der Fortpflanzung desselben erwiesen* (The Divine Order of Mankind, Proven from the Birth, the Death and the Propagation of Same). 1741. [Fourth ed. Berlin: 1775, ed. by his son-in-law Christian Jacob Baumann.]

Thomlinson, Ralph. *Population Dynamics: Causes and Consequences of World Demographic Changes*, 2d ed. New York: 1976.

United Nations. "The Population Debate: Dimensions and Perspectives." *Papers of the World Population Conference, Bucharest, 1974.* 2 vols. New York: United Nations, 1975.

Westergaard, Harald. *Contributions to the History of Statistics.* London: King, 1932.

Chapter 2

How Many People Could Live on This Earth? Changes of an Argument

Introduction

Anno 1741, Johann Peter Suessmilch computed in *Die Goettliche Ordnung in der Veraenderungen des Menschlichen Geschlechts, aus der Geburt, dem Tode und der Fortpflanzung desselben erwiesen* (The Divine Order in the Changes of Humankind, Proven by the Birth, the Death and the Procreation of Same) that the world's population amounted to approximately 1,000 million (today we think that the number may have been closer to 750 million), but that the earth could actually feed 13,932,000,000 million. Considering the slow rate at which the world's population then increased (0.3 percent annually, compared with 2.0 percent around 1970 and about 1.7 percent today in 1980, Suessmilch concluded "that the earth has not yet reached the limits of its population by far, and that therefore it did not require Plague or War or Famine in order to maintain the Balance" (Suessmilch, 4th edition, Berlin, 1775, p. 175f.).

Barely sixty years later, Robert Malthus, in his *Essay on the Princi-*

From Werner Obrecht, ed., "Weltgesellschaft und Sozialstruktur." *Festschrift fuer Peter Heintz*. Diessenhofen, Schweiz: Verlag Rueegge, 1980, pp. 173–90.

ple of Population (London, 1798), propounded the very opposite: that humans had an innate tendency to increase their numbers faster than they could increase their food supply, and that therefore from time to time Mother Nature had to interfere with plague, war, and famine in order to restore balance.

Ever since, optimists have repeated and are still repeating with Suessmilch that the earth could still feed many times more people than it is feeding now, whereas pessimists join with Malthus in the claim that from time to time catastrophes will and do occur because human beings keep on multiplying beyond the limits set by nature. The optimists point to the steady improvements in agricultural technology and the addition of new agricultural lands that obviously have sufficed to feed mankind, which has meanwhile grown to 4,300 million—and many of them at a higher standard of living than before. They also note that there seems to be no basis for assuming that this could not continue for a long time yet to come. They point out especially that even though at the beginning of industrialization the population of Europe did at first increase quite drastically, its rate of growth began to slow down again as the standard of living improved—in some countries even to almost zero, and that one could more or less naturally expect a similar development in the newly developing countries. In fact, say the optimists, this slowing down of the rapid growth of population can already be observed in some of these countries.

The pessimists for their part argue that even at their highest point, around 1870, these rates of increase in Europe never exceeded 1 percent, whereas in the developing countries since 1950 the annual rates of increase have been between 2 percent and 3 percent almost everywhere, and in some countries up to 3 1/2 percent and more. It certainly must take several generations until the annual increase of populations in these countries falls back again to at least that 1 percent per year that was the maximum in Europe in 1870. In countries like India and Pakistan, most of the potential agricultural land is already in use as such, and there is but little scope for increasing agricultural acreage. The "Green Revolution" of the 1960s was barely enough to keep pace with the increasing population. It must be doubted whether the grain surpluses in the United States, Canada, and Australia can still cover the deficits in other areas for any length of time into the future. Considerable portions of these surpluses during the last few years went to the Soviet Union and to China to counterbalance weak harvests in those countries. It is easy to compute, but difficult to imagine, what must occur, if at some future time a few years in a row of unusually weak harvests in Asia and Africa should coincide with similar weak harvests in North America, such as the years of unusual drought in 1934–36 that brought out the "dustbowl" in the Middle West of the United States.

The modern discussion takes place in two forms: one form is the World Models, which in addition to agricultural production also take into account raw materials, productive capacities, and the like, as well as the manner in which they are mutually interlocked and influence one another. These models do not directly ask, or answer, the question, "How many people could live on this earth?" An implicit answer in Meadows et al.'s *The Limits to Growth* is discussed below.

In the other form of the discussion, only the agricultural carrying capacity of the earth is being examined, and then computed: How many people could possibly live on what could possibly be produced? The answers vary, particularly in regard to three aspects:

1. How much potential agricultural land is to be reckoned with? Only as much as can be added through minor additions of agricultural utensils and with these additional land being put to the plow? Or should new agricultural land be included in the computations—land that can only be gained as the result of huge investments of capital—new dams, canals, whole networks of new roads, new settlements, new means of transportation, and so on?
2. What yields per acre are to be assumed in these computations? Present-day averages, which result from the present-day worldwide mixture of primitive and advanced agricultural methods? Or yields that could only be expected under worldwide application of the more advanced methods in use today in North America or in Holland? Or perhaps yields such as could be expected only with the very best and most advanced methods already in some places today, or perhaps even methods that are today only contemplated by scientists or so far at best in a mere laboratory stage?
3. What standard of living should be underlying these computations? From the absolute minimum that is necessary for survival, through the miserable standard of living on which millions of people in the developing countries are forced to survive, up to computing with today's standard of living in North America and Holland as a basis?

Most authors bypass as a matter of course the social and political organization that would be necessary to effect the kind of yields and standards of living that are part of their computations. Including within these computations such things as turning great tropical forests into agricultural land, or making wide areas of desert fertile, requires, of course, that the necessary raw materials, the necessary productive capacity, and the necessary political and social organizations are available.

In the next three sections three different sets of estimates of how many people could live on this earth are discussed:

1.   Estimates from 1890 to 1925—that is, some thirty to sixty years before the modern "population explosion," a time when the worldwide annual growth rate was still less than 1 percent;
2.   Estimates since 1950, with the worldwide annual growth rates already around 2 percent;
3.   Some very recent estimates that count on algae as a main basis for food and on population densities that by today's concepts would appear intolerable and that put the whole discussion on an altogether different basis.

1890 to 1925

In 1890 the English geographer E.G. Ravenstein assumed that the altogether 28.3 million square miles of fertile land on this earth could on the average feed 207 people per square mile; the 13.9 million square miles of semiarid land could on the average feed 10 per square mile; and the 4.2 million square miles of desert on the average could feed 1 person per square mile. Together, $5,858 + 139 + 4 = 6,001$ million people (Ravenstein, 1891, pp. 29, 30).

Assuming a population increase per decade of 8.7 percent in Europe, only 6 percent in Asia, but 20 percent in North America, and similarly for other regions this figure of 6,001 million would be reached by the year 2072—that is, 182 years from Ravenstein's date of computation (1890). Today we are expecting more than that for the year 2000: a population of about 6,300 million.

Ravenstein assumed that "all usable agricultural land will actually be used" (Ravenstein, 1891, pp. 29, 31).

A few years later A. F. v. Fircks criticized Ravenstein's assumptions as being much too low. For the fertile lands, he counted on 100 (versus Ravenstein's 70) people per square kilometer, for the semiarid lands, 20 (versus Ravenstein's 5), and for the deserts 5 (versus Ravenstein's .4) people per square kilometer. The main basis for Fircks's criticism was that "Ravenstein had not taken into account future improvements in average agricultural yields and had omitted the products of fishery and that he had in addition considered the tropics as unsuitable for white man's habitation."

With all of these increases in the assumptions, Fircks came to a total of 9,272 million, adding that the actual limit could perhaps be even higher "because up to now nowhere have all the means, be they plant or animal, that could be used to fulfill man's food requirements, been fully used for that purpose" (Fircks, 1898, p. 295).

A few years later, Hermann Wagner pointed out some faults in Fircks's computations, especially while converting square miles into square kilometers: "thus Ravenstein's 'fertile region' of 73.2 million square kilometers gets by a stroke of the pen transformed into 84.1 million square kilometers, etc." According to Alois Fischer (see below), Fircks could have come only to 7,800 million (Wagner, 1923, p. 889; Fischer, 1925, p. 842).

In 1912 Karl Ballod assumed that there were about 56 million square kilometers arable land on this earth, only about half of which (28 million square kilometers) were actually so used (Ballod, 1912, p. 99). He assumed that in order to provide food for one person with an American standard of living, 0.9 ha were required for grain and another 0.3 ha for everything else (e.g., for draft animals, for the production of fibers for clothing, and the like). Thus, 28 million square kilometers could fed (by the 1912 American standard of living) 2,333 million people.

Germany at that time had 66.3 million people, 50 million of which lived on food grown in Germany for which there was, on the average, about 1/2 ha available per person. Thus, the 28 million square kilometers of arable land actually used as such could, with the German standard of living, feed 5,600 million people.

Japan at that time needed on the average only 1/10 ha to feed one person and only little more for draft and other animals. "Even if we take into account that the Japanese, having on the average about 20 percent less bodyweight, thus also need on the average only about 20

percent less food, we come to only .125 ha land necessary per capita."
With that in mind, one can conclude that with the Japanese standard of
living, those 28 million square kilometers could feed 22,400 million
people. Ballod himself, however, voices some skepticism about this
computation and rather assumes that the 5,600 million mentioned
above could, with the German standard of living, live under humanly
acceptable circumstances (Ballod 1912, p. 99f.).

In addition, Ballod saw as a potential limit for future growth of the
world's population the limits of phosphate deposits. If additional deposits could be found, that would not only replace what was being used
up but would add more phosphate to the soil, then the maximum number of people that the earth could feed could be assumed to be about
twice as high—that is, about 11,200 million. At the same time, however, he emphasized that "the known deposits of phosphate could, at
the [1912] rate of consumption, be exhausted within about 100 years"
(p. 99f.). This consideration could well be seen as an early forerunner
of the manner of computation that in our own time would become
characteristic of the world models of Meadows and others.

In 1925 Alfred Penck determined for each of eleven climatic zones
of the earth the population density for the most densely populated
country in that region. Assuming that potentially the whole zone could
be populated with the same density as this one country, he came to a
potential world population of 9,000 million.

The most pessimistic of all the estimates in this group is that of Hermann Wagner. In the tenth edition of his *Textbook on Geography* (1923)
he points out that the real limit for the future growth of the world's
population probably does not lie in the potential amount of agricultural
land, but in the total amount of (sweet) water—quite a remarkable anticipation of later ecological discussions. "Thus," says Wagner, "even with
the rather incomplete knowledge that we still have of many areas, the
question can already be raised, whether this earth could even feed twice as
many people as it does today" (1923, p. 888). Twice the population of
1923 would be twice 1,800 = 3,600 million people. Considering the annual growth rate of the world's population at that time, of about 0.9
percent, this limit would have been reached by the year 2001. Little could
he anticipate that it would be surpassed only forty-seven years later (in
1970 the world's population was 3,632 million).

Also in 1925, Alois Fischer, after briefly presenting most of the
estimates discussed above, set forth his own estimate: that the earth

could feed about 6,400 million. His estimate rested on very detailed computations concerning types of fertility, differences in the kind of food being used in various areas, and other factors: for example, "Areas planted with rye, but also those planted with rice, have, speaking in terms of calories, only 3/4 of the food potential of areas planted with wheat, whereas areas planted with potato produce on the average one 1/3 times as much food" (Fischer, 1925, p. 845). Talking about peoples with higher, with more moderate, and with little consumption of meat, and bringing in some other considerations, he eventually discusses six different types of standards of living (North American, West European, Central European, East European, South European, Asiatic-African). With all of this, he presents a map of the world that shows for the most important great areas the population at his time and the population that it could potentially feed. Together, his computations gave the then population of 1,860 million and the potential limit of 6,400 million.

With the prevailing annual rate of growth of about 0.9 percent, this limit of 6,400 would be reached within about 140 years—that is, by the year 2065. Fischer assumes, however, as do most of the other authors cited above, as a matter of course, that within that time there would be improvements in agricultural technology that would then increase the agricultural carrying capacity of the earth.

Fischer, however, is more cautious than his predecessors in the manner in which he approaches the whole problem of estimating the potential maximum of the world's population: "Against all earlier attempts it must first of all be emphasized that it is altogether impossible to make a once and for all valid estimate of the world's carrying capacity because we do not know the technical means of the future" (Fischer, 1923, p. 843).

In 1931, Otto Neurath took over Fischer's estimate, with some minor changes, but with the same assumption that Fischer made: that future improvements in agricultural technology would increase the agricultural carrying capacity of the earth.

Since 1950

In 1960, Fritz Baade assumed 4 billion ha potential arable land and 2 billion ha potential grazing land, including half of the tropical forests as arable land. Assuming worldwide use of modern agricultural methods (and taking into account climatic and geographic differences), he assumes a potential average of 3 to 4 tons of grain per ha arable land and 1 1/2 tons per ha grazing land. That would make a total production of 12 to 16 billion tons from the arable land and of 3 billion tons from the grazing land, together 15 to 19 billion tons grain equivalent.

Then he starts with the actual fact that India feeds an average of "four people with one ton of grain [per year], many of them, however, on the brink of starvation," most of them with an unbalanced diet of too much carbohydrate and too little protein. In the Federal Republic of Germany the per capita consumption is 0.5 ton and in the United States 0.8 ton per year (in the United States a great deal of this estimate constitutes feed for pigs, chickens, and cattle). Baade assumes that the average grain consumption in Germany of 0.5 ton per capita, supplemented with protein from the oceans, would constitute an acceptable food standard for the future world population. Thus, the potential total production of 15 to 19 billion tons of grain equivalent could feed about 30 to 38 billion people at a very adequate standard as far as food is concerned (Baade, 1960, pp. 54–55). Baade, however (like some of the other authors), assumes that the world population will stabilize long before it reaches that number (p. 56).

In 1957, Colin Clark assumed that the earth could feed about 28 billion people; in 1970, he estimated that it could feed 35 billion, assuming worldwide application of agricultural technology and also of Holland's standard of living. The difference between his 1957 estimate (28 billion) and his 1970 estimate (35 billion) is due to improvements in agricultural technology in Holland in the meantime (2 percent per year) (Clark, 1957, p. 13; 1970, p. 153 and tables 154–55).

In a later computation, Clark assumes an average yield of 4.4 tons of grain equivalent per ha arable land, which, as he states, corresponds to "very productive farms in Europe," and is higher than the average for the United States (Clark, 1973, German ed. 1975, p. 39). (By way of comparison, Baade assumed in 1960 a worldwide average of 3–4 tons per ha.) At the same time, Clark criticizes the Club of Rome (actually he means Meadows et al.'s *The Limits to Growth*) for an "egregious error in fact. They begin with the assumption that 4,000 square meters (= 0.4 ha = 1 acre) are necessary to cover the normal food requirements of one person. Actually 2,000 square meters (= 0.2 ha = 0.5 acre) are sufficient to provide not only the minimum for one person, but food (and fibers) at the consumption standard of the United

States" (Clark, 1975, p. 35). The assumption of 0.4 ha = 1 acre of arable land per capita was for a long time, and is in part still today, one of the most common assumptions, although Osborn assumed, in 1948, that one acre per person is not enough (Osborn, 1948, p. 42).

Another estimate of the same magnitude as that of Clark's 1970 estimate—namely 35 billion people—can be found in Nathan Keyfitz (1969). A slightly higher estimate occurs in the report of the Population Division of the United Nations to the 1974 International Population Conference in Bucharest: 38 to 48 billion people (United Nations, 1975). (The report, however, assumes that the world's population will stabilize around the year 2140 at about 13 billion.)

The U.N. report assumes 2.4 billion ha potential arable land, which, however, considering double and triple harvests in some areas, are counted as the equivalent of 4 billion ha. After discounting 10 percent for "fibres, alcoholic liquids, and other non-food purposes," there remain 3.6 billion ha. It is assumed that 1 ha yields 60,000 kg/cal per day (i.e., $6 \times 10^4 \times 365$ per year). Discounting 10 percent for general losses and 3 percent for seed grain, the "remainder would suffice for a minimum diet necessary for survival of 2,500 calories per day for 76 billion people." But in order "to secure adequate nutrition, including protective foodstuffs like vegetable and fruit, the equivalent of 4,000 to 5,000 calories per person and day would have to be the goal. The potential total area (already counting in double and triple harvests) would then suffice for 38 to 48 billion people—that is, 10 to 13 times the current world population." (These "4,000 to 5,000 calories per person per day," however, do not mean twice the usually assumed 2,500 calories per person per day; rather, they refer to foodstuffs that are not yet processed as they are still standing in the fields. To the latter then correspond the usual 2,500 calories per day and person.)

The U.N. report emphasizes that "any considerable increase of arable land . . . would require immense investments of capital, on the order of 500 to 1,000 [1974] dollars per ha . . . [= $1,250 to $2,500 per acre]. For bringing to agricultural use all potential arable land outside of the tropics . . . some 500 to 1,000 billion [1974] dollars. The larger of the two figures corresponds to about one total annual national product of the United States [in 1974] and to about two times the total annual national product of all developing countries together for one year" (United Nations, 1975, p. 84f.).

Meadows et al.'s The Limits to Growth (1972) implicitly contains a figure that is quite comparable to the various more recent estimates cited above. Meadows et al. warn that, should both the world's population and its per capita consumption of nonreplaceable resources keep increasing as they have during the last few decades (2 percent annual increase of the world's population, 1.5 percent annual increase of per-capita consumption of irreplaceable resources), then a general catastrophe could be expected within 100 to 120 years (within 100 years, if mankind has at its disposal five times, and within 120 years, if it has at its disposal ten times as much as all already known deposits of raw materials).

To an annual increase of the population by 2 percent corresponds a doubling time of thirty-five years. Thus, 120 years would imply about three and a half such doubling times. Starting with 3.6 billion people in 1970 (the beginning year of Meadows et al.'s computations), that would amount to a world population after 120 years of 38 to 39 billion. It seems remarkable that this figure coincides with the upper limit of Baade's 1960 estimate (32 to 38 billion), although Baade based his estimate only on the agricultural carrying capacity of the earth, while Meadows et al. take into account the mutual effects of a great number of factors, including the consumption of irreplaceable resources.

Among the more recent estimates that take into account only the earth's agricultural carrying capacity, perhaps the highest is that of a project that is currently (1980) still under way: the "MOIRA project" under Hans Linneman at the Vrije Universitet in Amsterdam (its preliminary report was published in 1977). Taking as their starting point the "computation of the absolute maximum of food production of the world," prepared by the Dutch Agricultural University in Wageningen, the authors conclude that the earth could feed about 100 billion people. This is based on the following computation: first, the total land area of the earth is divided into 222 categories, according to conditions of soil, climate, geographic position, and other factors. Then for each of these categories, the maximum production (in grain equivalent) that could be produced on it with the best agricultural technology known today is computed. That leads to a maximum of 49 billion tons per year. Assuming that in the future, as is currently the case, only about two-thirds of all land in agricultural use is being used for the production of food, then about 32 billion tons of grain could be produced annually, which is about twenty-five times as much as is being produced in the late 1970s. Since about 4 billion people are living on this current production, the 32 billion tons so computed would suffice for feeding 100 billion people at current standards of living.

Recent Estimates of an Unconventional Kind

In *Dynamische Weltwirtschaft* (Dynamic World Economy), Fritz Baade asks what the absolute limits of living space on this earth might be and concludes that these absolute limits are not set by the amount of food that could be produced, but by the potential living space (Baade, 1969, p. 247). To that end, he first discusses "menschenwuerdiges Wohnen" ("dwelling under humane conditions"). The dwelling density of greater New York seems to him a suitable basis for such a computation, because the great majority of its inhabitants spend their lives within that area and apparently find it quite suitable. There are currently (at his time of writing, i.e., late 1960s) 14 million people living within an area of 10,250 square kilometers, which amounts to an average of 715 square meters per person; this might be considered the maximum dwelling density for "humane dwelling conditions."

"If one-half of the total land area in the world were populated at that density—and one would presumably prefer for that purpose the most beautiful landscapes with good climate—then 65 billion people could live on earth in this fashion" (Baade, 1969, p. 248). "These 65 billion people would then have to be fed with what the other half of the earth's land area could produce, which would undoubtedly be possible, as can be seen from a simple computation." Baade's "simple computation" is based on the following consideration: that "all the vegetation upon this globe, including all the plants that are growing in the oceans, are converting only one thousandth of the total solar energy that continuously reaches the earth into organic mass. Of this one thousandth part, in turn, again only one thousandth part is converted into food for humans, so that actually only one part in one million of the incoming solar energy is being used for feeding humanity" (Baade, 1969, p. 249).

After some computations concerning the production of fat and protein with the help of algae chlorella (based on some laboratory experiments), Baade states, "the production of the required amount of food for one person does not need by far 715 square meters [the average amount of space per person in the greater New York area—P.N.]. . . . it would be quite possible to feed one person on what can be produced on 71 square meters if they were used for food production."

Thus, our globe could, if the incoming solar energy were satisfactorily utilized, feed not 65 but 650 billion people. "But," writes Baade, "enough of these astronomical figures! It is enough to know that the limits for space on this earth on which to grow food would in the maximum case still be ten times as large as the limits for dwelling space" (1969, p. 249f.).

The Russian author K.M. Malin (as quoted in an OECD publication by Goeran Ohlin) made a similar computation in 1960: that, to begin with, by 1960 only 1.5 billion ha arable land were being used; that, under considerable capital investment, this acreage could be doubled; and that in addition the yield per acre could be increased four- to fivefold. Thus, instead of the 3 billion people living in 1960, 10 to 20 billion could be fed. With further investment of capital, the agriculturally used area could be enlarged to about 9.3 billion ha; in addition, the yields per ha could be further increased, so that in the end 65 to 130 billion people could be fed. "Under much more speculative assumptions concerning future possibilities of converting solar energy into food, these estimates could still be increased much further to a multiple of these figures up to about 143 to 933 billion and even more than that if it should become possible also to utilize the immense quantities of solar energy that are falling upon the oceans" (Malin, quoted in Ohlin, 1967, p. 32).

In principle, the same kind of computation (converting solar energy into food with the help of algae) is carried out by C. Marchetti in his 1978 paper "On 10^{12} (= 1,000 billions): A Check on Earth Carrying Capacity for Man." By his own words, however, Marchetti's main purpose is not to arrive at an estimate of the maximum number of people that the earth could possibly feed, but to demonstrate that the quest for such a maximum is absurd, by demonstrating that the earth could in principle feed an absurdly large number of people. He hoped to set the questions about population growth and possible resource depletion on a more rational basis. If mankind is willing to live on algae and other as yet unknown nonconventional kinds of foodstuffs, recycling everything, like astronauts in a space capsule, and on exceedingly narrow space, perhaps in skyscrapers on swimming islands or in the depth of the ocean, then one-tenth of the earth's surface would be more than enough to feed and house 1,000 billion people. The rest of the world could remain wilderness or serve as area for excursions.

Marchetti demonstrates that "it would indeed be possible to sustain these multitudes without exhausting important resources, including ecological ones. That is admittedly amazing, and may, even if not seen as an invitation to increased procreation, lead at least to some doubts concerning the reliability of investigations into the depletion of resources within all too narrow assumptions about man's ability to adapt to changing conditions" (Marchetti, 1978, p. iv).

But should anybody protest that the kind of life described in Marchetti's computations is "inhuman," without also proving it impossible on sheer "technical" grounds (meaning, that there would not be sufficient food and other resources to sustain these multitudes), then this would only support Marchetti's argument that the question, "How many people could live on this earth?" is a matter of social, economic, and political organization, and not one of agricultural carrying capacity and resource depletion. (Concerning energy and other resources, Marchetti comes to the same answers.)

Here the circle of argumentation is closed, in a rather nonpolitical manner—because no particular political ideology, or even a particular form of organization is advocated or presupposed—to the arguments of Third World representatives and advocates of the political Left, that hunger and material misery in this world are not caused by overpopulation but by the wrong distribution of food and other goods both between and within individual nations. This is a kind of argumentation that can be found not only on the political Left, but also with some classical and bourgeois, but at the same time anti-Malthusian, economists and political scientists. If one did not know in advance that the following two quotations come from two different political camps, one might easily assume that they both come from the political Left:

> This hysterical clamor that population increase leads to poverty, hunger, and uncontrolled ecological destruction is not only false—it also carries with it a certain danger: it effectively diverts attention from political questions, which are the real problems of this world.

> Rapid increase of population has nothing to do with the real reasons for backwardness; pointing at this growth of population only serves to divert attention from necessary changes of society.

The first of these two quotes is the closing of Colin Clark's *Der*

Mythos von der Ueberbevoelkerung (Engl.: 1973, German trans. 1975, p. 143); the second is from a speech by Lev Volodarsky, deputy minister of health of the Soviet Union, at the World Population Conference of the United Nations in Bucharest, 1974 (quoted in *Time*, September 9, 1974, p. 9).

Changing the Form of Argumentation—Two Phases

Most of the estimates discussed above of the possible number of people that could live on this earth—both those made between 1890 and 1925 still before, and those made after 1950, already during the current "population explosion"—have one thing in common: that the maximum population estimated to be possible would, based on the respective contemporary world population and its then prevailing annual growth rate (around 1 percent in 1925 and 2 percent after 1950)—be reached only after about 200 to 300 years. The only exceptions are Hermann Wagner's 1923 estimate, which would be reached already after 78 years, and Alois Fischer's 1925 estimate, which would be reached after 140 years; Dennis Meadows et al.'s (implicit) limit would be reached in about 120 years.

Generally, it seems that, as the actual world population increased from one estimate to the next, subsequent authors did not come up with a correspondingly shorter remaining span of time within which the world's population limit would be reached, but rather, they typically came to a higher figure for the earth's potential agricultural carrying capacity—apparently because improvements in agricultural technology led in the meantime to higher yields per acre. Thus, a remaining time span of some 200 to 300 years always offers a good basis for an optimistic outlook that more improvements may yet be following.

This, however, raises a difficult question: Do the authors arrive at their optimistic results in a perfectly objective manner, and do their results then make them optimists? Or do they perhaps approach the question itself as optimists and therefore come to optimistic conclusions?

Presenting the issue this way is not meant as an exercise in sophistry but as an attempt to formulate a real dilemma that many readers face: How do we judge those various estimates?

Before World War II, when annual growth rates were still only around 1 percent and the corresponding doubling time was around seventy years, a conclusion that "there is room for at least ten times more people than there are now" still sounded like talk of a far-out utopia, at least 200 to 300 years away—too far away to worry about today! But with annual growth rates of 2 percent and doubling times of one thirty-five years, "room for ten times as many" means the limit will be reached within only 100 to 120 years—a time frame that is likely to affect one's own grandchildren or great-grandchildren. And in countries with annual growth rates of 3 percent and more, and corresponding doubling times of twenty-three years or less, a population "ten times as many as now" would be reached within seventy-seven years, maybe sooner. (In 1979, of the world's 4,300 million people, 165 million live in countries with growth rates of 3 percent or more.)

Anybody who still wishes to be an optimist in view of such figures must either be able to contradict the computations or the underlying assumptions, or must shift the discussion to a plane where computations of this kind lose their meaning. Historically, it seems that we are in the process of a change in the form of argumentation.

The first phase of this process was essentially a matter of disputing the figures and computational methods of the pessimists by claiming that the growth rates would soon decline again, and also that there were still large, potentially arable areas as yet undeveloped. This form of argument, however, remains within the magnitude of the current debate: the question is merely a matter of one or perhaps two more doublings—perhaps sixty years instead of thirty, perhaps 120 billion people instead of 60 billion.

At this point, apparently, the second phase is beginning, as the discussion moves to quite another plane, with orders of magnitude that lie beyond all reasonable expectations: computations based on what are today as yet unimaginable population densities, provision of nourishment on a grand scale through nonconventional foodstuffs, production of raw materials out of unimaginable depths, production of the required energy for all of this with methods that are so far at best under theoretical contemplation, and so on (Baade, 1969; Malin, 1960 [in Ohlin, 1967]), and, finally, computations assuming within themselves closed stationary systems, deliberately involving populations of quite unrealistic orders of magnitude (Marchetti, 1978: 1,000 billion). Compared with these, optimistic estimates like that of Clark (35 billion) and others—including what is currently the most optimistic computation that still stays with conventional assumptions, that of the MOIRA project (100 billion)—appear pitifully pessimistic. One certainly can expect that even this second phase will some day be replaced by a third one—as is already taking shape in science fiction: the settling of distant planets or of huge platforms with large self-provisioning cities that circle the earth in orbits, continuously accepting the population surplus of the earth (and their own population increases as well).

But, if one then reacts to this kind of spherical music of the future by pointing at today's actual rate of growth of the world's population of some 200,000 people each day (note: that was in 1980; as of 1991 it is 250,000 each day—P.N.), and asking whether, within any reasonable length of time, we shall have enough of these huge platforms and enough space rockets and interplanetary buses with which to resettle another 200,000 to 250,000 surplus people from this earth every day, does this make one merely a prosaic earth-bound pragmatist?

The true pessimists, of course, like Paul Ehrlich (1968) and Fairfield Osborn (1948) before him, who are already considering a catastrophe as unavoidable, do not even enter the field of such computations. For them the earth is already or is at least about to be overpopulated, and every single day brings us closer to catastrophe. The precarious food situation of South Asia, and parts of Africa, is for them sufficient proof of their view.

In order to provide at least a somewhat more realistic basis for this whole discussion, let me cite a few fairly plausible figures and a few sentences from a demographic publication of the World Bank, which in turn refers to a few figures in a United Nations (1973) publication. This U.N. report assumes that, as a result of declines in fertility, the annual rate of increase of the populations in the developing countries will decline from 2.4 percent in 1970 to about 2.1 percent by the year 2000. About this, the World Bank report remarks:

> The lower fertility implies that the total population of developing countries in the year 2000 would be about 760 million less than if fertility remained unchanged. At the end of the century, the growth rate of developed countries is expected to be 0.6 percent and that of the world as a whole is expected to be 1.8 percent. (Actually it had already fallen to 1.8 percent by 1979.) Recent population growth has been concentrated in eight large developing countries (People's Republic of China, India, Indonesia, Brazil, Bangladesh, Pakistan, Nigeria, Mexico) inhabited by about 1,800 million people representing nearly 70 percent of the population of the developing countries. . . . these countries added nearly

600 million people to the world during the 20 years between 1950 and 1970. Of these eight large countries, only three—Brazil, China, and Mexico—have attained death rates below 13 per 1,000. Mortality has also fallen in the other five countries but death rates are still above 16. These death rates are expected to continue to fall; unless fertility also declines, their growth rates could rise significantly. [World Bank, 1974, p. 10]

Past rapid rates of population growth have created a young age structure which provides a built-in momentum for future growth. Even with the most antinatalist policies conceivable, fertility will not drop to replacement levels quickly. Even when it does, population will continue to expand for approximately 70 years from now. . . . For instance, even if fertility in the eight largest developing countries were to drop to replacement level today—and it is not likely to reach that for some time—their combined population would be about 60 percent larger 70 years from now. Thus policy makers must take a very long-term view of the relation between population size and resources, even in countries which do not seem densely populated today. [World Bank, 1974, p. 2]

Afterword, in 1994

This paper was originally written in 1979. Preparing it for republication in 1994 allows me to compare the projections of population figures twenty years ahead in the 1973 United Nations report with the actual twenty-year figures.

The U.N. report projected that the population of the eight largest developing countries—China, India, Indonesia, Brazil, Nigeria, Pakistan, Bangladesh, Mexico—which in 1970 had together about 1,800 million people, would have increased by 950 million in twenty years (i.e., by 1990), to a total of 1,800 + 950 = 2,750 million. In 1990, they actually had almost that many: the actual figure was about 2,740 million.

One must remember that during the intervening twenty years, China has instituted the most decisive antinatalist population policy ever undertaken by a major country: it began in 1971 with a big propaganda campaign using the slogan: "One child would be ideal, two is enough, three is already too many." When that did not suffice, in 1979 China enacted the well-known policy of "only one child per family." (This is described in detail in chapter 8.) This policy apparently brought down the annual growth rate for China from 1.5 percent to 1.4 percent. With a population of about 1,000 million, a reduction of the annual growth rate by .1 percent amounts to a reduction in annual births of one million.

In retrospect, both the strengths and the weaknesses of this kind of population projection become visible: on the one hand, it seems possible to come (over a period of twenty years into the future) remarkably close to actual figures as long as one need consider only the normal processes of social change in regard to the whole complex of social attitudes and traditions about procreation and family size. On the other hand, we cannot see what active government interference with these developments will take place in the future, and the extent to which such interference may be enforceable and thereby influence changes in the relevant figures.

References

Asimov, I. *Earth Our Crowded Space Ship.* Greenwich, CT: Fawcett, 1974.

Baade, F. *Der Wettlauf zum Jahre 2000—Paradies oder Selbstvernichtung* (The Race to the Year 2000—Paradise or Self-destruction). Oldenburg: Gerhard Stalling Verlag, 1960, 1967.

———. *Dynamische Weltwirtschaft* (Dynamic World Economy). Munich: Paul List Verlag, 1969.

Ballod, K. "Wie viele Menschen kann die Erde ernæhren?" (How Many People Can the Earth Feed?). *Schmollers Jahrbuch fuer Gesetzgebung, Verwaltung und Volkswirtschaft im Deutschen Reich*, *36* (1912): 81–102.

Brown, H. 1954. *The Challenge of Man's Future.* New York: 1954.

Buringh, P.; J.D.J. van Heemst; and B.J. Staring. "Computation of the Absolute Maximum Food Production of the World. A Contribution to the Research Project on 'Problems of Population Doubling and Food Supply' (MOIRA-Project)." Agricutural University Wageningen, The Netherlands, 1975.

Clark, C. "World Population." In *Nature, 181* (1957) (Cited in Reid and Lyon [eds.], *Population Crisis—An Interdisciplinary Perspective.* San Francisco: Scott, Foresman, 1972, 23.)

———. *Starvation or Plenty.* New York: Taplinger, 1970.

———. *The Myth of Overpopulation.* Melbourne: Advocate Press, 1973. [German ed.: *Der Mythos von der Ueberbevoelkerung.* Cologne: Adams Verlag, 1975.]

Ehrlich, P.R. *The Population Bomb.* New York: Ballantine, 1968.

Fischer, A. "Zur Tragfaehigkeit des Lebensraumes" (The Carrying Capacity of the Living Space). *Zeitschrift fuer Geopolitik, 2,* 1 (1925): 762–79; 2: 842–58.

Fircks, A. F. v. *Bevoelkerungslehre und Bevoelkerungspolitik* (Theory of Population and Population Policy). Leipzig: Hirschfeld, 1898.

Keyfitz, N. "Population Problems." In P. Cloud (ed). *Resources and Man.* San Francisco: W.H. Freeman (1969). [German ed.: *Wovon Können Wir Morgen Leben?* Frankfurt: Fischer (1973).]

Linnemann, H., et al. MOIRA Model of International Relations in Agriculture. North Holland, Amsterdam: 1979.

Malthus, R. *Essay on the Principle of Population*. London: 1798.

Marchetti, C. "On 10^{12}: A Check on Earth Carrying Capacity for Man." International Institute for Applied Systems Analysis, Wien-Laxenburg, paper No. RR–78–7, May 1978.

Meadows, D.H.; Meadows, D.L.; et al. *The Limits to Growth. A Report to the Club of Rome's Project on the Predicament of Mankind*. New York: Universe Books, 1972. [German ed.: *Die Grenzen des Wachstums*. Reinbek: Rowohlt, 1973.]

MOIRA. See Linnemann.

Neurath, O. "Das gegenwaertige Wachstum der Producktionskapazetaet der Welt" (The Current Increase of Production Capacity throughout the World). *Bericht des World Social Economic Congress*, Amsterdam, 1931, pp. 105–41.

Ohlin, G. *Population Control and Economic Development*. Paris: Development Centre of Organisation for Economic Cooperation and Development (OECD), 1967.

Osborn, F. *Unsere ausgepluenderte Erde*. Zurich: Pan Verlag, 1950. [American ed.: (1948): *Our Plundered Planet*.]

Penck, A. "Das Hauptproblem der Physischen Anthropogeographie" (The Principal Problem of Physical Anthropogeography). *Zeitschrift fuer Geopolitik, 2* (1925): 330–47.

Ravenstein, E.G. "Lands of the Globe Still Available for European Settlement." *Proceedings of the Royal Geographical Society, 13* (1891): 27–35.

Suessmilch, J.P. *Die Goettliche Ordnung in der Veraenderungen des Menschlichen Geschlechts, aus der Geburt, dem Tode und der Fortpflanzung desselben erwiesen* (The Divine Order in the Changes of Humankind, Proven by the Birth, the Death and the Procreation of Same). Berlin: 1741, 1775.

United Nations. *Demographic Trends in the World and Its Major Regions*. New York: United Nations, 1973.

————. "The Population Debate: Dimensions and Perspectives." *Papers of the World Population Conference, Bucharest 1974*. New York: United Nations, 1975.

Wagner, H. *Lehrbuch der Geographie*. Allgemeine Erdkunde. Hannover: Hahnsche Buchhandlung, 1923.

World Bank Staff Report. *Population Policies and Economic Development*. Baltimore: John Hopkins University Press, 1974.

Chapter 3

The "Limits to Growth" Debate: From Malthus to the "Club of Rome" and Back

The Club of Rome and Its Critics

Ever since its publication in 1972, a slender volume by Dennis Meadows and others, called *The Limits to Growth,* but better known as "The Club of Rome Report," has taken center stage in the debate concerning the "population explosion," especially that occurring in the Third World—whether this be a danger to the future of mankind, threatening to exhaust the food supply and necessary raw materials and to precipitate catastrophic air and water pollution as a consequence of overindustrialization, or whether this is all nothing to worry about because there is still enough of everything to last us for a very long time.

Ever since that time, the Club of Rome, under whose auspices Meadows et al.'s book was published, has come under attack; it is

Paper presented before the Columbia University Seminar on "Content and Methods of the Social Sciences," November 12, 1975, augmented with materials from a similar paper before the Queens College Social Science Division on May 10, 1976, on occasion of the author's thirtieth anniversary as a member of the Queens College faculty. Published as "Zur Debatte ueber die 'Grenzen des Wachstums'." *IBE Bulletin-Bildungsforschung-Entwicklungshilfe* (Vienna) *23–24* (December 1976), pp. 32–53.

often sinisterly referred to as "that mysterious Club of Rome," as if it were a kind of international conspiracy of some big-time capitalist-imperialist plutocrats who, warning of big catastrophes if the steady growth of population continues and if the production and consumption of irreplaceable materials does not come to a standstill within thirty to sixty years, intend to stop the development of the Third World and to maintain their own economic and in part also political hegemony over those regions of the world.

Let me briefly present a few facts about the Club of Rome, culled in part from its own publications and in part from those of its critics.

Its founder and chairman is Aurelio Peccei, former director general and chairman of the board of Olivetti, still a member of the board both of Olivetti and of Fiat, head of Italoconsult, a management consulting firm that is a subsidiary of Montecatini Edison. In 1958 Peccei published *At the Edge of the Abyss*, which dealt with general problems of population, pollution, development, and the like, and the mutually interlocking relations between them. In 1968, he obtained the sponsorship of the Giovanni Agnelli Foundation for a major research project in that direction. Agnelli himself, also an Italian industrialist, is a member of the board of Montecatini.

After a first meeting of some thirty economists, geneticists, planners, sociologists, political scientists, industrial managers, and others in the Academia dei Lincei in Rome in April 1968, Peccei and a few others decided to set up a more permanent organization for further discussion and to organize research in this general direction. From the place of its first meeting, the organization took its name—"The Club of Rome."

By 1974, the Club had about eighty members from some twenty different countries, mostly economists, educators, civil servants, humanists, and industrialists. In order to keep the organization from becoming too unwieldy, membership was limited to one hundred, but an effort was made to include representatives of widely different cultures and value systems. In Peccei's own words:

> Although its members do not participate in political decisions, and although the Club as a whole is not bound by any ideological, political or national commitments, it has access to decision makers and has assembled a great fundus of knowledge and information. In spite of great diversity in their backgrounds and their origins, the members of the

Club share one conviction: that the problems confronting mankind today are too complex and too interwoven to be overcome with traditional strategies and institutions. [Peccei and Siebker, 1974, p. 19]

The Club has a secretariat in Rome and additional offices in Geneva and Tokyo. For financial support it relies on the Batelle Memorial Institute and on Italian business companies.

In addition to Peccei, the directors of the Club were in 1973: Alexander King, scientific director of OECD (Organization for Economic Cooperation and Development) and former scientific secretary to the British Cabinet; Saburo Okita, head of the Japan Economic Research Center in Tokyo; Eduard Pestel, professor at Technische Hochschule in Hannover and a member of the Volkswagenstiftung in Germany, which funded both the first and the second report to the Club of Rome (Mesarovic and Pestel, 1974); Hugo Thieman, head of the Batelle Institute in Geneva; and Caroll Wilson, professor at the Massachusetts Institute of Technology.

Harvey Simmons, one of the authors of *Models of Doom*[1]—to date probably the soundest critique of *The Limits to Growth,* written by a group of scientists at the University of Sussex in England—points out some interesting similarities and dissimilarities between the Club of Rome and the "Technocrats" of the 1930s:

> Whereas Technocracy claimed that the economic problems of the United States could be solved through the use of scientific engineering techniques, and that political institutions alone stood in the way of maximizing the enormous amount of untapped energy in the USA, Forrester and his men [referring to Professor Jay Forrester of MIT, author of *World Dynamics,* the first of the World Models, and former teacher of Dennis Meadows—P.N.] take the completely opposite view, stressing that political solutions will be needed to prevent world disaster. [*Models of Doom*, p. 193]

Simmons points out as a similarity between the two groups:

> the link between scientists and a disinterested but prominent and influential elite. In the case of Technocracy this elite was composed of businessmen; in the case of the system dynamic group [Forrester, Meadows, and their coworkers—P.N.] . . . this elite is composed of men who are at the top of various knowledge institutions: research institutes, foundations, or management consulting firms. [*Models of Doom*, p. 193]

And now for the attack: In a German volume of articles pro and contra the Club of Rome called *Wachstum bis zur Katastrophe?* (Growth toward Catastrophe?), edited by H.E. Richter (which also includes contributions by Dennis Meadows), Henrich von Nussbaum, a well-known German author, states:

> The most harmless explanation for this aberration is this: that a group of somewhat belated natural scientists and well-meaning dilettantes got hold of the wrong topic. Enthused by goals that do them honor but that go beyond their capacities, they approached this world as a biocybernetic organism managed in a mechanical manner without any consciousness. Lacking any genuine method, they fell back upon biomechanical analogies similar to those in medieval cosmologies or in the cultural morphologies of the nineteenth century. [Richter, 1974, pp. 53–54]

And, a dozen pages later:

> The question after the identity and motivation of the 75 to 86 members . . . we can bypass at this point. These gentlemen presumably have their reasons for wanting to remain hidden. What could be discovered in this respect I have presented elsewhere. [p. 66][2]

And again further down:

> Only against this background could this Rome report become a sensation. Its factual information was launched and perceived through that screen of personal and technological nimbus of secrecy and revelation. It is the computer that gives the assertions of this study its flair of authority; the Club of Rome, an "invisible collegium" of unknown composition into which any degree of prominence, any authority can be interpreted, endows it with that notion of worldwideness and superiority that cannot be outdone.
>
> I may be forgiven the heresy, it certainly is not meant as the ultimate weapon for defaming a cause against which nothing else could be presented: the structure of consciousness to which the publicity of the Club of Rome addresses itself and that helped its report to an effectiveness unheard of up to now for surveys of this kind is either *pre-* or *post-fascist*. It was not the argumentation, it was the mumbo-jumbo that created all that excitement, that well-apportioned mixture of unquestionable authority and impenetrable anonymity. [p. 91, emphasis added]

After this, von Nussbaum hammers at the fact that, even after eighteen months of worldwide debate, the data volume with the computer programs has not yet been published, obviously in order to continue the secrecy. In retrospect, this sounds rather funny, because that volume did indeed appear under the title *Dynamics of Growth in a Finite World* only a few months later. Thus, while von Nussbaum was writing his accusation, the authors and their secretaries must already have been sweating over the galleys for this volume of 637 pages. In addition, *The Limits to Growth* already carried in the back an announcement that well over a dozen papers with the technical details, written by the original *Limits to Growth* team, could be ordered directly from the publisher and appeared soon thereafter as *Toward Global Equilibrium: Collected Papers for* The Limits to Growth (from Wright-Allen Press in Cambridge, MA.)

Further, the authors of the *Models of Doom,* the University of Sussex group, report that while they were preparing their critical analysis, the *Limits to Growth* team provided them, even before *The Limits to Growth* was published, with all the computer programs so that the Sussex group could carry through their own computations with varying numerical assumptions corresponding to their own criticism.[3] The book of the Sussex group originally appeared in England under the title *Thinking about the Future.* When it appeared in America soon thereafter under the title *Models of Doom,* it carried as an appendix an eighteen-page paper by Meadows, "Response to Sussex."

The Debated Books

Meadows et al., *The Limits to Growth*
Mesarovic and Pestel, *Mankind at the Turning Point*
Forrester, *World Dynamics*

When the Club of Rome decided in 1968 to sponsor some research concerning the "predicament of mankind," meaning the potential threat of catastrophe from population explosion, resources depletion, and general pollution, the question arose: What might be the best method for the analysis of the relations between and the probable future development of the large number of interlocking and mutually influential variables involved in these problems? Already well-established methods such as multiple correlation and regression of time series or general input–output analysis did not seem adequate for the purpose.

At that point, Caroll Wilson, one of the directors of the Club of Rome, himself a professor at MIT, suggested the method of "systems dynamics" developed by Jay Forrester, his colleague at MIT, for the analysis of complex problems in industrial and city planning. "Systems dynamics" itself was an outgrowth of "Cybernetics" which had been developed by Norbert Wiener, also at MIT, during the 1940s, originally starting with the analysis of a certain medical problem in connection with Parkinson's disease. Wiener's concern at that time was to examine the adequacy of certain theoretical notions about the disease and the involvement of certain malfunctioning of the brain and/or the nervous system, through translating these notions into a computer model and comparing the outcome in the form of certain mathematical curves with actual observations.

This basic idea of Wiener's "Cybernetics"—of translating a rather complex process involving a large number of mutually influential variables into a computer model—Forrester developed into his "Systems analysis" for the study of quite different kinds of problems: those of industrial and city planning. After Forrester presented his method of analysis at the Club's June 1970 meeting in Geneva, a delegation of the Club spent ten days with Forrester and his staff at MIT. The upshot was twofold: first, Forrester worked out a set of equations and computer programs for a preliminary study of his own that resulted in the book *World Dynamics*, which he described in the preface as "a dynamic model of world scope, a model which interrelates population, capital investment, geographical space, natural resources, pollution, and food supply" (Forrester, 1971).

Although written without any mathematics, *World Dynamics* was nevertheless not written in a language for a wider public but essentially in one for experts in the field and for those accustomed to complex problems presented in computer language. Thus, while its novel approach certainly created a stir among the experts, it might easily have disappeared from the scene again, as have many other pioneering works before it.

The second consequence was that an international team of experts was assembled at MIT, headed by Dennis Meadows, a former student of Forrester, to work out a more comprehensive model involving many more factors and the mutually interlocking relations between them.

This larger study was funded with a $250,000 grant from the Volkswagen Foundation. Its first published report became *The Limits to Growth* (1972), followed within the next three years by a whole series of books and papers with all the necessary data and computer programs, the "keeping secret" of which had served von Nussbaum as so much proof of a deliberate intention to mystify the public.

Although based on a much larger model of a total of 121 factors or variables in five major subsystems—resources, population, pollution, capital investment, and agriculture (compared with only 43 individually numbered factors within the same five subsystems in Forrester's book)—*The Limits to Growth* was written in nontechnical language that any educated layperson could read. The authors tried to reach as wide a public as possible with their general warning of an imminent collapse of the life-supporting system on earth, unless mankind soon changed its ways of rapid growth of population, rapid depletion of resources, and rapid pollution of the environment.

The book spread like wildfire. Within the first year, it was translated into twenty-five languages and became a subject of debate in literally hundreds and hundreds of articles in newspapers, magazines, and learned journals and in books written about it by experts, journalists, and others the world over.

In essence, at least to my reading, *The Limits to Growth* was *World Dynamics* all over again—although with many more variables and factors included. Indeed, Forrester himself indicates as much in the preface to *World Dynamics*, when he refers to the then already progressing work of Meadows.

Both models begin with the development (and interlocking) of these 121 or 43 factors, respectively, during the preceding seventy years (1900–1970) and then project this under varying assumptions into the future.

They both do it on a global basis, that is, without reference to special regional problems, including problems of transportation of goods from region to region, and inequalities of production and productivity or regional consumption patterns, and particularly without reference to differences between social and political systems. This led to a good deal of criticism by those who considered all of these differences as essential parts of the discussion. Some of this, however, was later taken up by Mesarovic and Pestel in the so-called Second Club of Rome Report, *Mankind at the Turning Point* (1974).

Both books project the further development of those respective 121 or 43 mutually interlocking variables into the future under varying assumptions concerning rates of growth and rates of consumption under varying assumptions of available supplies. Since we obviously cannot know how much more iron, copper, zinc, and other resources, as well as how much more oil the earth may still hold and that may yet be discovered, *The Limits to Growth*, for example, makes its computations under two separate computational assumptions: that mankind has at its disposal five times, and that mankind has at its disposal ten times as much of all these minerals as the total by 1970 of all known (or with reasonable assuredness estimated) deposits on earth, based on the then current estimates of the U.S. Bureau of Mines. Few points have aroused as much criticism as these assumptions, as discussed below.

The Limits to Growth then computes the consumption of these supplies on the basis of two alternative assumptions: once on the assumption that the annual rate of consumption per capita (worldwide) remains the same as in 1970 (so that increasing consumption comes only from the increase in world population—about 2 percent per year); and a second time on the assumption that per-capita consumption is growing as well, at the rate at which it is currently growing—about 1.5 percent per year. (Under this latter assumption, total consumption rises each year by 2.0 + 1.5 = 3.5 percent per year).

Both books come more or less to the same devastating conclusion: if mankind keeps on growing at the current rate of 2 percent, and keeps increasing its per-capita consumption of irreplaceable goods at the current rate of 1.5 percent per year, then the assumed total available supplies (of, in the one computation, five times, in the other ten times as much as all known deposits worldwide in 1970), a general breakdown of the system would have to be expected, according to the one assumption within about 100 years, and according to the other assumption within about 120 years. (The continuous overheating of the atmosphere as a consequence of the continuously increasing energy consumption is not yet considered in these computations.)

Let me emphasize, because this point has been misunderstood again and again in all the discussions that I have ever seen: this is *not a prediction* that the authors are making of things to come, *but a warning of what would happen if* mankind were to continue to grow its own numbers and its per-capita consumption at the rate at which they are growing now and have been growing for the last few decades.

The authors add that these dire consequences *could be avoided*— that is, no catastrophe were to be expected, *if* both the growth of population and the increase in per-capita consumption of irreplaceable resources were to be slowed down systematically and brought to a virtual standstill within thirty to sixty years. This, of course, takes into consideration that both population growth and increasing rates of per-capita consumption could not be brought to a halt all at once, either by political or by social action—but implies hope that this could indeed be accomplished within thirty to sixty years. The world's population, especially in the Third World, is bound yet to grow for several decades because of changes in the age structure in recent decades, when as a consequence of improved health and living standards, infant and child mortality have decreased considerably. Thus, at present, larger cohorts than ever before are coming into the procreative age every year.

Both Forrester in *World Dynamics* and Meadows and his team in *The Limits to Growth* refrain from offering any recommendations as to how to accomplish this slowing down and eventual halting of population growth and increase in per-capita consumption of irreplaceable resources and further industrialization. They even refrain from discussing the social or political changes that might follow from this. Rather, they limit themselves to their warnings of threatening catastrophes and leave it to whatever responsible decision makers there are the world over to decide on what measures need to be taken and how they are to be effectuated. In particular, they refrain from such ethical questions as who is to be allowed to have children and who is not, and who is to produce and to sell and who is to receive what materials and what products. Theirs is meant as a strictly nonpolitical computation about total resources available and total numbers of human beings who will need them—even though the implications must of course be political in nature. But those are for the political decision makers to consider.

Meadows and his team do, however, make a few statements in the vain hope that they will not be misunderstood as advocating that the present dramatic differences between "haves" and "have-nots"—that is, between industrialized and developing countries—should become permanent. They point out that even within this thirty- to sixty-year deceleration and halting of population growth and industrialization, there is ample room for the industrialized countries to help the developing ones so that the latter can still attain about half of the standard of living of the former within a few decades.

Although, realistically speaking, in view of the present situation of most Third World countries, this would certainly sound like a far-far-out utopia, it led nevertheless to an outcry from critics in those countries: They won't ever let us have more than half of what they themselves are having—down with the imperialists!

It is almost pathetic to read the outburst of a member of the audience during a 1973 panel discussion in Germany, on the occasion of *The Limits to Growth* receiving the "Peace Prize of the German Booktrade" (Friedenspreis des Deutschen Buchhandels), trying to give the whole matter a political turn:

> Or is this an apocalypse concerning the condition of imperialism. . . . is this study a call to peace, such as people want, or is it a call to war? . . . those who don't sit in this room, those who get the bombs thrown at their heads [Note: this refers to the then still ongoing war in Vietnam— P.N.] as is happening in Indochina, those who are supposedly concerned by it and who will afterwards have to suffer it all, they are not addressed. . . .
>
> . . . this book that receives the Peace Prize suggests to the capitalist nations the conclusions that it is not so much the norms of economic growth that are touched by it, as that the problem of limits to raw materials is one of distribution: therefore, the book is an invitation to exploitation and to war. [Richter, 1974, p. 32]

Another participant commented that

> what must be slowed down is not the growth of population but the principle that is at work here, i.e., the profit principle: that capital is being exported to India on the basis that there is a cheap labor force there. [Richter, 1974, pp. 37–38]

A third discussant added that most of the long-range programs at MIT are financed by the Pentagon, which only goes to show that they are already preparing for the day when they can no longer exploit the Third World, once these nations have followed the example of Vietnam and sent the Americans packing with all their supposedly friendly development aid, which really seems to be a sign that imperialism is at long last coming to an end (Richter, 1974, pp. 90–91).

In response, Meadows, who participated in the same discussion, could not refrain from shooting back: "when *my* group works toward cutting down the demands of the rich countries upon the raw materials of the poor, then this is an indication of the last gasp of capitalism and its stupid games. But when *you yourself* are expressing the same wish, then this is the struggle against imperialism and a proof of your humanitarian motives." (Richter, 1974, p. 91)

And so it goes.

In addition to criticizing the model makers for daring to include as a matter of computational practicality the assumption that mankind has at its disposal in one computation five and in the other computation ten times as much irreplaceable resources as were known or reasonably estimated to exist in 1970, the critics most frequently took the model makers to task for treating mankind and its resources as one single global unit, thereby neglecting all regional differences in population, resources, and political and social management of these resources, among other factors. The most often-cited example was China, which had been able to conquer hunger and was about to improve its general standard of living with large-scale industrialization. India, on the other hand, was apparently unable to do so, in spite of its huge Community Development program and its vaunted "Green Revolution."

The natural response to this could be that, should Forrester's and Meadows's computations really be correct, as far as their total worldwide figures are concerned, then there is nothing to gain from pointing out that some regions are certainly better off than others and might be able to last a bit longer than less-favored ones. The question under discussion must obviously be whether the threat of exhaustion of available resources is realistic at all—not whether the catastrophe will befall all regions of the globe at exactly the same moment.

At any rate, the second report, *Mankind at the Turning Point* (Mesarovic and Pestel, 1974), took account of a good deal of regional differences by dividing the world—or, rather, their computations about it—into ten major regions: North America, Western Europe, Japan, Australia plus South Africa, Eastern Europe and the Soviet Union, Latin America, North Africa and the Middle East, Tropical Africa, South Asia, and China. In this division, they paid special attention to differences in internal development, import and export among regions, different population densities, different densities of industries, and of raw materials, and the like.

For some overall comparisons they considered differences among three superregions: the developed world, the socialist world, and the developing world. In addition, *Mankind at the Turning Point* considered a much larger number of variables and the mutual relationships among them than did *The Limits to Growth.*

With its attention to some human factors and a less grating language for pronouncing its nevertheless quite dire conclusions, the second report soon earned itself a reputation as more humane and for backing away from the merciless impending-doom posture of the first report. Actually, of course, the main difference is only a matter of time horizon: Forrester and Meadows let their model run until its curves showed a general breakdown of the system and then simply read off the time that it took until that moment: some 100 to 120 years. Mesarovic and Pestel only asked: What would the situation be like after fifty years? Of course, neither they nor Forrester and Meadows before them expected a complete breakdown within fifty years.

Otherwise, the conclusions of the second report are, if anything, even more grim than those of Forrester and Meadows. For example, they point out that within the last two decades (i.e., ca. 1950–70), the United States has changed from a net exporter to a net importer of important raw materials, and then raise the specter of an interregional transportation problem of enormous magnitude: as the population of South Asia grows at its current 2 percent per year (which would mean doubling in thirty-five and quadrupling in seventy years), a huge deficit of food grains must develop, even if all arable land is utilized with the most advanced agricultural methods (including large-scale irrigation and use of artificial fertilizer, which in turn requires enormous amounts of machinery and of oil).

The region already imports large amounts of food grains, especially in times of "weak monsoons." Now the only major region that still has large areas of unused arable land and is a major producer of exportable grain is North America (as well as some parts of Australia). Disregarding for the moment such often-discussed possibilities as the conversion of the huge forests in the Amazon basin and, with the help of irrigation, large parts of the Sahara into arable land, Mesarovic and Pestel raise the following question: Assuming that North America could and would produce for export the huge amounts of grain necessary to cover the expected grain deficit in South Asia (and disregarding for the moment all problems of payment and similar concerns), could these huge amounts of grain be transported from where they are grown to where they are needed? Mesarovic and Pestel's devastating answer (supported by the necessary computations) is "No." The total tonnage required would by far overtax the intra-American transportation system. There would not even be enough transportation available to ship the grain from the Midwest, where it grows, to the harbors—not to mention the ships that would be necessary to transport it across the ocean or the unloading and transport facilities that would be needed within the various countries to bring the grain from their harbors to where it will be needed.[4]

They go through the same types of problems concerning oil and various other minerals and for various regions, including the cost of investment and the materials needed for producing all of these materials, and finally address the question of energy, especially atomic and solar energy.

Let us not forget pollution, to which Mesarovic and Pestel pay little attention, although this constitutes one of the major subsystems with Forrester and with Meadows, who deal also with the general pollution caused by the steady increase in industrialization and its attendant well-known chain of destruction: pollution destroys the oxygen in the water, which kills the plankton on which the fish feed, which man in turn used for food, and so on.

One may classify in a rough and ready manner, as I have done elsewhere (Neurath, 1975, p. 209), the discussants of problems of population increase and resources depletion as "optimists" and "pessimists." The optimists see no reason for serious worries since mankind so far has always been able and always will be able to overcome its difficulties as they arise—how else could we still be here? The pessimists, on the other hand, whether or not they compute a fixed time limit for impending doom, assume that the race between man and his food supply and his ability to produce materials cannot go on much longer before it will be lost.

Within this rough classification, the authors of all three books discussed here—Forrester, Meadows et al., and Mesarovic and Pestel—all belong in the category of pessimists. The fact that Meadows et al. make their computations—that is, let their model run—until they indicate a breakdown of the life-supporting system, while Mesarovic and Pestel let theirs run only over a period of fifty years, and thus do not include a time limit for the depletion of resources, may make readers see the latter as less gloomy; certainly many journalists have seen them as such. But the difference is only a psychological one for the reader, who finds talk of a complete breakdown here and only talk of expected difficulties there. Had Mesarovic and Pestel run their model over an additional fifty or one hundred years into the future, they would undoubtedly have come to the same kind of a breakdown, whether or not it would be indicated after the same "100 to 120" years the other models predicted, or perhaps a little later. "A little later" could in this case be only a question of another few decades, certainly not enough to change the essential point of the discussion: that continued rapid population increase and continued increase in per-capita consumption of irreplaceable natural resources must lead to a breakdown of the life-supporting system within a rather limited span of time that is not measured in millennia or even in centuries, but only in so many decades—whether ten or twelve decades, as in the Meadows model, or a few decades more.

Basically, these authors all agree in their fundamental outlook and give essentially the same warning: danger is afoot unless mankind cuts down, and cuts down quite drastically, on the rapid increase of its own numbers, on the rapid increase in the per-capita consumption of irreplaceable natural resources, and on the worldwide pollution in the wake of its rapid industrialization.

Whether or not one agrees with their computations, or their numerical and other assumptions, they certainly have made an important contribution through giving new and massive impetus to the general discussion of certain basic topics. Even if one considers their warning of impending doom somewhat exaggerated, as most critics do, there is no denying that much more serious concern about the issues so raised is in place than was the case before *The Limits to Growth* set in action this worldwide discussion.

The Old Malthusian Problem in a Newer Form

The main argument against the "doomsters" seems fairly unbeatable: for hundreds and hundreds of years mankind has grown in numbers from about 550 million in 1650 to 4,000 million today—and if mankind has been able to grow all this time, then its food supply must have grown with it as well, or else how could we all be here? And, historically speaking, when mankind could no longer live on its method of feeding itself at a given point of its development, it invented a new method: when hunting and gathering of berries no longer sufficed, man invented the tilling of the land and the growing of animals, the rotating of plants and fertilizing them with cow dung. When his own strength was no longer sufficient to do all the tilling, he began training animals to pull his plow; when that no longer sufficed, he learned to drive his plow with oil and gasoline, and eventually to seed huge plains from flying airplanes and to harvest what grows with huge harvester combines. And so on. And so on.

While there can be no denying that eventually there must be some end to it, because a limited earth can in principle hold only a limited number of people, the end is certainly not yet around the corner or anywhere near in sight. There is still plenty of time and space for making new inventions to last us yet a long, long time.

Who would have thought as recently as 200, 150, or even 100 years ago that, with massive irrigation and artificial fertilizer, with oil and electricity as sources of energy, semiarid lands that had seemed forever to be barren could be made arable?

Thus goes the conclusion of the optimists: there is absolutely no reason to expect that the world will come to an end within 100 to 120 years; the whole prediction or computation is just a figment of the imagination of a few computer-crazy professors who like to play games with exponential equations, or with patient computers that can spit out reams of doomsday computations in no time flat if only the professors have first programmed such into them.

Not to speak of the sinister political implication, that all of this scare talk of the need to stop further industrial growth in order to forestall great dangers is only intended to perpetuate the huge gap between the "haves" and the "have-nots" in this world.

The model makers try in vain to explain that theirs is *not a prediction* of the end of mankind within the next 100 or 120 years, but *only a warning* of things that are bound to happen unless we take measures to prevent them.

This argument back and forth between the "doomsters" and their opponents has been reported in the previous section. Now let me come to a point that has not yet come up, and is not discussed in the books themselves either, although implicitly it is of course there: that in times way back in the historic and even more so in the prehistoric past, mankind grew in numbers so slowly that generally each generation found essentially the same relation between population numbers and food supply as the generation or generations before it; changes took place only slowly and almost imperceptibly. For long periods in the past, births and deaths must have been more or less in balance, even if there were occasional periods of large-scale famine and starvation, and then again periods of better supplies and again a slightly faster growth in numbers. Thus, if new inventions were made for increasing the food supply (and perhaps the supply of other materials as well), they could always help toward alleviating existing problems and shortages or even toward improving general living conditions. If one were to extend the Mesarovic and Pestel model, say, for another 40 or 100 years beyond those 50 years they computed, of necessity the same breakdown would occur, regardless of whether it would happen in exactly the same 100 to 120 years as in the Meadows model or perhaps a little later.

Now let me start with a few figures to illustrate the point. I shall not go back so far as the transition, say, from mere food gathering to tilling of the soil but only a few centuries. Although the earlier figures to be used must of course only be estimates, I shall start with the 550 million in 1650, which Carr-Saunders estimated in his classic, *World Population* (1936, p. 30)[5]—a figure that has not come under too much debate by later demographers with access to better means of estimation.

By 1850, the world's population had about doubled, from 550 million to about 1,200 million, at an annual rate of growth of about 3 per 1,000 or 0.3 percent at the beginning and about 5 per 1,000 or 0.5 percent toward the end of that 200-year period. That means a fairly stable relation between population numbers and food supply with a slow growth of both from one generation to the next, of about 10 percent around the year 1650 and about 17 percent toward 1850. At least at the beginning of that 200-year period there was still enough untilled arable land that, if one generation needed 10 percent to 17 percent more food, it could take that much additional land to the plow. If, meanwhile, improvements in agriculture could increase the yield per ha, all the better: less new land would be needed or more food could be grown, and thus life could be made a bit easier.

After 1850 the pace quickened: it took only 100 years more (instead of 200) to double the world population from 1,200 to about 2,500 million. Annual growth rates increased from about 5 per 1,000 in 1850 to 9 per 1,000 in 1950, or to about 30 percent within one generation. At that rate, additional land could no longer be put to the plow to keep pace with population growth. Man had to begin to make haste with that vaunted ingenuity that in the past always had enabled him to make the inventions needed to produce the necessary ever-increasing amounts of food to keep feeding his ever-increasing numbers. Still, as far as the global relation between world population and food supply was concerned, 1950 did not look all that different from, say, 1920. New inventions or the spread of established inventions to lands where they had not yet been applied, especially to countries of the Third World, still make up more or less for the growing numbers.

Then the real population explosion began: within only twenty-five years, from 1950 to 1975, the world's population grew by 60 percent, from 2,500 million to 4,000 million, at a current rate of 2 percent per year—that is, more than twice as fast as only twenty-five years ago. If this rate of increase were to continue for some time, it would mean a doubling of the world population within thirty-five years, to a level of about 8,000 million by the year 2010.

It appears patently impossible to produce the huge quantities of food needed for a population growing that fast from generation to generation by putting that much additional land to the plow. Even where there may still be huge semiarid or even arid tracts of land that could be made fertile through appropriate irrigation and other technology, this patently cannot be done in sufficient quantities fast enough to keep up with the growing numbers of people.

This means that by now mankind has become almost completely dependent on its ability to invent and to spread ever new methods of food production, whether they are altogether new or represent improvements of existing methods, and to do so from generation to generation in order to fend off mass starvation. It really does not matter whether the necessity for improvements and the danger of mass starvation or other catastrophe is indicated with a few simple figures that everybody can grasp at once or with the help of complex computer models comprehensible only to the experts—the danger simply is there.

Next comes the consideration that even more food and everything else is needed to raise the abysmally low standard of living of large masses of humanity, even if only by relatively small increments. Just to make sure that there is no misunderstanding, "raising the standard of living" generally means quite different things in different parts of the world. Where to many an American this may mean such things as two cars instead of one, two television sets in the home, more and better plumbing, more and better gadgets, more vacation travel, and many other things that can make life more pleasant, to many people in the poorer parts of the Third World, this may mean going hungry a little less often, having two pieces of loincloth instead of one, two storm lamps or two bicycles in a village where before there was only one, and so on through the simplest necessities of life. Or, in agriculture, it might mean iron-tipped plows where there were only wooden ones; "eight-inch plows" (which can cut an eight-inch furrow) where there were only four-inch plows before (which in turn requires oxen strong enough to pull an eight-inch plow and enough fodder to feed this stronger oxen, instead of the much smaller and weaker creature needed before, which needed less fodder); two small water pumps in a village where there was only one, or perhaps none, so that women had to carry water on their head for miles from a faraway pond or river. And so on and so forth.

To all of this we must add the need for enough energy to keep all the industries going that produce the machinery that keep these industries going, and to get the necessary materials out of the ground; to produce and to maintain the necessary means of transportation, and all the innovations necessary for the necessary recycling of the ever-growing quantities of used materials both in order to prevent them from polluting the whole sphere of life and in order to help slow down the depletion of ever scarcer, nonreplaceable raw materials.

It is an old and much beloved parlor game to twit the demographer's tail by extending his projections a little further into the future, demonstrating what astronomical figures will be reached within a relatively short time and then using that as a "proof" of the impossibility of really making such computations or to demonstrate that such calculations are nothing but the idle play and nonsense with which demographers, model makers, and similar people like to amuse themselves or scare other people.

We can all play this game ourselves with great mathematical accuracy by looking up in a compound interest table what happens to a capital X if it is invested at a given annual interest rate Y in Z years. If we then assume some maximum number of people that can live on a square mile, it is easy enough to compute the maximum number of people that can live on this earth—and how fast that number would be reached if mankind were to continue its growth at the present rate of 2 percent per year. The limit would be reached soon enough.

The game can be refined by setting aside certain amounts of land for the growing of food, adding some assumptions about the expected increase in the amount of yield per acre.

Still, the game must reach its limit within a length of time not too outlandishly beyond the horizon. If the critic then gets obstreperous by pointing out that people can live in much higher densities than was assumed in the computations—just have a look at how densely they manage to live in Hong Kong or Calcutta—well, one can always extend the computations by a generation or two or even three until the whole world is computed to be a single Hong Kong or Calcutta—then what? If the critic points out that four people can live where we assumed that only two could live, or perhaps even eight where we assumed two, then at the present rate of growth, with a population doubling time of thirty-five years, the limit will be reached thirty-five or perhaps seventy years later— does the critic really think that this shows there is no danger at all?

The game is old. Malthus played it, without inserting the figures, when he wrote in the first edition of his *Essay*, in 1798:

> Through the animal and vegetable kingdom, nature has scattered the seeds of life abroad with the most profuse and liberal hand. She has been comparatively sparing in the room and the nourishment necessary to rear them. The germs of existence contained in this spot of earth, with ample food and ample room to expand in, would fill millions of worlds in the course of a few thousand years. [Malthus, 1959, p. 9]

In his preface to the Ann Arbor reprint (1959), of Malthus, Kenneth Boulding provides some figures:

> The crucial principle is that there must be some limit to the number of mankind, and that growth of population, at no matter how slow a rate, must eventually bring the number to this limit. Even more dramatic illustrations of the power of growth at a constant rate can be devised than Malthus imagined.
>
> Thus, if the present world population of 2,500,000,000 people were to continue to grow at about its present rate of 2 percent per annum, in only 765 years the whole surface of the earth (land and water) would be covered with a solid mass of people, and in a mere 8,000 years the whole known astronomical universe, two thousand light years in radius, would be solid with humanity.
>
> Long before this time it is not unreasonable to postulate limits of the growth of population which will bring it to an equilibrium at a zero rate of growth. [p. vi]

Let us cite just one more player in this game: L.D. Stamp (1953) provides a carefully computed table where everybody can look up exactly how much humanity there would be at the growth rates of 0.25 percent, 0.50 percent, 0.75 percent, 1.0 percent, 1.15 percent, and 1.50 percent by the years 1960, 1975, 2000, 2500, 3000, 5000, and finally he adds as his punch line that the last figure at the growth rate of 1.5 percent, by the year 5000 would be $1{,}237 \times 1020 =$ 123,700,000,000,000,000,000,000 (Stamp, 1953, p. 29).

The tragedy is that the growth rate of 1.5 percent for 1950 was already well overtaken when Stamp's book was published in 1953, at which point it was already 2.0 percent; and what he computed as his highest estimate for 1975—namely, 3,410 million—is already way behind us (as of November 1975), with about 4,000 million already alive. What Stamp computed as his very biggest assumption for the year 2000—namely, 4,947 million—is already some 1,500 to 1,700 million less than the current estimate of the Population Division of the United Nations for the year 2000, which is 6,500 to 6,700 million.

What distinguishes the builders of the world models—Forrester, Meadows, and Mesarovic and Pestel—from the older players of this parlor game is that instead of considering only one limit—namely, humanity standing on the earth tightly packed side by side—they consider a few other limits at the same time: so much land, so much food capacity on that land, so much food required per person, so much water and air per person, so much need of various minerals all through the alphabet from aluminum, chromium, coal, cobalt, and copper, through silver, tin, tungsten, and zinc. They therefore come to their computed limit earlier than those players who measure the limit only in terms of how much standing room humanity would need if standing tightly packed, without setting aside sufficient land on which to grow the food so that they will have enough to eat in order to be able to keep on standing there, plus adding some computations for the raw materials and the machinery for producing some overhead cover should rain or snow or hail come down on them while standing there waiting for their food. Not to speak of the problem of transportation to get the food from where it may be growing to where they may be standing and waiting for it. A problem, to which at least Mesarovic and Pestel in *Mankind at the Turning Point* have addressed themselves.

Let me shorten the game somewhat by comparing its older version—the one that dealt only with space and food—with the newer version, just to show that they are not all that different from each other. I must preface this comparison, however, with a quote from Meadows to show that the newer players are not claiming any unwarranted priority for themselves but acknowledging what connects them with the older ones, especially with Malthus:

> There are physical limits to population and capital growth. As we have already indicated, the world models are built upon the assumption that the earth is finite, and that some change in current exponential growth processes will thus be necessary to accommodate man's physical presence and activities to the earth's limits. The purpose of the models is to investigate what kinds of changes might and should occur. Professor Freeman [in *Models of Doom*—P.N.] is correct in categorizing the models as "Malthus in, Malthus out." . . . our own impressions suggest that the world is finite in several important ways. . . . *We are indeed Malthusians* at least in a broad total-systems sense. [*Models of Doom*, 1973, p. 227; emphasis added]

We have now, in 1975, about 4 billion people on this earth. If they continue to increase at the current 2 percent per year, which would mean doubling their number every thirty-five years, this adds up to 8,000 million after thirty-five years, 16,000 million after seventy years, and 32,000 million, or 32 billion, after 105 years, and about 43 billion after 120 years. Another ten years, or 130 years altogether, would bring this to 52 billion.

Now let us compare these figures, reached by simple exponential expansion by 2 percent each year, with actual computations and estimates made by various authors in two steps: first, we compare them with some estimates of the earth's capacity to feed humanity, and we then compare them with the limits that are implicit in the Forrester and Meadows models, particularly in *The Limits to Growth*.

Fritz Baade, director of the Institut fuer Weltwirtschaft in Kiel, comes to the following estimates and conclusions (Baade, 1967): The total of arable land on this earth may be estimated at about 4 billion ha, the total of grassland at about 2 billion ha. The total yield per ha of arable land may be estimated, as a worldwide average, at some three to four tons of grain or its equivalent, and that for grassland at about 1.5 tons of grain equivalent per ha. That adds up to a total of some 15 to 19 billion tons of annual yield of grain or grain equivalent. These averages take into account differences in agricultural technology, and in climate, as well as noting that some areas will yield double or triple harvests.

At the time of Baade's writing (the mid-1960s), the total amounts of grain and grain equivalent available to India came in an ordinary year (in other words, there were no especially low harvests in the wake of weak monsoons, as happens from time to time), and Baade took into account what was needed for seed grain as well as ordinary losses—to about one-quarter ton per capita per year. That, of course, was an average covering a wide range of living conditions from millions of people on a near-starvation diet to a small elite living in luxury. For Germany, that same kind of overall average came to about one-half ton per capita per year, and for the United States it was about four-fifths ton per capita per year. In Germany and especially in the United States, this included large quantities of grain or grain equivalent used for animal feed, as well as for the production of beverages—factors that played but a minor role in India.

Taking the figure for Germany as a kind of guideline, Baade (1967, p. 55) states:

> [I]t may be considered a well founded estimate to assume that with one ton of grain equivalent, produced on arable or grass land, and assuming that the need for the protein food will be complemented with what the oceans will give, two people can be fed with one ton of grain equivalent (per year).
>
> This attempt at an estimate thus leads to the result that with a total world production of about 15 billion tons of grain equivalent (per year), about 30 billion people, and with a production of 19 billion tons about 38 billion people can be fed upon this earth.[6]

Baade emphasizes that this, of course, was not a prediction of how many people there ever will be, but merely an attempt to assess the total number of people that the earth could feed. This was all based on the current agricultural technology as it was being used in various parts of the world. And, falling in my broad classification among the optimists, he assumes, as do most of the other optimists, that as time goes on, new developments in agricultural technology and new ways of making land arable will further extend the total number of people that the earth can feed.

To which we might add: whether Baade's or anybody else's figures are exactly accurate, or whether on closer scrutiny they might be adjusted a bit upward or downward, is not relevant for our discussion, as long as there are no obvious reasons to doubt the overall magnitude. Whether one reckons with four or with five tons of grain or its equivalent per ha of arable land or perhaps with three instead of with only two people to be fed on one ton of grain or its equivalent per year will in the end only increase the total number that the earth could feed by, say, about 50 percent, or at a maximum by 100 percent. Assuming, as we have done throughout this discussion, a 2 percent annual increase of the world's population, this would only mean a twenty-five- or thirty-five-year difference before we reach the limit of people the earth can feed.

All other computations I have ever seen that try to estimate how many people the earth could feed are of a similar order of magnitude. For example, the Population Division of the United Nations estimated at its 1974 Population Conference in Bucharest that the earth could feed about 38 to 48 billion people. The largest estimate I have seen so far came to 50 billion. This does not mean that there might not be other, somewhat higher estimates, but the order of magnitude seems to stay within this range of some 30 to 50, possibly perhaps up to 55 or 60 billion.

Let us recall that Meadows et al. came to the conclusion in *The Limits to Growth* that if mankind were to go on increasing its numbers at the current rate of 2 percent per year, and its consumption per capita of irreplaceable materials at the current rate of 1.5 percent per year, this would lead to a general catastrophe within 100 to 120 years—100 years if mankind has five times, and 120 years if it has ten times as much irreplaceable materials at its disposal as known or as reasonably assumed deposits the world over in 1970. This then coincides fairly well with the estimates, based solely on the earth's capacity to feed mankind: Baade's limit of 30 to 38 billion would be reached (again, assuming the current rate of growth of 2 percent per year) within 98 to 115 years; the limit estimated by the Population Division of the United Nations of 35 billion would be reached in about 110 years, and the largest estimates I have seen so far, of 50 billion, would be reached in about 128 years.

To repeat once more: these latter computations all are based only on the capacity of the earth to feed mankind, with no consideration of any other problems and questions after raw materials industrialization and pollution. In view of this, it makes but a limited amount of sense to pick apart every single numerical assumption in the world models, many of which are certainly debatable, and then to believe that one could thereby prove that the overall result and warning of the model makers could be dispelled as senseless and superfluous scare-mongering.

Now let me round out the picture by restating the one point to which neither Malthus nor the "food only" computers nor the model makers paid any special attention: man's capacity to keep on making all the many inventions that will be necessary to increase food production and the production of all the minerals, machinery, and other things necessary actually to bring new land to the plow, to make new arid lands fertile, to increase the yields per acre, and so on.

I am not in a position to offer you any figures just now, but I do recall seeing some such figures in *Science* or elsewhere, indicating that the total number of inventions also tends to increase at an exponential rate, as might be expected on the simple assumption that an exponentially increasing mankind will bring forth an exponentially increasing number of inventors, and with them also an increasing number of inventions.

I have no quarrel with those who expect that some day we shall be able to irrigate the Sahara desert and farm the Amazon basin or the Congo basin (except to ask what effect cutting down the rain forests may have on man's ability to survive on this earth), or that we shall be able some day to dig minerals out of the earth through shafts three and four times as deep as the deepest today. But I do have some quarrel, or at least some serious questions, with those who take it for granted that we shall be able to accomplish all of this within the short time left, some 100 to 120 or may 130 or so years, while mankind grows at current rates from its present size of 4 billion to some 30 to 50 billion—that is, unless we heed the warning of the model makers and others, that mankind simply cannot keep up for long its current 2 percent per year rate of growth, and its current ever-growing rate of consumption of irreplaceable materials. My quarrel is with those who take all of this for granted on no better basis than their own optimism and the fact that so far mankind has indeed managed—neglecting to heed the fact that through most of its history mankind managed with very small growth rates, that even as recently as 300 years ago, the growth rate amounted to only some 3 to 5 per 1,000 per year, compared with our current 20 per 1,000, and in fact in wide regions of Africa, 30 and 35 and more per 1,000 per year.

True enough, it is not difficult to punch holes in the model makers' computer programs—their numerical assumptions about what may be available and the rate at which things can be developed and will be consumed and so on. The World Bank, for example, makes the point in its criticism of *The Limits to Growth* that, if, for example, the pollution factor in Meadows's computer program were reduced to five-eights of its currently assumed value, there would be no breakdown of the system on this specific count (Haq, 1972). But it is not all that easy then to claim that mankind can therefore cheerfully keep on increasing at 2 percent per annum without soon running into bigger problems than have ever beset it in the past. That is really the essential message of the model makers, regardless of their individual figures: that mankind will have to slow down on both these counts in order to regain enough breathing space without being threatened by starvation or extinction at every moment or at every turn of the road.

Back to Malthus

With that we are actually back at Malthus. If we forget about the well-known, ever-quoted, and ever-refuted mumbo-jumbo about man's supposedly innate propensity, if unchecked, to multiply his own numbers at a geometric, while being able to increase his food supply only at an arithmetic progression, what did Malthus really say on this point?

First of all, he said that man indeed has the biological capacity to increase his own numbers faster than he can increase his food supply so that whatever limits there may be on the latter must also act as limits on the former. Malthus based his assertion concerning the geometric ratio at which man tends to multiply his own numbers on the fact that in the British colonies in North America (which had only recently become the United States), the population had indeed doubled about every twenty-five years during the preceding 150 years. (We might add that doubling every twenty-five years corresponds to an annual rate of growth of 2.8 percent, which is considerably less than current annual rates of growth in many countries in Africa, where the rate ranges up to 3.5 percent and more, with 4.1 percent in Kenya as a maximum, amounting to a doubling time of under eighteen years. Generally, the doubling time for all of Africa is twenty-seven years, for all of India, Pakistan, Bangladesh, and a few smaller countries in Southeast

Asia together it is about twenty-nine years [less in a few smaller countries], and it is twenty-six years for all of Latin America [Population Reference Bureau, 1975]. Thus, there can be but little sense in disputing whether Malthus did or did not give enough consideration to the role of immigration during those 150 years and some other details.)

While it was well and good to pooh-pooh Malthus throughout the nineteenth and the early twentieth century—and to lambaste him into the bargain for his moralizing attitude when he claimed that the poor were the cause of their own poverty because they produced more children than they could feed, and to reproach him for the cruelty in that famous passage in the edition of 1803, that "a man born into a world already possessed, if he cannot get sustenance from his parents, upon whom he has a just demand . . . has no business to be where he is. At nature's mighty feast there is no vacant cover for him. She tells him to be gone"—this did nothing to defeat his main argument.

In fact, the entire argumentation against Malthus had to lose ground when countries with populations counting by the dozens or in the case of India by the hundreds of millions proved unable to sustain their own populations with their own food production while at the same time they were too poor and too lacking in exportable raw or other materials to pay for large-scale food imports.

In the 1950s and 1960s, when "weak monsoons" threatened wide parts of India with famine, it was still possible to stave off the worst by shipping a few million tons of American wheat—initially at very favorable loan conditions, of which later, when it became too difficult for India to pay, large parts were simply wiped off the slate. But at that time there were still major surpluses in storage in the United States, and in addition there was land in the so-called soil bank—meaning land that lay fallow under a governmental price support system that paid farmers for *not* producing. Meanwhile, however, the storage bins have for the most part been emptied and most of the former "soil bank" is back in production. Thus, should another major shortage of food grains occur in India or anywhere else, it might not be possible to cover the deficit with American grain.

And old Malthus, wherever he may be residing, may nod his head: Yes, that is what I have been expecting all along. At first I was surprised that they were able to stave it off for so long—but with one industrial or agricultural revolution or another they still managed. But now I am surprised that with all those inventions and improvements it did not take more than twenty-five years for the food situation the world over to get as tight as it is now. I wonder how long they will be able to keep it up before it gets really bad.

What Malthus asked was essentially one simple question: What is bound to happen if at some given point in time there simply is not enough food in a given area? As an answer, he could only see that people would have to die—whether of starvation, or of pestilence, or of war. And since obviously people would not bring these things voluntarily upon themselves, he concluded that it must be Mother Nature who from time to time will institute these as "positive checks," as he called them, in order to restore the balance between population and food supply which man in his propensity to procreate has disturbed.

That, if you will forgive the oversimplification, is in essence what Malthus said to this point, if we omit his moralizing interpretation that Nature obviously rewarded those who exercised wise and moral restraint in regard to procreation and punished those who did not. The latter, of course, agitated his critics, who saw in all of this a defense of the status quo, a justification of poverty on the one end and of wealth on the other. However, I shall not deal here with Malthus's social philosophy or with that of his critics.

And what is the essence of the claims and statements of the model builders in this context? It is basically the same, minus the moralizing, except that they add to Malthus's concern with land and food production other problems such as the depletion of raw materials and the pollution of the biosphere, things that Malthus and his contemporaries never considered in danger of exhaustion. Otherwise, the model makers, too, are essentially pointing out the impossibility of man continuing to multiply his numbers as he has been doing during the last few decades. Unlike Malthus, they do not stay with general theoretical discussions, but go on to make actual computations about how long it would take until, under certain assumptions about available land and food and raw materials and the like, there simply will no longer be enough to supply the ever-increasing multitudes with the necessities of life. Malthus himself gave no concrete or even nearly concrete answers but stayed with generalities because he saw as his task not to compute limits but to explain the general problem of increase in numbers and what "Nature" was doing about it.

The model makers, on the other hand, assume that man, if properly warned in time, would take the necessary measures by himself without waiting for Mother Nature to apply her disciplining "positive checks"—in other words, that people, if warned in time, would on their own cut down their high birth- and growth rates (as they have indeed done in most of the industrialized countries) as well as slowing down and eventually bringing to a standstill the ever-growing use rate of irreplaceable raw materials.

Had the model makers come to the conclusion that it might take some 10,000 years, probably not much would have happened. Had they said "1,000 years or so," perhaps some eyebrows might have been raised. But they said "within 100 to 120 years." And they said it so that the statement did not disappear, like so many others, on library shelves. It was the psychological effect of thinking that "100 to 120 years is not farther away than our grandchildren or at the most our great-grandchildren The world can't come to an end with them already!" Just to think: I myself am now, in 1975, not more than 110 years away from the time when my grandfather was twenty-five years old. "And within such a short span of time, counting from now on into the future, it should be all over? Ridiculous! Nobody but a few computer-crazy professors could dream up such a thing!" Not to speak of the political implications that people in the Third World and on the political Left especially saw in the model makers' call for a halt to further population increase and further industrialization, just when the Third World is beginning to emerge from its misery and low standards of living with the help of industrialization.

What wonder that, when two years after *The Limits to Growth*, *Mankind at the Turning Point* appeared with computations only about how the situation might develop during the next fifty years, with no definitive announcement of the end being nigh within so and so many or rather so and so few years, people took comfort from its lack of talk of impending doom. Or that journalists and others gladly stated that the "Club of Rome" had distanced itself from its original pessimistic prognosis. The fact that, were one to continue Mesarovic and Pestel's computations over an additional fifty to seventy years, one would reach conclusions similar to those of Meadows et al., went beyond the horizon of most readers.

Limiting themselves to a time horizon of fifty years also relieved Mesarovic and Pestel of the necessity to make any kinds of even only computational assumptions about how much of the various irreplaceable raw materials mankind might have at its disposal, since whatever the unknown quantities might be, they would certainly last for another fifty years. The possible exception is oil, which for several decades experts had been saying could only last another thirty years or so— while actually over the decades new deposits have been repeatedly discovered, so that now, in spite of dramatically increased consumption, the remaining deposits are still bigger than ever before. This, in one of those simple logical jumps to which mankind is prone in the search for easy solutions, has served many people as a "proof" that the same must be true for all the other raw materials. So what was all the fuss about?

Now at long last, back to Malthus: he, who for almost 200 years has been decried as one of the worst pessimists, now appears, in comparison with the modern model makers, almost as some kind of optimist. No matter how bad the situation might be getting in a certain area, according to Malthus, Mother Nature would always interfere with her "positive checks" of famine, war, or pestilence long before man in his unreasonable and untamed urge to procreate could finish off his own kind for lack of food.

It was left to the modern model makers to put the handwriting on the wall for mankind—the modern Nebuchadnezzar, telling man that, if he will not instantly bethink himself and change his ways, then this will soon be the end of him and his kind.

And so, let me repeat once more what might pass for a newer formulation of the old Malthusian problem: although no one can tell what as yet unknown quantities of raw materials the earth may hold, or what new technologies may enable us at some future time to dig ever deeper into the ground for them, or to increase the productivity of the soil for food, or to discover new sources of energy to accomplish all this, if mankind keeps increasing its numbers at the current rate, then whatever limits there may be for the earth to support ever larger numbers must be reached not within far away millennia but within at best a low single-digit number of centuries. Whether this will be within 100 or 200 or perhaps even 300 years will, of course, be relevant for those who are living 100 or 200 years from now, but it is not really relevant for the one point at issue here: that the time has come, especially in regard to population increase, to slow down, for policy makers to set measures in this direction, whatever these measures may suitably be within each country, each political system, each religion, and each culture.

While there is every reason to look with grave concern at current developments and what the future may bring in regard to further increases in the world's population, there is one ever so slight ray of hope that I do not want to hide from you: at the recent World Population Conference in Washington, DC (November 26–30, 1975), a strange undercurrent of at least a few hopeful figures could be observed: in one or another paper figures turned up, such as that the annual rate of population growth for India had dropped from 2.2 percent a few years ago to 2.0 percent now—this would mean that the population of India could be expected to double not in thirty-two years, but only in thirty-five years. While this does not make too much of a difference for the problems on hand, still, if true, it would be a first ray of hope that perhaps the upward trend of annual rates of population increase might be coming to a standstill. It is all the more hopeful a prospect since one or another figure in that direction turned up in some other papers as well. Though received by the great majority of the audience, practically all of whom were experts themselves, with considerable skepticism, still, with all the frightening figures that fill the annual "World Population Data Sheet" of the Population Reference Bureau and the annual estimates of the Population Division of the United Nations, it was good to hear that at least some, even if only a small minority, of the assembled experts thought that they could discover a flicker of light on the very dark horizon. Certainly not enough yet to be cheerful, but perhaps a first indication that it might not yet be too late for a turnaround.[7]

Note in 1994

When this paper was written, in 1975, the world's population stood at about 4,000 million, with an annual growth rate of 2.0 percent, or 80 million people per year. By 1993, it stood at about 5,500 million, with an annual growth rate of 1.65 percent or 91 million per year. Thus, those who had predicted at that meeting in Washington in 1975 that the peak of the increase of the growth rate had been reached were apparently right.

It ought to be noted, however, that this reduced annual rate of growth of 1.65 percent is an average of widely disparate figures. For the "more developed" countries (with over 1,200 million people), it is 0.5 percent (or 6 million), and that includes 0.2 percent for all of

Europe (excluding Russia), with some 500 million. For the "less developed" countries, with together some 4,300 million people, the annual growth rate is 2.0 percent (or 86 million each year). But that, too, is an average of widely disparate figures: the rate is 1.2 percent for China (with 1,179 million) and 2.3 percent for all less developed countries without China (compared with about 2.6 percent back in 1975). Thus, while the ray of hope some saw at that meeting in 1975 is actually there, it is, where it really counts—in the developing world outside of China—still rather thin. In fact, in many of the very poorest countries of Africa, which are closest to the brink of starvation or where famine actually covers large areas, the annual growth rates are still well above 3.0 percent—in fact, it is as high as 3.5 percent in quite a number of them (Côte d'Ivoire with 13 million, 3.5 percent; Kenya with 28 million, 3.7 percent; Malawi with 10 million, 3.4 percent; Tanzania with 28 million, 3.1 percent; Uganda with 18 million, 3.1 percent; and Zambia with 9 million, 3.1 percent.

Annual growth rates of 3.5 percent correspond to a doubling time of only twenty years, and for countries with even higher growth rates, the doubling time is even shorter. In a few smaller countries in Central America growth rates are almost as high, but generally for all of Latin America the average annual increase is down to 1.9 percent.

Notes

1. Throughout this chapter, *Models of Doom* will be used to refer to Cole et al., 1973.

2. Concerning this question of the Club of Rome's membership supposedly being kept a dark secret, Henrich von Nussbaum claimed that he had to go to great length to uncover who they were. I reported on my own experience in that regard in a paper that I gave on May 10, 1976, at Queens College, New York, to the Social Science Division under the title: " 'The Limits to Growth' Debate" as follows:

> No sooner had *Limits to Growth* been published . . . [than] political opponents . . . began accusing the Club of Rome, that nobody had ever heard of before, as being a secret organization of international industrialists, banded together for the preservation of their hegemony over the world's economy, operating in the dark with sinister motives and connections.
>
> One should think that the recent meeting of the Club in Philadelphia may have helped to change that picture. As to the often claimed deep dark secrecy abut who its members are, I can only report that if we had time enough, I could read you names, titles, and organizational or business affiliations of 1/3 of its members—namely, of all those who happened to be at the meeting in Philadelphia.

How did I find out? Well—together with about three or four dozen others I snuck into the press room and picked up one of the mimeographed lists of participants, i.e., members and specially invited guests, and looked for those who had the mysterious symbol "CM" standing next to their names. From a footnote, hidden at the bottom of the first page, I had learned that this meant "Club Member." There were 27 of them, from 20 different countries, including—I repeat: members, not simply guests—people from Ethiopia, Egypt, Indonesia, Senegal, Mexico, and even one from Yugoslavia and two from Poland.

In fact, one of the more amusing moments of the conference came when Adam Schaff, a political scientist from Poland, told the meeting how he had always been bemused, where all these attacks on the Club as a secret organization for the preservation of capitalist hegemony left him—since he was a representative of a socialist country and at the same time one of the oldest members of the Club of Rome. Whereupon he turned to Aurelio Peccei and Alexander King and complimented them for having organized this meeting in a manner that would surely help to dispel that strange myth.

By way of identification let me add: Adam Schaff is currently the director of the International Institute for Social Science Research in Vienna, one of those East–West Institutions that the United Nations created for the exchange of ideas between scientists from communist and noncommunist countries.

Even more impressive in this direction was a panel discussion in which Mesarovic and Pestel, the authors of *Mankind at the Turning Point,* reported on their later work in which they developed models for use by individual countries; followed by reports of representatives from Iran, Egypt, and Venezuela, each one either the planning minister or the head of the planning commission for his own country, on how, in close cooperation with Mesarovic and Pestel, they had used these models for actual planning.

3. See the acknowledgments in *Models of Doom,* where the authors (the Sussex group) thank Meadows and his group, especially Dennis and Donella Meadows, for answering numerous questions and criticism of the part of the Sussex group "when they visited us in July 1972 and also for presenting us with an early version of the Technical Report of the *Limits to Growth.*"

This preceded by two years the publication of von Nussbaum's attack in *Wachstum bis zur Katastrophe* (published in 1974) against the authors of *The Limits to Growth* for keeping their database a secret.

4. But more overwhelming even than these economic figures are the quantities of food to be transported. These would presumably consist first of all of grain, which means that the annual grain import would, by the year 2025, reach about 500 million tons. This is more than the total grain production of the industrialized world (or more than twice the total grain harvest, annually, of North America). [Mesarovic and Pestel, 1974]

The authors are assuming that the average annual increase of population of 2.5

percent for the South Asia region will have declined by the year 2025 to only 1.0 percent—i..e., a return of the growth rate to its level before the current population explosion began around 1950. But the shift in age structure due to this population explosion, with ever larger cohorts coming into the procreative age during the next few decades, would nevertheless let the total population of the region grow from 1.3 billion in 1975 to 3.8 billion by 2025.

> This amount [500 million tons] would be about twice the total tonnage of all goods that are presently shipped across the ocean from the United States.
>
> If one considers that grain must be shipped from the Midwest to the harbors over an average of 2000 km, this would require a transportation effort of about 1000 billion ton-kilometers to transport these huge quantities . . . to the shipping harbors . . . corresponding to about the annual ton-kilometers of the total transportation of all goods in the United States. [Mesarovic and Pestel, 1974, pp. 113–15]

An article in a special issue of *Science* (1975, table 2) on food lists for the United States, Canada, and Australia, the only major net exporters of wheat and coarse grains, the following figures for production and net exports (in million tons):

	Production	Net export
1971–72		
All three countries together	283.3	70.6
United States alone	232.4	41.6
1974–75*		
All three countries together	245.2	85.0
United States alone	198.6	60.0

*1974–75 was a year of smaller harvests in most countries.

5. Annual growth rates from 1650 on are taken from David Heer (1968), who in turn took his figures from Carr-Saunders and from the *United Nations Statistical Yearbook* for 1965 (p. 24).

6. This passage appeared with exactly the same wording in the first edition of Baade's book (1960), which makes his estimate already fifteen years older than those cited in the present paper.

7. The most important of the papers referred to in this context, indicating that the peak of the rising annual growth rates of the world's population may already have passed, is R.T. Ravenholt (1975). He was the director of population at AID (Agency for International Development, U.S. Department of State). Ravenholt showed that for several countries the annual growth rates were already lower than ten years before. Skeptics objected that the most telling of these figures referred only to small countries with well-known successful program for population control.

References

Baade, Fritz. *Der Wettlauf zum Jahre 2000. Paradies oder Selbstvernichtung* (The Race Toward the Year 2000. Paradise or Self-destruction?). Oldenburg: Stalling Verlag, 1960. [2d ed., Berlin: Non-stop Buecherei, 1967.]

Boulding, Kenneth, ed. Robert T. Malthus, "An Essay on the Principle of Population" (1798). Ann Arbor: University of Michigan Press, Ann Arbor Paperback editions, 1959.

Carr-Saunders, A.M. *World Population: Past Growth and Present Trends.* Oxford: Oxford University Press, 1936. [Rept. London: Frank Cass, 1964.]

Cole, H.S.D.; Christofer Freeman; Marie Jahoda; and K.L. Pavitt, eds. *Models of Doom: A Critique of the Limits to Growth.* New York: Universe Books, 1973.

Forrester, Jay. *World Dynamics.* Cambridge, MA: Wright-Allen Press, 1971.

Haq, Mahbub ul. "Die Grenzen des Wachstums. Eine Kritik" (The Limits to Growth. A Critique). *Finanzierung und Entwicklung, 3,* 4 (December 1972) [A journal of the World Bank].

Heer, David. *Society and Population.* New York: Prentice-Hall, 1968.

Malthus, Robert T. *An Essay on the Principle of Population,* ed. Kenneth Boulding. Ann Arbor: University of Michigan Press, 1959. [Originally published, London: 1798.]

Meadows, Dennis, et al. *The Limits to Growth. A Report to the Club of Rome's Project on the Predicament of Mankind.* New York: Universe Books, 1972.

———. *Dynamics of Growth in a Finite World.* Cambridge, MA: Wright-Allen Press, 1974.

———. *Toward Global Equilibrium: Collected papers for* The Limits to Growth. Cambridge, MA: Wright-Allen Press, 1974.

Mesarovic, Mihajlo, and Eduard Pestel. *Mankind at the Turning Point: The Second Report to the Club of Rome.* New York: E.P. Dutton, 1974.

Neurath, Paul. *Zwischen Pessimismus und Optimismus* (Between Pessimism and Optimism). In "Wissenschaft und Weltbild: Festschrift fuer Hertha Firnberg" (Science and World View. Papers in honor of Hertha Firnberg). Wien: Europa Verlag, 1975.

Peccei, Aurelio, and Manfred Siebker: *Die Grenzen des Wachstums. Fazit und die Folge-Studien* ("The Limits to Growth"—Sum Total and the Follow-up). *Der Club of Rome ueber Initiativen, Ergebnisse, und Vorhaben bei der Erforschung der Weltproblematik.* Reinbeck bei Hamburg: Rowohlt, 1974 (Rororo).

Population Reference Bureau. "World Population Data Sheet." Washington, DC: 1975.

Ravenholt, R.T. "World Population Crisis and Action toward Solution." Paper presented at the International Population Conference, Washington, DC, November 1975.

Richter, Horst E., ed. *Wachstum bis zur Katastrophe?* (Growth toward Catastrophe?) Stuttgart: Deutsche Verlagsanstalt, 1974.

Science. "Special issue on food." *188* (May 9, 1975).

Stamp, L. Dudley. *Our Undeveloped World.* London: Faber, 1953.

Chapter 4

Models of the World's Problems and Problems with the World Models

Introduction

When *Limits to Growth* first appeared with its message of impending doom, it hit the world like a bolt out of the blue. Its main points were that the current growth of world population at 2 percent per annum was rapidly endangering mankind's ability to feed itself, that some of the world's nonrenewable resources were about to be exhausted, and that even if we managed to avoid these two dangers, we would pollute water and air so much that if we didn't starve to death we could surely choke to death. These problems had been discussed with increasing intensity at least since the end of World War II. Paul Ehrlich's *Population Bomb* had been a bestseller since 1968 and the Paddocks' *Famine 1975!,* with its suggestion of "triage" for whole nations, had stirred up a storm since 1967, as had other books in a similar vein. Pollution had been the battle cry of environmentalists for decades.

From Joseph Grunfeld, ed., *Growth in a Finite World.* Philadelphia: The Franklin Institute Press, 1979, pp. 107–35. (Originally presented in March 1976 at a series of seminars on "Growth in a Finite World" at the Franklin Institute in Philadelphia.)

For a possible explanation of the effect, let me first remind you that Thomas Robert Malthus's "An Essay on the Principle of Population" (1798) met with a similar reception. Anonymously written and presented originally as but another entry in an ongoing discussion about the causes of human misery, it "attracted immediate attention and the warfare of pamphlets instantly commenced [with] more than a score [of them] . . . even in the first five years before the second edition" (Keynes, 1963, p. 99).

Part of the reason for this reaction may be seen in this quote from John Maynard Keynes:

> The importance of the essay consisted not in the novelty of the facts but in the smashing emphasis he placed on a simple generalization arising out of them. Indeed his leading idea had been anticipated in a clumsier way by other eighteenth-century writers without attracting attention. [Keynes, 1963, p. 100]

That "simple generalization" was Malthus's claim that man, if unchecked, has a tendency to increase his numbers faster than his food supply, and that from time to time Mother Nature has to interfere with "positive checks" such as war, pestilence, and famine to restore the balance. *Limits to Growth* also placed its main emphasis on a "simple generalization": If man and his consumption of nonrenewable resources keep on growing at their present exponential rates, a total collapse of the life-sustaining system must shortly follow. All else is elaboration and supporting detail—gilding the lily, as it were.

It seems that there are two reasons for the impact that Malthus and Meadows had:

First, both Malthus and Meadows happened to present their respective generalizations in the most authoritative form known to their contemporaries. Malthus's was in the form that was considered (whether rightly or wrongly is not relevant at this point) to be a mathematical law, and this at a time when mathematical formulations were first seen as the best way to state the fundamental laws of nature. Meadows presented his formulation as a computer model, when his contemporaries were just getting used to the awe-inspiring powers of the computer.

Second, the conclusions drawn from their respective generalizations intensified the political and social controversy of their time. Malthus concluded that the poor were the cause of their own poverty, that their inconsiderate incontinence caused them to produce more offspring than they could feed, and that any aid given to them would only make matters worse since they would reproduce even more. He himself argued these points quite forcefully in opposition to the British Poor Laws, and he was immediately attacked for condemning the poor to eternal misery and for siding with the rich in defending the social and political status quo.

Meadows's call for a total halt to population growth was similarly interpreted as an attack on the modern poor, that is, the peoples of the Third World. He seemed to think that their current growth rates (2.5 percent and 3.5 percent per annum) were the cause of their poverty and again there was the implication that any aid would only make matters worse as long as those people were unwilling to reduce their high birth rates. The peoples of the industrialized West, with growth rates of 1 percent or less, appeared to be reaping well-earned rewards. Meadows called for a worldwide halt to industrial growth within thirty to sixty years, that is, long before most of the Third World countries could hope for a decent standard of living, let alone reach the standard of the West. This was seen as a parallel to Malthus's siding with the rich. It seemed to be an effort to preserve the worldwide social and political status quo with its ever-widening gap between haves and have-nots and to lock the latter forever in their present misery and second-class citizenship. Meadows furiously denied these inferences and cited his own writings to the contrary, but to no avail.

Flaws found either in his data or in his assumptions were given sinister interpretations either as intentional falsifications or as a deliberate misleading of the public; perhaps he and his coworkers had been bribed by the powers that be. Were not the leading members of the Club of Rome, which had sponsored their survey, present or former big-business leaders? Had not the Volkswagen Foundation financed their research? Had not Meadows and his coworkers studied or taught at MIT and similar institutions, which are maintained in part by big business for the training of future managers who would then run society on their behalf? Surely these poor creatures had been so brainwashed and deprived of all critical social thought that one need not even bribe them any more: They produced their writings in support of the capitalist-imperialist system all by themselves and then even proudly showed them off as the products of what they thought were their own independent minds.

Against this background I shall try to answer two questions: One, what are the merits and some of the flaws of these world models? And two, what could or should be their function in the ongoing discussion about what the Club of Rome calls the "problematique humaine"? I shall first deal with certain conceptual and methodological problems arising from the Forrester-Meadows model, from the Mesarovic and Pestel model, and from a comparison between them; then I shall consider the "Latin American" or the Bariloche model, with its quite different approach and purpose.

The Forrester and Meadows models were, of course, the great pioneering efforts, and no amount of subsequent criticism can detract from the merit of having set the whole train in motion. In fact, most of the many later models would probably never have seen the light of day, had they not had *World Dynamics* and *Limits to Growth* to lean on or to inveigh against. I sketch out some problems with them and some of the debate around them primarily to have a benchmark for discussion.

"Cause-Effect" versus "Goal-Seeking" Models

Earlier models, especially demographic ones, described the future of changing systems by programming into the computer variables with either constant or varying rates of change plus some relations between them. That procedure assumed that a model could neither produce by itself any changed conditions other than those directly programmed into it nor adjust to any changes that took place while it was in operation.

Forrester in *World Dynamics* (1971) and Meadows in *Limits to Growth* (1972) drastically changed this approach. They built into their world models systems of positive- and negative-feedback loops corresponding to the mutual impact of the variables on each other. Through these feedback loops a continuous series of changes was set in motion, both in the parameters and in their rates of change. These were fed back into the system, which thereupon adjusted itself to its own changes while the model was in operation.

Most impressive for the outsider was the ability of the model to produce changes that the model builder himself could not foresee directly because they resulted indirectly from the feedback loops built into the model. In principle the changes and the outcome are already built into the model, but the computer is necessary for calculating the result.

Since the outcome is in principle foreseeable in spite of its complexity, the Forrester and Meadows models have often been attacked as wholly deterministic. One criticism is that, because of the conditions and assumptions built into the model and its modus operandi, the model must predict total collapse after a relatively short time and has no bearing on the possible future of the real world about which it is meant to provide some insights. As Christofer Freeman put it succinctly in *Models of Doom* (the well-known critical analysis of *Limits to Growth* by the University of Sussex team), "Malthus in—Malthus out" (Cole et al., 1973, p. 8). If you build Malthusian assumptions into the computer, assuming exponentially growing population and resource consumption and limited supplies, then the model of necessity spits out reams of Malthusian catastrophes. Not because catastrophe is a real possibility, but simply as a consequence of the equations built into the model.

Another criticism sees the model as a kind of Newtonian world where every particle has its fixed initial position and the magnitudes and directions of all the forces affecting the particle are defined in advance. With all these data, it is possible to foresee all future states of the system, including any potential collapse; they are completely predetermined. Any indeterminacy is only an illusion arising from the incompleteness of our information or our inability to absorb it.

However, men trying to elicit concerted action to deliberately change the course of history can't be determinists—that is a contradiction in terms. To insist then, "Maybe they are not, but there models are," is only a gratuitous insult.

On the other hand, this kind of a model, once set in motion, produces a unique solution for any given moment in time despite the feedback loops built into it, and the observer can do nothing but wait for the outcome. In that sense, Mesarovic and Pestel called this a "cause-effect" model.

Their own radical improvement was the "interactive" or "conversational" mode of analysis. With that they enabled the observer to interact directly with the model, within certain built-in constraints. Either he can at a suitable point change one or more of the parameter values, or he can select one of several alternative scenarios built into the model.

The observer is in a position similar to that of the politician or decision maker in the real world, who can affect the course of events, but is also limited by the political, social, economic, and other constraints of the system. Unless, of course, he can change the whole structure of the system through revolution or in some other way. Since the observer-politician presumably makes his changes with some actual or hypothetical goals in mind, Mesarovic and Pestel called theirs a "goal-seeking" model.

Except for their own "standard scenario" in which the model builder himself has already made the necessary choices, the "goal-seeking" model does not lead to unique solutions for any given moment. The observer himself, by choosing parameter values and scenarios at various points during the run of the model, determines the outcome. The outcomes are only provisional; if the observer-politician makes additional choices down the road, the "foreseeable" future changes. What is "unforeseeable" is only the choice or combination of choices he is going to make in pursuit of his actual or hypothetical goals.

Hence, the functions for these two different models are quite different. The "cause-effect" type tries to project what happens if events take the course indicated by the initial conditions and the parameters, equations, and feedback loops built into the model. It remains a purely mathematical projection so long as these initial conditions are assumed to be purely hypothetical. It is a prediction only to the extent that initial conditions, parameters, equations, feedback loops, and built-in rates of change approximate present and anticipated conditions in the real world. The "goal-seeking" model is by definition not a tool for prediction or "predictionlike projection." Because of the observer's role, it is a tool to aid him in making his own decisions (within the built-in constraints of the model) by trying alternative combinations of parameter values and scenarios and observing their consequences; he can then select the one whose outcome seems best to fit his intended goals. He must decide how or to what extent he can persuade the real world to adopt those changes in parameter values or scenarios that he considers best, such as a change in the capital investment ratio or a shift from more industrial to more agricultural output or vice versa.

Some Problems with the Choice of Variables

The model maker, of course, chooses the variables he considers relevant for describing the world situation or those particular aspects of it he is interested in. Accordingly, the model is subjective, explicitly or implicitly. This would be a trivial point were it not for the critics from the Third World and from the political Left who tend to make this very point a basis for criticism. The choice of variables and the underlying basic assumptions is, of course, influenced by the model maker's background. Critics claim that the modelers have a capitalist-imperialist world outlook. In the minds of these critics, this prevents the modelers from seeing the world as it "really" is. With this point of view, the choice of every single variable and every single assumption can be debated on political and ideological grounds. I shall come back to this argument when discussing the Bariloche model, which rests on quite different social, political, and ideological assumptions.

For the present, however, I shall not criticize the modelers for failing to see the world in the same way as their counterparts in New Delhi or in Moscow or as the makers of the Bariloche model do. Instead, I shall limit myself to certain inevitable technical problems that arise whatever the choice of variables and whatever the social or political orientation of the model maker. I shall take pollution as a convenient example to make my point.

Forrester's model has a subsystem called the "Quality of Life" that is a function of crowding, pollution, and other factors. This has been criticized for being fuzzy, fraught with unreliable data and subjective judgments, and generally unmanageable. Since the model indicates a total collapse when the "Quality of Life" becomes intolerably low, the whole model is open to criticism.

The Meadows model does not have such an omnibus variable. Instead, pollution is itself one of the five basic subsystems of the model. In one of many alternative runs, Meadows demonstrates that, even if all other problems are solved, the system nevertheless collapses because of the enormous amounts of pollution. I summarized this position earlier: If we don't starve to death, we shall surely choke to death. The University of Sussex team severely criticized this variable, saying it was based on insufficient data available only for the last ten to twenty years. They cheerfully cited Professor Thompson's inaugural lecture (1970) that:

> In 1900 just before the advent of the private motor car large British cities had reached beyond their abilities to absorb horse manure, with consequent public health implications. [Cole et al., 1973, pp. 82, 89]

This point *The Economist* made famous with its irreverent crack that "in 1872 any scientist could have proved that 1972's quantum of urban transport and travel within London was impossible (and therefore a city the size of London was impossible) because where were Londoners going to stable their horses and how could they avoid being asphyxiated by the manure?" (*The Economist,* March 11, 1972, p. 20).

A study team of the World Bank observed that:

> if the ratio of pollution to capital stock . . . were to be reduced to three-eights of the value originally assumed—an adjustment well within the error range of the data—the prediction of catastrophe would be erased. [Haq, p. 38; German transl., 1972, p. 6]

These considerations lead to two important questions: One, should a (world) model include variables concerning which information is as scanty as it now is for pollution? And two, should it include variables that have error margins so wide that the outcome depends on where within these margins one chooses the numerical values for the parameters?

Forrester at one point says that one should include such variables rather than leave them out altogether. I advise against it except for in-house experimentation with the model. If there are too many such variables with such overly wide error margins, then we simply can't have a model.

Mesarovic and Pestel decided not to include a pollution variable in their model. Their nonetheless impressive account of the "problematique humaine" is ample proof that that particular variable is irrelevant for some aspects of the problem. Of course, critics may afterward complain about its absence and call the model builder incompetent for omitting it or impute more sinister motives to him: perhaps he wanted to protect the polluters.

Population Growth and Nonrenewable Resources

Next to the famous warning of impending total collapse within 100 to 120 years, nothing has stirred up as much criticism and outright ridicule as two statements that Forrester and Meadows never made: that the world population would keep on growing at 2 percent per annum until the final collapse and that all the nonrenewable resources left in the world amounted to not more than five times today's known reserves.

What Forrester and Meadows really did was make a mental experiment under these two assumptions to demonstrate what would happen if these assumptions were true. No more, no less.

Most critics also agree that the current 2 percent per annum growth in world population cannot possibly be sustained for many more decades. The difference comes with the critics' belief that "demographic transition" will decrease the birthrate and population growth by itself and in due time without any special action. If we provide high enough standards of living and sufficient security for old age, large numbers of children become less desirable. The cite the demographic history of the West over the last 300 years and particularly the aftermath of the Industrial Revolution as near proof for their claim.

The most recent figures seem to indicate that in most countries, including many of the faster-growing Third World countries, the growth rate may indeed have already passed its peak. The worldwide average seems to stand now at about 1.8 percent per annum or even slightly less, rather than at the 2 percent of a few years back. United Nations projections, presented at the World Population Conference in Bucharest, already are based on this lower figure (Table 4.1). Most relevant for our discussion is the time lag of fifty to seventy years between reaching a new reproduction rate of 1.00 and reaching zero growth. Forrester and Meadows might have saved themselves a few brickbats by assuming a world population growth rate of 1.8 percent instead of 2 percent (a doubling time of thirty-nine instead of thirty-five years). This would not have weakened their argument, but it might have been criticized for being too optimistic.

In estimating nonrenewable resources, both Forrester and Meadows took the 1970 estimates of the U.S. Bureau of Mines. These were a compilation of data from scientific journals and industry sources, and they were, for better or for worse, probably the best estimates available even though some of the figures are certainly open to debate.

In a first run they asked: If we had available five times the estimated resources and if both the current 2 percent per annum population growth and the 1.5 percent to 2 percent growth in annual per-capita consumption are maintained, how long would it all last? The answer was their famous "about 100 years," which disregarded for the moment the fact that some resources would last longer and others less than that.

In a second run they asked: How long would it all last if we had not five times but ten times the nonrenewable resources? Answer: about

Table 4.1

United Nations Population Projections

	More developed countries	Less developed countries	Total
Peak of growth rate	1.3%	2.4%	1.9%
	1950s	1970–1980	1980–1990
Growth rate by year 2000	0.6%	2.2%	1.8%
Year net reproduction of 1.00 is reached	2020	2070	2070
Year zero growth is reached	2070	2140	2140
Time lag between 1.00 reproduction rate and ZPG	ca. 50 yr	ca. 70 yr	ca. 70 yr
Projected population for A.D. 2000 (in millions and percent of total)	1,368 (21.4%)	5,039 (78.6%)	6,407 (100%)
Projected population for A.D. 2100 (in millions and percent of total)	1570 (12.8%)	10,687 (87.2%)	12,257 (100%)

Source: United Nations, 1975, "Bucharest I," pp. 5, 12.

120 years. (Although the results of this second run are more optimistic, they were usually completely ignored by most critics.)

I won't discuss whether the supposition that five times today's estimated resources are available was a good starting point; the authors were sufficiently lambasted by critics who thought that it was not. Instead, I want to discuss two implications of their answer that have been either little understood or noticed.

First, assuming that five times the known nonrenewable resources will be used up in 100 years implies that during each of the next five twenty-year periods we shall be able to discover, mine, and utilize as much as we know or estimate to exist today. This is an average consumption: somewhat less will be consumed during the earlier periods, and correspondingly more during the later.

Compared with the pace at which we have been discovering new resources during the last twenty years, that seems to be a tall order. According to Philip Abelson (1975), "World consumption of oil had [by 1974] reached the level of fifteen billion barrels a year, while discoveries had dropped to the level of five- to eight-billion barrels per year." Current reports seem to indicate that all the new oil in Alaska, under the North Sea, in Venezuela, and in Mexico is less than that already known to lie under Saudi Arabia and the Persian Gulf. It is possible that deposits in Siberia may match today's known reserves. What other big discoveries have we made these past twenty years? And what can we realistically expect to discover during the next twenty years? And the next, and the next?

Similar figures could be cited about other raw materials, although other authors of course delight in citing contrary figures.

Second, the claim that with ten times the estimated nonrenewable resources available, only twenty more years of total consumption are possible (total collapse after 120 instead of 100 years) has puzzled many readers. This is simple enough: Combining an annual population growth of 2 percent with an annual increase in per-capita consumption of about 1.5 percent yields a total increase of about 3.5 percent in total annual consumption, which corresponds to a doubling time of about twenty years. Hence, doubling all available resources would indeed add only another twenty years.

Seen in this light, the "five-times supposition" seems less pessimistic than at first. It is still possible to be an optimist and think that either we shall be able to discover and utilize this much at the necessary pace, or that the world's birth rate will drop off in time so that we don't have to make our new discoveries quite so rapidly, but the ridicule heaped on this particular mental experiment is less deserved than was thought by its critics. (Let me add in passing that the "ten-times supposition" implies that we would discover and utilize within each of the next six twenty-year periods about 1.6 times today's known resources, again somewhat less during the earlier and more during the later of these six twenty-year periods.)

The whole problem is formulated wrong. The question is not: "How great are resources in the earth?" This we cannot really answer. The question should be: "Regardless of the amount the earth holds, can we realistically expect to discover, utilize, replace, or recycle for more than a few more decades the enormous quantities required to keep pace with a steady 3.5 percent increase in annual consumption?"

One can consider many possible schemes about irrigating the Sahara, farming the Amazon basin, mining the ocean floors and desalinating their waters, utilizing nuclear fission or fusion or solar energy, and so on, providing one talks not only about these possibilities but also about a reasonable time scale.

Forrester and Meadows considered this impossible and therefore called for a slowdown of both population and industrial growth. Mesarovic and Pestel, though not projecting so far ahead, also painted a grim picture for the next few decades and beyond. They raised the alarm, but there is nothing wrong with that. (I do hope that others might demonstrate that the situation, although dangerous, is not hopeless.) What the authors of these models are implying is that to simply trust that "demographic transition" and new technologies alone will take care of our problems seems too great a gamble; if we really expect the pattern to be a repeat of Western history, then this will take at least another two or three generations. But the West never had the general long-term high growth rates that the developing countries have today. And the period of fifty to seventy years needed to reach a net reproduction rate of 1.00 and then zero growth supports their warning, while indications of demographic transition, the recent deceleration of the growth rate, and new technological developments seem to support the opposite view.

Now all of this, especially the possibility that the rate of new discoveries cannot keep pace with the growth of population and consumption, is a Malthusian formulation in slightly more modern garb. But what purpose does the label serve?

The Time Horizon

The choice of a time horizon for projections presents a serious dilemma: To reach the long-range planners one must speak in terms of many decades, but to reach the actors and decision makers on the political and social scene one must keep in mind that their time horizon is in most cases limited by their term of office, usually only a few years and seldom more than a decade or two.

For Forrester and Meadows the problem did not have this particular form. Once they had programmed their computer, they let it run until all available resources were consumed or air and water were totally polluted and the system collapsed. Then they simply looked at the time scale. Had this read "100,000 years," I doubt whether that would have attracted much attention; "10,000 years" might perhaps have raised an eyebrow here and there; "1,000 years" might have provoked some ridicule. But "100 to 120 years" could produce nothing but disbelief and outrage.

Mesarovic and Pestel decided on a time horizon of fifty years, up to A.D. 2025 (a few of their projections up to A.D. 2100) and explained their decision as follows:

> If during this coming half century a visable system emerges, an organic growth pattern will have been established for mankind to follow thereafter. If a viable system does not develop, projections for the decades thereafter may be academic. [Mesarovic and Pestel, 1974, p. 17]

Judging from their fifty-year projections, it is easy to surmise that, if they had let their standard scenario run without a fixed time limit, it would probably have led to quite impossible situations, similar to the total collapse in the Forrester and Meadows models and within a similar period. Their description of the impossible grain deficit from South Asia after only fifty years of a 2 percent annual population growth (see below) is a case in point. It is strange, then, that *Limits to Growth* provided such an outcry, but *Mankind at the Turning Point* didn't. On the contrary, aside from some criticism here and there about their methods or assumptions Mesarovic and Pestel were called optimists and good guys, while Forrester and Meadows were pessimists and bad guys.

There is, however, another aspect to the choice of a time horizon. Let me again quote Mesarovic and Pestel:

> As we will demonstrate time and again . . . the dynamics of the World system require twenty years or more for the effects of change to be accurately measured and fully revealed. . . . Given these delays (of the effects involving changes of human attitudes and social adjustment) a twenty-five year period cannot accurately reveal the dynamics of the system. What appears to be a minor deviation in a twenty-five year assessment can become a major upset after forty years. . . . [Mesarovic and Pestel, 1974, p. 16–17]

That is why choosing a shorter time horizon to cater to a narrow range of vision of political actors and decision makers may be worse than just an exercise in futility. Not making them sufficiently aware of the time-lag problem may help create a sense of complacency that could lead to disaster.

I say this primarily because the forthcoming Leontief report, *The Future of the World Economy* (1977), apparently uses A.D. 2000 as the break-off point for most of its projections. With its brave suggestions that we can (with great effort, to be sure) safely manage at least until the end of the century, which is certainly true enough, it provides too short a range and thereby induces too much complacency about the real difficulties in the decades ahead.

Beyond that, we can either be optimists and deride the pessimists for their fear of faraway ghosts that may never materialize, or be pessimists and sneer at the optimists for their shortsightedness. But I fear that too much unwarranted optimism is likely to do incomparably more harm than equally unwarranted pessimism. Any wrong measures taken because the pessimists panicked too soon can usually be corrected within a few years at the most. But the consequences of too much complacency—for example, in regard to population growth—even if for only a few years, may take decades to repair, and we don't have enough decades to spare. That, in a nutshell, is the message of both *Limits to Growth* and *Mankind at the Turning Point.*

Some Differences between *Limits to Growth* and *Mankind at the Turning Point*

One of the least popular aspects of *Limits to Growth* was its high level of aggregation, treating all of mankind as one monolithic producing and consuming unit somewhat in the spirit of Wendell Willkie's "One World or None." Thus, the food problem is formulated as: How long can a unit of four billion people, growing by 2 percent (80 million) each year, continue to feed itself with a limited amount of arable land and a given average yield per acre? The critics had a field day pointing out the important differences between regions that this approach bypassed or omitted, but lost sight of what seems to me the book's most important contribution: the daring not only to formulate in concrete terms, however arguable, the generally recognized truism that in a finite world mankind can't grow forever, but also to show that those limits may be dangerously near. This time is so near, in fact, that decisions can no longer be postponed or left for future generations to worry about.

Mankind at the Turning Point divides the world into ten regions, each somewhat homogeneous in geographic, economic, social, and political terms. This makes it possible to treat both differences and relations between various regions, including the unequal distribution of population, food supply, nonrenewable resources, problems of transportation, and so on. Whereas in *Limits to Growth* the collapse of the system occurs (computationally) for the total system all at once, in *Mankind at the Turning Point* it threatens individual regions only one by one, not all at the same time, and not all for the same reason. This leaves open the possibility that other regions might come to the aid of one threatened with collapse, an altogether more realistic and psychologically more acceptable picture of the world.

Nonetheless, the authors demonstrate more impressively what unsolvable problems would arise if the current 2 percent annual growth of world population were to continue for only a few more decades. For instance, even with fairly optimistic assumptions about the development of agriculture (additional land and higher yields per acre), South Asia would have an annual deficit of some 500 million tons of grain by A.D. 2025. Even if these huge quantities could still be grown in North America for export, the sheer task of moving them from the Middle West to the harbors would completely overtax America's internal transportation system (Mesarovic and Pestel, 1974, pp. 121–22).

With regionalization the authors were able to introduce a new concept: the distinction between "undifferentiated" and "organic" growth. The former is described as a cancer on the world that must be stopped, while the latter should be cultivated. "Organic" growth implies more growth where it is necessary to satisfy basic needs and less growth where it only adds to luxuries or waste. With that concept the authors moved away from the rigid "no growth" stance of *Limits to Growth,* a move that was seen as a complete turnabout by the Club of Rome. It certainly makes the presentation of the whole problematique and its impending dangers more acceptable to the common reader.

I regret the particular label that the authors chose to give to that concept, not for any semantic reasons but because of the organic analogy. The authors themselves explain it in terms of undifferentiated single-cell division versus differentiated cell growth within a functioning organism (Mesarovic and Pestel, 1974, pp. 3–4), but the organic analogy has been abused since time immemorial for political and ideological purposes. According to Livy, Menenius Agrippa (about 500 B.C.) told the plebeians of Rome his story of the fight between the stomach and the limbs and persuaded them to stop their rebellion and to go home and continue their work in good old organic growth fashion. It has served all kinds of authoritarian regimes as a handy ideological tool ever since.

Since I seriously disagree with the authors of *Mankind at the Turning Point* on the next point, I prefer to let them explain it in their own words:

> The regional development systems are represented in terms of a complete set of descriptions of all essential processes . . . physical, ecological, technological, social, etc. These descriptions are related through a multi-level hierarchical arrangement reflecting the relevant scientific disciplines. [Mesarovic and Pestel, 1974, p. 36]

Under a diagram representing the various strata, the authors explain:

> The behavior of the world system is represented in five levels, termed strata . . . : individual, group, demo-economic, technological and environmental. Each level provides a representation of the world system using knowledge as embodied in different sets of scientific disciplines, from psychology and nutrition to ecology and geophysics. All strata are interrelated in a total model. [p. 42]

I come from a discipline that delights in classification schemes for the description of human behavior, and far be it from me to deny the same pleasure to colleagues from another discipline, particularly since theirs appears quite defensible on logical grounds and makes sense in its own right. But I can't see where this somewhat complex scheme fits into their model. How is it needed or helpful for a better understanding of the whole problematique that it sets out to analyze? I can't find any place where the authors themselves used or needed it.

At the 1976 Club of Rome meeting in Philadelphia, we heard from the heads of the planning commissions in Iran, Egypt, and Venezuela how they used, in cooperation with Mesarovic and Pestel, localized versions of the model for the analysis of economic planning problems in their respective countries. Professor Pestel told of a similar operation for the West German government. It all sounded very encouraging. So did the experimental demonstration of the model, with all those green spaghetti curves cheerfully wriggling across the computer screen as members of the audience called for changes in parameter values.

I hope and expect that the next development will be a more probabilistic treatment of the whole process, perhaps in the form of probable ranges of outcomes for a given choice of parameters or scenarios. That, however, is a rather tall order, and I can't hold it against the authors that they did not come up with it in the first round.

Testing the Models

In the literature there are essentially two kinds of tests of the world models. One is to vary, within presumably plausible ranges, the parameter values to see whether the results remain essentially the same or whether those plausible changes lead to drastically different outcomes. The other is either to run the model backward from its starting point to see whether it can correctly retrodict or to start it in the past and run it up to the present.

I came across many such reruns and tests of the Forrester and Meadows models, but not of the Mesarovic and Pestel model. Perhaps I did not keep track sufficiently of the literature, but the task would anyhow have been too formidable. Mesarovic and Pestel have some 100,000 relations stored in their computer, compared with only a few hundred in other models.

The double claim of the World Bank team that reducing the ratio of pollution to capital stock to three-eighths of its value (in the Forrester model) would obviate the collapse of the system, and that this change lay well within the error margin of this variable is a somewhat extreme case. If they can make both claims stick, then we can't use this particular pollution variable. And if they can make similar claims stick about several variables, then we simply can't have a model.

There is also a claim that much smaller changes can have similar effects. Vermeulen and de Jongh (1976) developed an appropriate system of sensitivity functions and inflation factors and came to the following conclusion:

> We have found that if the three parameters [below] are all given a change of ten percent in the year 1975, the disastrous pollution collapse, which is the main thesis of the Meadows study, is avoided. Furthermore, this result was confirmed by employing the standard run of the Meadows technical report and changing the parameters by hand. This is in direct conflict with Meadows where he says (in *Dynamics of Growth in a Finite World*) " . . . we have come to the conclusion that the standard behavior of the model of overshoot and decline exhibited by the model is remarkably insensitive to variation in estimates of most system parameters." [p. 30]

Here are the three variables and their changes:

Variable	Original value	Change	Changed value
Fraction of industrial output allocated to consumption (FIOAC)	0.43	+10%	0.473
Average lifetime of industrial capital (ALIC)	14 yrs.	−10%	12.6 yrs.
Industrial capital output ratio (ICOR)	3.0	+10%	3.3

The authors mention specifically that Meadows in *Dynamics of Growth in a Finite World* also experimented with this last variable (ICOR), increasing it at one time from three to four, and reducing it at another from three to two.

The authors of *Models of Doom* also take issue with the variable industrial capital output ratio (ICOR). According to them, Simon Kusnetz found that from country to country for the years 1900 and 1970, ICOR varied between two and eight. Then, noting that Meadows had taken his value of three from an estimate by Samuelson for the American economy, they question his application of that estimate, made for a single and rather stable industrialized economy, on a world-wide basis over the total run of the model (Cole, et al. 1973, p. 71).

The ordinary reader is, of course, in no position to judge this argument, but he can raise a serious question: If it is true that such comparatively small changes in given parameter values can throw the system out of kilter, how reliable is the model? And more, how can the experts (Vermeulen and de Jongh versus Meadows) come up with such contradictory conclusions when rerunning the same model?

A related method of testing the model involves using variables representing factors that the critics maintain should be included or given more consideration. For example, Boyd criticized Forrester's model for its pessimism about the possibilities of technological change:

> To test the sensitivity of the World Dynamics model to changes in assumptions I have altered the model to conform to the technological optimist's view. This involved adding a new state variable, technology, and multipliers to express the effect of technology on the other state variables. [Boyd, 1972, p. 517]

With these and other modifications the model does not lead to collapse.
Boyle claims:

> during the translation step using the Meadows model, a typographical error was noted in the original program listing—one number in a sequence was larger by a factor of 10 than its companions; this was

> corrected. During validation, major discrepancies were found between
> the results from the translated program and those originally published in
> three of the twelve runs reported. [Boyle, 1973, p. 127]

I have not found this claim repeated or referred to in any of the other
critiques of the model that I have seen. I cannot judge its validity
without knowing exactly what error Boyle is referring to and then
tracing out its consequences myself. But I can state that this kind of a
claim (reported in *Nature*) tends to shake one's trust in the published
results regardless of whether one is inclined to accept the original model.

The second method of model testing, to see if the model can correctly retrodict or if it can run from the past and predict the present, has
meanwhile become a lively parlor game, producing at times startling
results. This one comes from *Models of Doom:*

> World 2 [that is, the Forrester Model] will not run backward from 1900
> for a little over 20 years. Figure 2 [*Models of Doom*, p. 113] is obtained
> by first running the model back to 1880 and then running it forwards
> from that date, using the parameter values so obtained. The curves are
> curious—they seem to indicate that the twentieth century lies in the
> aftermath of a catastrophic population collapse (from a previously infi-
> nite population) dated about 1880, with population still decreasing as
> late as 1904. [Cole et al., 1973, p. 113]

Making it quite clear that "even if this exercise is an indication of
Forrester's 'guesswork,' it does not necessarily mean [that] his model
is totally ridiculous," the authors proceed to tell us that

> if he had started his model run at 1880 with initial values based on his
> argument in *World Dynamics,* the collapse predicted by the standard
> run model would be brought forward by 20 years. And if he had started
> the model at 1850, the collapse would be predicted around 1970. [Cole
> et al., 1973, pp. 113–14]

Again, the reader cannot directly judge the correctness of the claim. He
can only note that if both the claim itself and its numerical interpretation
by the authors are correct, then there is something wrong with the model.

For fairness, let me present some conclusions from two recent papers in support of Forrester. Both take issue with the previously quoted
passage from *Models of Doom*. Both papers are quite mathematical, so
I will cite their verbal conclusions, which will suffice for the point I
wish to make.

In the first paper, "Backward Integration Tests of Dynamic Models," Richard W. Wright points out that

> stability of dynamic models is very different in forward than in backward integration. These models are not only dynamic . . . but *feedback dynamic* (emphasis the author's]. . . . From the feedback loops structure comes asymmetry in backward vs forward integration stability. [Wright, 1976, p. 132]

In addition he makes a second point that is also taken up by Britting:

> A dynamic model is constructed to be adequate over a specific range of values of its state variables. If, in a time period earlier (or later) than that for which the model was designed, substantially different values of state variables hold, then the model cannot be expected to behave like its referent system. [Wright, 1976, p. 137]

It is well known from common regression analysis that extrapolation too far beyond the range of the data can sometimes lead to quite paradoxical results. My favorite illustration is the main regression example in my own statistics text where I extrapolate a regression line far beyond the range of the data and find that a boy of exactly zero height weighs exactly −93.86 kg (Neurath, 1966, p. 395).

Wright then tells us that the failure of Forrester's model to retrodict back to 1880 comes primarily from "poor formulation of death rate and capital investment rate as functions of 'Material Standard of Living.'" He explains that both functions are in error whenever the numerical value of "Material Standard of Living" falls below 25 percent of its 1970 value. Wright claims in passing that Forrester was just plain lucky that between 1900 and 1970 (the period on which the model is based), this never happened, so that the errors in the formulation of these two variables do no harm to his conclusions. Wright then points out that prior to 1900 this was indeed the case. But then he demonstrates how comparatively small modifications in the multipliers linking those two subsidiary variables to the "Material Standard of Living" correct these errors, after which the Forrester model does indeed retrodict quite well to 1880 (Wright, 1976, pp. 131–32, 136–39).

While it may give some comfort to Professor Forrester to see his model thus rescued from failure, and with the help of two such minor corrections at that, the very ease of this rescue maneuver and the smallness of the necessary corrections are a source of discomfort for me because it brings back the question raised above: If it is that easy to produce major changes in the model—in this case to make it retrodict for twenty years with minor modifications within the error or plausibility range of the data—how trustworthy is the model?

The second paper, "Backward Integration of System Dynamic Models—A Useful Validation Test?" by Kenneth Britting (1976), makes the following point: The DYNAMO computer language in which these models are written employs "a very simple rectangular integration algorithm" that, through its stepwise integration mechanism, produces results somewhat different from those obtained through analytic integration. According to Britting, the errors accruing from this procedure are considerably more serious in backward than in forward integration and lead to great divergencies between the retrodictive results so obtained and those for backward analytical integration. That alone would account for a major part of the failure of the model to retrodict (Britting, 1976, pp. 143, 145).

Again I am disturbed by the comparative ease with which the model can be thrown out of kilter or be corrected. But I am even more disturbed since this time the trouble doesn't even arise from the construction of the model itself (the choice of variables or the parameter values of the whole logical structure), but instead from a purely mathematical issue having to do with the integration algorithm used by the computer language (DYNAMO) in which the model is written. This certainly tends to undermine seriously one's confidence in the results obtained with that model.

Now, back to the failure of the model to correctly retrodict or to correctly predict from the past. Wright has noted the dangers of extrapolating too far beyond the database (backward in this case). That is a great danger even with a fairly homogeneous database. In this case the situation is worse, since the database runs from 1900 to 1970 and includes two rather different periods: essentially slow growth before World War II and fast growth afterward (e.g., worldwide population growth of 1 percent worldwide before and of 2 percent after the war). Thus, in this case backward extrapolation is applied to a purely slow-growth period; and either parameters or mutual relations (including feedbacks) are derived from this mixture of slow- and fast-growth periods. Wright's findings about the death rate and capital investment rate as functions of a "Material Standard of Living" are just one particular illustration of this point. Failure to predict the present from the past is essentially the obverse of the same coin. Let me illustrate with a deliberate exaggeration: If we applied to the 1850 world population of some 1,200 million the 2 percent growth rate of 1970, the projected 1970 population would be some 13,000 million.

I would be even more worried if a model with this kind of a heterogeneous database retrodicted correctly over an appreciable length of time into a purely slow-growth period or if it correctly predicted in that manner.

The model makers brought this criticism on themselves by using this heterogeneous two-part database. However, one must admit that they hardly had much choice in the matter; could they have used only a fairly homogeneous database, say, the postwar period of 1948–70? There may be consolation in the fact that it won't be long before we have a sufficiently long postwar period to serve as a more homogeneous database for new models. Then, we all can play some of these backward and forward games that the model makers themselves invited and the critics enjoy so much.

To be fully consistent, one must add: If its heterogeneous database prevents the model from correctly retrodicting into a slow-growth period, it must also prevent it from correctly predicting into a fast-growth period. This is certainly true, but in this case it would tend to err on the conservative side.

All the model makers say is that continuing for a few more decades with a 2 percent population growth and a 1.5 percent growth in per-capita consumption will lead to disaster. And a model that works demonstrably well over the period 1900 to 1970 does, if projected ahead with today's growth rates, indicate such disaster after some 100 to 120 years.

The Bariloche Model

In spite of their differences in method and purpose, the two models discussed above at least stand on the same side of the ideological divide. Let me now present a model from the other side.

The "Latin American" or "Bariloche" model was developed at the Fundacion Bariloche in Buenos Aires under the direction of Amilcar Herrera. Work on the model began in 1970 after a meeting sponsored by the Club of Rome and other organizations. The Club of Rome supported its feasibility study. Later on it was financed by others, including the International Development Research Center in Ottawa, which also published (in 1976) the preliminary report *Catastrophe or New Society? A Latin American World Model,* written by Herrera and nine teammates. For most of what follows I shall rely on the report itself. Occasionally I shall take a detail from a paper by Peter Fleissner (1975) of Vienna, a model specialist with the Austrian Academy of Sciences, who wrote it after a presentation of the model by Herrera at the International Institute of Applied Systems Analysis (IIASA) in Vienna (Laxenburg) in October 1974.

Herrera et al. (1976, p. 7) specifically oppose the view "prevalent in the developed countries" that the main problems facing humanity are those of physical limits, and also oppose "the solutions proposed in some of the most influential circles in the developed countries," namely, to contain rapid population growth "especially in the Third World." They likewise oppose "the basic characteristic of this position," which is "that it accepts in a totally uncritical manner the central values of society as it is now." Instead, "the stance of the present authors is radically different: that the major problems facing society are not physical but socio-political, . . . based on an uneven distribution of power, both between nations and within nations" (pp. 7–8). This, incidentally, is no different from the assumptions of the basically nonideological, but otherwise equally radical, RIO report, the third report to the Club of Rome by Ian Tinbergen (1976) and his team.

> The model presented here is quite explicitly normative. It is not an attempt to discover what will happen if present trends continue but tries to indicate a way of reaching a final goal, the goal of a world liberated from underdevelopment and misery. [Herrera et al., 1976, p. 7]

> Our conceptual model of the "ideal" society is based on the premise that it is only through radical change in the world's social and international organization . . . proposed is a shift toward a society that is essentially socialist, based on equality and full participation of all its members. [Herrera et al., 1976, p. 8]

The model is designed to answer essentially one question: Assuming that in 1980 the necessary political and economic reorganization of society and the necessary reordering of priorities take place, how long would it take until certain basic needs (such as: 3,000 calories and 100 grams of protein per person per day; 12 years of basic education from age 7 to 18; a certain minimum amount of living space per family, varying somewhat from region to region) are assured for everybody? The model is in addition designed for obtaining "an optimum distribution [of capital and manpower—P.N.] . . . so that life expectancy at birth is maximized at each point during the run . . . instead of maximizing some economic indicator—GNP for instance" (Herrera et al., 1976, p. 9).

Beyond assuming for computational purposes that the necessary political conditions obtain in 1980, the report is as little concerned with direct political discussion as are *Limits to Growth* and *Mankind at the Turning Point.*

The purpose of the Bariloche model is essentially to demonstrate that, as far as physical requirements are concerned, it is entirely feasible to reach this minimum goal within a manageable length of time. It also showed how much faster this goal could be reached with an egalitarian income distribution than with the present income distribution.

The report is mainly concerned with the needs of the developing countries, and it divides the world into developed and underdeveloped portions. Since the report stresses a maximum of regional autarchy, it subdivides the latter into three regions at different stages of development. These therefore have different requirements for achieving the goal. The regions are as follows:

I.   Europe, North America, Japan, Soviet Union;
II. Latin America;
III. Africa, Asia.

The level of aggregation appears rather high, considering all the criticism that had been raised against *Limits to Growth* (which had no regions at all, only one global world); it is certainly higher than that of *Mankind at the Turning Point* (with its ten regions) which is still criticized on that point. In fact, Mesarovic and Pestel have already provided more subregionalization in later versions of their model (Mesarovic and Pestel, 1975).

With its reliance on regional autarchy, the model bypasses the kind of interregional problems illustrated by Mesarovic and Pestel's discussion of the grain deficit in South Asia and the corresponding problem of transporting grain from North America. Only in the last section on "international solidarity" shall we see the authors coming back to this issue.

I shall not discuss the details of this model any more than I did those of the others beyond mentioning that it is rather optimistic about resources, trusting fully in man's ingenuity to discover in due time new ones, to recycle used ones, and to find replacements for those that are exhausted (it assumes oil to be exhausted after about 100 years). Its assumptions about arable land and its yield are in line with those of other optimists (e.g., the late Fritz Baade of the Institute of World Economy in Kiel) which were considered sufficiently realistic by other experts. There is, however,

> one major characteristic of the model that distinguishes it from most others . . . that population size is generated endogenously by a sub-model that relates demographic variables to socio-political variables . . . one of the basic hypotheses [is] . . . that *the one truly adequate way of controlling population growth is by improving basic living conditions* [Herrera et al., 1976, p. 8, emphasis added]

Thus, demographic transition is a carefully spelled-out, integral part of the model itself. It seems to me that if one replaced its estimates with those of the United Nations Population Division (see below) as presented to the World Population Conference in Bucharest in 1974, then at least regional, if not total collapse would be indicated in a manner similar to that of the other models. In fact, to some extent this does happen even with the more optimistic assumptions of the Bariloche model.

The United Nations estimates presented in Table 4.2 are annual growth averages by decades with ranges indicating variation between subregions. The difference between "Asia, first run" and "Asia, second run" in the model is caused by assuming first four tons, then six tons of average yield per acre (Herrera et al., 1976, p. 93).

It is worth noting that the Bariloche estimates for the year 2060 (0.43 for Latin America, 0.37 for Africa, 0.55 for Asia, second run) come surprisingly close to the call for a worldwide halt to population growth within thirty to sixty years for which *Limits to Growth* has been decried.

With these expected declines in the growth rate, it is assumed that the developed countries will be able to fulfill the minimum goal of basic needs for all people within a few years: Latin America by the early 1990s, Africa by 2008 (Herrera et al., 1976, pp. 97, 89, 91).

The situation is entirely different for Asia: It will achieve 2,800 calories per person per day by 1992, remain at that level until 2020,

Table 4.2

Estimates of Annual Population Growth

	U.N. estimates 1990–2000	Bariloche model estimates				U.N. estimate of year when zero growth is achieved
		2000	2020	2040	2060	
Latin America	2.5–3.0%	1.27	0.89	0.56	0.43	2105
Africa	2.8–3.0%	1.93	1.19	0.79	0.37	2140
Asia, first run	2.3–2.7%	2.01	1.73	1.38	—	East Asia 2080 South Asia 2120
Asia, second run	—	2.04	1.16	0.82	0.55	—

Source: United Nations, 1975, "Bucharest I," pp. 5, 12; Herrera et al., 1976, pp. 89, 91, 93.

then drop back sharply, reaching by the year 2040 the 1960 level of only 2,150 calories. "Thereafter, the decline accelerates until levels are reached that are incompatible with survival" (Herrera et al., 1976, p. 93), which is what Mesarovic and Pestel computed for a correspondingly earlier year, assuming a 2 percent annual growth rate. Mesarovic and Pestel made their computation to demonstrate that 2 percent per annum growth can't be maintained.

The authors point to a paradox: "The runs were stopped at the year 2040 [Asia, first run] because after that date the indicators (particularly life expectancy) cease to have any meaning. Although the calories provided by the food sector drop below the minimum required for survival, life expectancy remains relatively high owing to the effects of education and housing" (Herrera et al., 1976, p. 93).

If that isn't a demonstration that there is something wrong with the basic construction of the model, then I don't know what such a demonstration would have to consist of. The problem under discussion is too grim for jokes, but Martial's famous quote comes to mind: *Difficile satiram non scribere* (It is difficult not to write satire). The other models certainly were taken to task by their critics for much less contradictory results.

As a way out, the authors tried a second run for Asia assuming six tons of yield per acre of arable land instead of the four tons in the first run. With that assumption, the situation holds out until the end of the run (2060). "In the last years of the run, however, the capacity to produce food is stretched to its limits, and it is inevitable that some years about 2060 Asia will not be able to feed its inhabitants adequately" (Herrera et al., 1976, pp. 94–95). This is about what *Limits to Growth* said: 100 to 120 years to a total collapse (remembering that the *Limits to Growth* model was computed in 1970, that would mean the threatened collapse around 2070 to 2090.) Let us remember that under these estimates, Asia by 2060 would have at least 60 percent, if not more, of the world's population.

The Bariloche authors assume that by that time the other regions will still have enough unused arable land with which to feed the people of Asia. However, they do not discuss the point that Mesarovic and Pestel made about the transportation problem.

The book ends with an appeal for international solidarity (as do the authors of *Limits to Growth* and *Mankind at the Turning Point)* and makes concrete quantitative suggestions about international aid. It also demonstrates how much faster the goal of satisfying basic needs for all mankind could be reached, and with how much smaller requirements of GNP per capita, through an egalitarian society.

In their call for international solidarity the authors suggest that, beginning in 1980, the industrialized nations donate a certain fraction of their GNP to Africa and Asia. The plan calls for a free transfer of capital amounting to 0.2 percent in the first year, 0.4 percent in the second year, and so on until it reaches 2 percent of GNP in the tenth year. This level is maintained until the two regions can satisfy the basic needs of their people. Once one of these regions can do so, the contribution from the industrialized countries is reduced at the same rate, by 0.2 percent of GNP each year, until it reaches zero after ten years (Herrera et al., 1976, p. 100). This aid would not appreciably reduce the time that Africa and Asia need to satisfy basic needs, except in housing. It would contribute toward a rise in per-capita income and with that to "a better level of general well-being" (pp. 102–3). (Let me note that 2 percent per annum is about three times the level of contributions currently suggested by the United Nations and about twice the highest contribution made by countries like Sweden.)

While one could in principle expect that future North–South negotiations (perhaps aided by OPEC-like cartels) might eventually produce substantial aid increases without major changes in the social order, the next set of computations is directly aimed at an egalitarian society for its own sake, "based more on a sense of basic justice and social solidarity than on technical economic considerations" (Herrera et al., 1976, p. 103). Comparisons for fifteen regions show that "in the underdeveloped countries the GNP per capita needed to satisfy basic needs in egalitarian conditions is something between three and five times less than that required if current income structures are maintained. Even in capitalist countries this factor varies between 2.6 for Japan and 4.4 for the most advanced Western European countries. Only in the socialist states, where income distribution is more egalitarian, is the factor lower than 2" (p. 104).

With an egalitarian income structure, basic needs could be satisfied for Africa around the year 2008 with an average GNP per capita of $558. With the present income structure, an average GNP of $2,000 per capita would be needed, which could be achieved only thirty-eight years later. Similar computations for Latin America lead to a fifty-year time difference (Herrera et al., 1976, p. 106).

Regardless of the criticism (including questions about its great optimism about demographic transition), the Bariloche model fulfills at least one demand raised by critics from the Left: It does away with the other models' acceptance of the world as it is organized today; it calls on all countries, be they capitalist or socialist, democratic or authoritarian, modern or backward, to cooperate in meeting a common danger. This may require (as the RIO report claims) a redistribution of the world's material goods and a different spirit for accomplishing it. While the designers of *Limits to Growth* and *Mankind at the Turning Point* may consider their models realistic and capable of dealing with the world's problems, their critics consider them conservative, if not reactionary defenders of the status quo. This is essentially the accusation leveled at Malthus. To these same critics the Bariloche model is a brave revolutionary design that boldly takes issue with the "real problems" of the world that the others are either too greedy or too blind to see. While to those others, in turn, the Bariloche model is nothing but an unrealistic fantasy, quite irrelevant for the problems of the "real" world.

This is a difference between social and political ideologies that cannot possibly be settled by detailed analysis and critique of the mathematics and assumptions of the models. The best that detailed critique can do is to make one see where facts are distorted or where plausible developments are misunderstood or misrepresented.

The Functions of World Models

Let me return to my original question: What could or should be the function of world models? Basically I believe that they should serve two main functions: to analyze the problematique and to help spread the message of their conclusions.

Let me begin with the second. I doubt whether models really spread their messages. I suspect that most people are awed, but don't understand all those diagrams and curves. They read what they can understand, and the message comes through loud and clear. The diagrams only lend the model authority, and trained readers gain additional insight from studying the diagrams.

Beyond that the models are still very vulnerable to criticism. They attempt to force issues with tight logical arguments, when, in fact, too many of the relevant considerations do not lend themselves to this kind of formulation. They demand trusting the model maker (or for that matter, the critic) because the whole argument is too involved for any but the best trained to follow. I fully understand the model maker's dilemma in this respect: If he tries to reach a wider audience by simplifying either the model or its presentation, he is criticized for omitting the important; if he tries to include all that his critics want him to include, he is criticized for obfuscation. Some are attacked from both sides. Hannes Hyrenius, demographer at the University of Gothenburg, Sweden, took the authors of *Models of Doom* (the Sussex team) to task for letting Meadows off too lightly in their twelve-page critique of his population subsystem. Then he presents a demographer's list of all the additional information necessary to make this a worthwhile variable (Hyrenius, 1975, p. 205). The authors of *Models of Doom* berated Meadows for the very opposite, claiming he needed a general input variable to indicate the overall influence of population growth of the system. They maintained that fewer variables would have been sufficient; too many only confuse the issue (Cole et al., 1973, p. 55).

What is the poor model maker to do? I am not citing laymen who are talking through their hats; both critics are experts.

My main concern is with the seeming vulnerability of the models vis-à-vis comparatively minor changes in the parameters or in the structure of the feedback loops. My concern is heightened by the contradictory statements of experts about the same variables or about the results of reruns of the same model. Hence, I doubt that world models are stable enough to be trustworthy, particularly for the general reader, who tends to see the discussion as just another squabble among scholars who don't know the answers themselves. This certainly undermines the credibility of the message.

Nevertheless, world models do serve useful functions. *Limits to Growth* has already fulfilled a historical task: It has put the "problematique humaine," as perceived by the Club of Rome, on the map. It stimulated worldwide discussion on the issues and reached an incredibly wide audience. This is an enormous achievement, and technical criticism of the model as such seems superfluous.

I am inclined to look on the Forrester-Meadows model not so much as a method (although certainly as the pioneer for a method) than as a historical event, in the sense of having created a worldwide interest in the main topic treated by the model makers: that continued population explosion and increasing resources consumption and pollution of the biosphere portend serious dangers for the future of mankind. In its technical aspects it has already been overtaken by the next generation of models (I am referring here to Mesarovic and Pestel) which will, in turn, be supplanted by a third. I anticipate that probability models will be the next stage. Only a model that combines a flexible interaction mode with an efficient probability statement can really constitute a useful analytical tool.

In my opinion, the greatest use for these models and their successors lies not with all-encompassing world models, but with the analysis of problems of more limited scope; recall those reports from Egypt, Iran, Venezuela, and West Germany with their much more localized applications. I expect similar applications to single industries or even to individual enterprises.

The world models' main impact is in my opinion primarily psychological and ideological; they do not lead directly to action. *Limits to Growth* created a new climate in which the issues can be discussed. It is a secondary matter whether such discussions take place with the help of complex computer models (I doubt that they will) or with the usual citing of a few key figures and tables and an occasional diagram that the participants can understand at a glance.

The Bariloche model, if it has any impact at all, can only have a purely ideological one. I just can't see any socialist nation deciding to slow down its industrial growth and to transfer massive aid to Asia just because of the Bariloche model's recommendations. Even though some leaders may subscribe to the model's premise that all men must have enough to eat before some should indulge in luxuries, and to its prerequisite of a worldwide socialist order for the rearrangement of priorities, a binding commitment to that effect is unlikely. What impact could this highly political model possibly have on the other side of the ideological divide? It may provide useful arguments for Third World ideologues and others to carry on their battles against the West or to try to persuade the developed world into increasing its aid.

Beyond the overall shock and propaganda effect, I rate the chances for direct impact of world models of any kind rather low. But the propaganda effect, if the model's message is widespread, can certainly be highly significant. While I can't envisage presidents and prime ministers sitting in front of computer screens trying out alternative parameter values and scenarios, I can see some of their advisers doing just that. The message that too great a population growth, too much resource depletion, and too much pollution are serious worldwide dangers is by now part of every decision maker's thinking and indirectly enters into their decision making. They could have learned all of this from other sources as well, but I am convinced that as a matter of fact many of them learned it from these particular sources, or rather, that many of them incorporated it into their thinking because these particular sources had stirred up all that discussion. If that can be accomplished through more and better world models, then regardless of methodological problems, let us have more of them.

The model maker has to face a major difficulty, whether his message is pessimistic or optimistic. He will be hailed as a great scientist and an ally by some, and as a charlatan and an enemy by others.

Let me give a parallel: A group of people in heavy trucks is about to cross a bridge. A man warns them that the bridge is too weak and will probably collapse. He cannot be 100 percent sure, but he is an engineer and knows such things professionally. If these people were ordinary tourists, they would probably think twice before risking the crossing. Now let them be a group of political activists in hot pursuit of the enemies or in urgent flight from them. Now the question is no longer "What are the chances that he is right?" but "What are his motives? Is he for us or against us? Is this a ruse to stop us from crossing?"

No matter how objective and politically neutral the model maker, his message becomes political and will be treated as such by virtue of its political consequences. The objectivity of the data and the methods and the intended political neutrality of the message cannot prevent that. Indeed, every single assumption entering the model explicitly or implicitly can and will be given a political interpretation. So will the modeler's acceptance or nonacceptance of the status quo.

These are major obstacles not only for acceptance but even for serious discussion of any model and its message. They limit the effectiveness of both a model's message and its appeal for cooperation between social groups or between nations.

That is something the model maker simply has to live with. But of course, if he feels that his work is his calling, then he will go on with it regardless of difficulties and consequences, as others have done before him in what they themselves conceived as their service to mankind.

References

Abelson, Philip H. *Energy for Tomorrow.* Seattle, WA: University of Washington Press, 1975.

Baade, Fritz. *Der Wettlauf zum Jahre 2000—Paradies oder Selbstvernichtung* (The Race toward the Year 2000. Paradise or Self-destruction?). Oldenburg: Gerhard Stalling Verlag, 1960. [2d ed.: 1967.]

Beckerman, Wilfred. "Economists, Scientists and Environmental Catastrophe." *Oxford Economic Papers* (November 1972), pp. 327–44.

———. *In Defense of Economic Growth.* London: Jonathan Cape, 1974. [American ed.: *Two Cheers for Growth.*]

Boyd, Robert. "World Dynamics: A Note." *Science, 177* (1972), 516–19.

Boyle, Thomas J. "Hope for the Technological Solution." *Nature, 245* (September 21, 1973).

Britting, Kenneth R. "Backward Integration of System Dynamics Models—A Useful Validation Test?" In C.W. Churchman and R.O. Mason, *World Modeling—A Dialogue.* New York: North Holland-American Elsevier, 1976 pp. 141–50.

Carter, Nicholas. "Population, Environment and Natural Resources—A Critical Review of Recent Models." In United Nations, "Bucharest II," 1975, pp. 222–31.

Churchman, C. West, and Richard O. Mason, eds. *World Modeling—A Dialogue.* New York: North Holland/American Elsevier, 1976.

Cole, H.S.D.; Christofer Freeman; et al., eds. *Models of Doom. A Critique of Limits to Growth.* New York: Universe Books, 1973. [English ed.: *Thinking about the Future.*]

Economist, The. "Limits to Misconception." March 11, 1972, pp. 20–21.

Ehrlich, Paul R. *The Population Bomb.* New York: Balantine Books, 1968.

Fleissner, Peter. "Ein Weltmodell aus der Sicht der Entwicklungslaender. Dag Modell der Fundacion Bariloche" ("A World Model from the Point of View of the Developing Countries. The Model of the Bariloche Foundation.") In Energy and Growth. *Energie und Wachsstrum* (Mitteilungen des Instituts fuer Gesell-schaftespolitik in Wien [Communications of the Institute of Social Policy.]), *16* (1975), 54–64.

Forrester, Jay W. *World Dynamics.* Cambridge, MA: Wright-Allen Press, 1971.

Freeman, Christofer. "Malthus with a Computer." In H.S.D. Cole, C. Freeman, et al. (eds.): *Models of Doom. A Critique of Limits to Growth.* New York: Universe Books, 1973, pp. 5–13.

Haq, Mahbub ul. "Reports on the Limits to Growth." By a World Bank team (Mahbub ul Haq, chairman). (Mimeo). [German translation: "Die Grenzen des Wachstrums—eine Kritik." *Finanzierung und Entwicklung* (December 1972). (Journal of the International Monetary Fund and the World Bank; also available in English), pp. 2–8.]

Herrera, Amilcar O., et al. *Catastrophe or New Society? A Latin-American World Model.* Ottawa, Canada: International Development Research Center, 1976. [Available through UNIPUB, New York.]

Hyrenius, Hannes. "On the Use of Models as Instruments in Formulating Population Policies." In United Nations, 1975, "Bucharest II," pp. 201–10.

Keynes, John Maynard. *Essays in Biography.* London: Horizon Press, 1951. [American ed.: New York: W.W. Norton, 1963.]

Leontief, Wassily. "Preface, Introduction and Summary." *The Future of the World Economy*. New York: United Nations, 1976.

Leontief, Wassily, et al. *The Future of the World Economy. A United Nations Study*. New York: Oxford University Press, 1977.

Malthus, Robert T. *An Essay on the Principle of Population*. London: 1798. [This is the first, anonymously published edition, actually a pamphlet. The second edition, of book length, and with the name of the author, appeared in 1803.]

Marstrand, Pauline K., and T.C. Sinclair. "The Pollution Sub-System." In H.S.D. Cole, C. Freeman, et al. (eds.), *Models of Doom. A Critique of Limits to Growth*. New York: Universe Books, 1973, pp. 80–89.

Meadows, Donella H.; Dennis L. Meadows; et al. *The Limits to Growth, A Report to the Club of Rome's Project on the Predicament of Mankind*. New York: Universe Books, A Potomac Associates Book, 1972.

Meadows, Dennis L.; William W. Behrens, III; et al. *Dynamics of Growth in a Finite World*. Cambridge, MA: Wright-Allen Press, 1974.

Mesarovic, Mihajlo, and Eduard Pestel. *Mankind at the Turning Point, The Second Report to the Club of Rome*. New York: E.P. Dutton, 1974.

————. *Motivation, Objectives and Conceptual Foundations*. Mimeo; Lecture at International Institute of Application Systems Analysis, IIASA, Vienna, Laxenburg, 1975.

Neurath, Paul. *Statistik fuer Sozialwissenschaftler Eine Einfuehrung in das Statistische Denken*. (Statistics for Social Scientists. An Introduction to Statistical Reasoning). *Stuttgart: Enke, 1966*.

Paddock, William, and Paul Paddock. *Famine 1975!* Boston: Little, Brown, 1967.

Page, William. "The Population Sub-system." In H.S.D. Cole, C. Freeman, et al. (eds.), *Models of Doom. A Critique of Limits to Growth*. New York: Universe Books, 1973, pp. 43–55.

Ravenholt, T.R. *World Population Crisis and Action toward Solution*. Paper presented at the International Population Conference, Washington, November 1975 (mimeo).

Tinbergen, Ian (coordinator). *RIO: Reshaping the International Order, A Report to the Club of Rome*. New York: E.P. Dutton, 1976.

United Nations. *The Population Debate: Dimensions and Perspectives*. Papers of the World Population Conference, Bucharest, 1974. New York: United Nations, 1975. [2 vols. cited as "Bucharest I" and "Bucharest II".]

Vermuelen, P.J., and D.C.J. de Jongh. "Parameter Sensitivity of the 'Limits to Growth' Model." *Applied Mathematical Modeling, 1* (June 1976), 29–32.

World Population Data Sheet. Washington, DC: Population Reference Bureau, 1976 and preceding years.

Wright, Richard W. "Backward Integration Tests of Dynamic Models." In C.W. Churchman and R.O. Mason (eds.), *World Modeling—A Dialogue*. New York: North Holland/American Elsevier, 1976, pp. 129–40.

Chapter 5

Comments at the 6th Global Modeling Conference, Vienna-Laxenburg, 1978

As a sociologist—and not even a mathematical one—I can't help feeling like an interloper at this conference. My reasons for being here are that I am a statistician and demographer, and I have studied and written about your work during the last four years. Still, as an outsider I am observing you and your world in a way that reminds me of a book that described how a three-year-old child experiences the world of the grown-ups. Its title is "Nunni among the Giants."

Now, meeting you at last with the naive and amazed eyes of a child, I am making an amazing discovery: the giants in their grown-up sphere, which ordinarily we children dare not enter, play games rather similar to ours. The same joyful playing with new ideas, the same formation of little groups that stake out their own turfs but then cheerfully play with others from other turfs, the same watchfulness about what the outside world is going to say about their play, and to some

These comments were made toward the end of the closing session of the 6th Global Modeling Symposium conducted by the IIASA (International Institute of Applied Systems Analysis), Laxenburg, Vienna, in October 1978. Published in Donella Meadows, John Richardson, and Gerhart Bruckmann (eds.), *Groping in the Dark: The First Decade of Global Modeling* (New York: John Wiley & Sons, 1982), pp. 266–68.

extent the same drawing together in search of identity as a group when the outside closes in or, worse, when the outside tends to treat them as nothing but little children playing some odd kinds of games that the grown-ups don't quite understand, or care to understand, because it is, after all, only child's play.

I am, of course, overstating the case, because I am fully aware of the enormous impact that global modeling has had (ever since the publication of *The Limits to Growth*) on the public debate about the issues of population explosion and resource depletion. Even if they never knew and never will know what a global model is or can do, millions of people acquired through the debate about the first model a feeling of possible impending doom—or at least the need to assert that they don't believe in such doom, in spite of what some of the model makers may be saying.

However, I do not intend to talk to you about the social importance or, for that matter, about the theoretical meaning of what you are doing. Instead, I want to make a few remarks in my role as an observer at your conference, that is, as "Nunni among the giants."

Let me preface what comes next by saying that, in a way, I went through this some thirty years ago at some of the earliest meetings of the American Association of Public Opinion Research and the American Institute of Mathematical Statistics.

A new science, or a new branch within a field of science, or, if you want to call it so, a new specialty within a given field, characterized by a set of methods, techniques, and theories too esoteric for the outsiders to follow fully, has been in the process of establishing itself. And, not too surprisingly for a sociologist, its practitioners, feeling lonesome in their places of work and insecure about their position in the world, are looking for others with similar interests; they come, they meet, they find help, security, and a sense of identity in each other's presence. Eventually, if the history of other cases allows a projection into the not-too-distant future, they will form their own society, with its own journal. I recall at an early meeting of the American Association of Public Opinion Research a formal motion to appoint a committee for the purpose of devising a name for the activity in which we were engaging and, more important, a professional title for its practitioners; the maker of the motion said that it should be a title ending with "-ologist" or "-ician" or "some such thing." You already have a name for your subject; I will not be surprised if, within a few years, I will attend a conference of the "International Society for Global Modeling." If you don't have the name for your society yet, take it as a free gift from Nunni.

To repeat: as an outsider I am, first of all, struck by the search for an identity among you, quite naturally coupled with a feeling of insecurity about the activity in which you are all engaged, whether it is worthwhile, whether it will help the world with its problems as you are hoping that it will, or whether what you are producing will be abused by others for power purposes. I also note search for agreement on basic theories, concepts, and methods, so that a group working on a new model will not need to establish its right to make a model before being allowed to proceed with its own special approach to its particular results.

Second, I am struck by the limited degree to which methods and results can be compared from model to model, and by the lack so far of a common language and a common set of concepts and basic canons in terms of which the quality of work and results can be judged. However, you have discussed these points at great length. We sociologists are now in the midst of similar difficulties, so we are not surprised when we see them elsewhere.

Third, I am, to some extent, astonished that so many of you skirt the essentially social, economic, and political nature of your work, of your results, and of the impact that it has on the social and political world around you. True, each of you is fully aware of this. Nevertheless, I find it amazing that so eminently political an activity can be discussed in such generally unpolitical terms.

This brings me finally to a more personal observation: I admire the spirit of cooperation among you and the genuine civility with which you are treating each other, even when there are obvious differences in approaches, results, and implications, including political ones. Too, I admire the dedication and enthusiasm with which you are going about your work. You have not yet become as professionalized as the scientists who started their branches many years earlier. There are still among you many who joined your organizations, not just in search of a job, but in search of a place to make a contribution to mankind. Your work is a joy for an old outsider to see.

To which I will add an observation from my position as a demographer: note how few of the people present are of my generation and how many are younger. This is, of course, no accident, but a by-prod-

uct of both population growth and the most recent industrial revolution. Anything concerned with computers is basically the province of
a younger generation with its own technology: hardware, software,
and new intellectual activities—of which global modeling is one of
the newest.

Welcome to the playground!

Chapter 6

On a Contradiction within the Bariloche Model (It computes for the people of Asia more years of average life expectancy than food on which to live that long)

In 1976, when the worldwide discussion of the so-called Club of Rome Models (*The Limits to Growth* by Dennis Meadows et al., 1972, and *Mankind at the Turning Point* by Mesarovic and Pestel, 1974) had just begun to slow down, an entirely different kind of model appeared on the scene: *Catastrophe or New Society? A Latin-American Model*, by Amilcar Herrera et al. (1976). Developed in close cooperation with and supported by the Fundacion Bariloche in Buenos Aires, it soon became known as the "Bariloche model." Since it is discussed at length in chapter 4, only enough of its purpose and content will be

---

Originally a supplement to the author's paper "Bevoelkerungsvermehrung, Resourcenverknappung und Weltmodelle" (Growth of Population, Depletion of Resources and the World Models), presented at a symposium of the Austrian Ministry of Science and Research in October 1978. The papers from that symposium were subsequently published by the ministry, but without the various supplements.

indicated here to facilitate understanding of the discussion of what appears to me as a serious contradiction within that model: *it computes a prolonged average expectancy of life at birth for the people of Asia for a time (ca. the year 2060) when, according to the computations of the same model, there will not be enough food to enable them to live that long.*

The Bariloche model, as distinct from the Club of Rome models, tries not to compute (and warn of) what would be likely to happen should the world continue, as it did during the last few decades, to increase its population annually by 2 percent and its per-capita consumption of nonreplaceable resources annually by 1.5 percent. (The answer, according to *The Limits to Growth* [Meadows et al., 1972], is that there would be a general catastrophe within 100 to 120 years.)

The Bariloche model tries instead to compute how long it would take under certain (varying) assumptions to secure for all people on this earth a certain minimum of basic needs, such as 3,000 calories and 100 grams of protein per person per day, twelve years of basic education from age 7 to age 18, and a certain amount of living space per family, varying somewhat from region to region. In addition, the model is designed to obtain "an optimum distribution of capital and manpower . . . so that life expectancy at birth is maximized at each point during the run . . . instead of maximizing some economic indicator— GNP for instance" (Herrera et al., 1976, p. 9).

Like the Club of Rome models, the Bariloche model does not deal with the various political and social changes necessary to obtain these goals, except to state at one point in the introduction that "what is proposed is a shift toward a society that is essentially socialist, based on equality and full participation of all its members in the decisions affecting them" (p. 8).

In its computations and numerical assumptions the model is construed under the overall assumption that, beginning with 1980, all societies are geared toward obtaining the minimum requirements of basic needs as stated above.

The point essential for the present discussion begins with this statement in the introduction:

> One major characteristic of the model that distinguishes it from most others built so far is that *population size is generated endogenously* [emphasis added] by a submodel that relates demographic variables to sociopolitical variables. This submodel permits the exploration of one

of the basic hypotheses put forward in this study, namely that *the only adequate way of controlling population growth is by improving basic living conditions* [emphasis by the authors]. (p. 8)

The Bariloche model deals with four regions: (1) Europe, North America, Japan, and the Soviet Union; (2) Latin America; (3) Africa; and (4) Asia. (It is interesting to note that after *The Limits to Growth* had been so heavily criticized, including by critics from the political Left and from Third World countries, for treating the world as one single global production and consumption unit without taking into account all sorts of regional differences, and after *Mankind at the Turning Point* had introduced ten different regions—which critics still considered insufficient—the Bariloche model, coming from the political Left and from a Third World country, Argentina, now deals with only four regions.)

The Bariloche model computes separately the possibilities for obtaining the minimum goals described above for each of the four regions. Of interest for the present discussion are the computations for Asia. Here follow the relevant passages (from p. 93ff.):

ASIA—The results of the run for Asia are very different from the results for other regions because basic needs are not satisfied to the desired levels.

In the food sector a consumption rate of 2,800 calories per person per day is achieved by 1992, and that level is maintained until the mid-2020s. It declines slowly after that and in 2040 reaches almost the same level as in 1960 (2,150 calories). Thereafter the decline accelerates until levels are reached that are incompatible with survival. . . .

The failure to attain the satisfaction of basic needs to the desired levels is reflected in the demographic indicators. . . . The rate of population growth is reduced very slowly and the population increases five-fold in 80 years, reaching 7,840 million in 2040. Life expectancy at birth improves, but is always below levels in other regions. . . .

The runs were stopped at the year 2040 because after that date the indicators (particularly life expectancy) cease to have any meaning. [Emphasis added.] Although the calories provided by the food sector drop below the minimum required for survival, life expectancy remains relatively high owing to the effects of education and housing; the function that links life expectancy to the socioeconomic variables is continuous, and no minimum value for food intake was established below which this indicator is reduced to zero.

. . .

The problem in Asia arises in the food sector. By 2010 all available land is being cultivated. . . .

. . . the rapid increase in the coast of producing food, due to the development of new land for agriculture, takes resources from the rest of the economy, causing backwardness and also hindering the satisfaction of the other basic needs. In summary, the delay in reaching adequate levels of well-being leads to a sustained high population growth rate, and *a vicious circle develops: increased population and the increased cost of producing food make it more and more difficult to satisfy basic needs.* [Emphasis added.]

At this point, the report mentions that other regions "still have great expanses of uncultivated land when their populations have become stable" (p. 93) but that, for reasons explained in the report itself, regions should turn to import of food "only as a last resort."

Thus far, the computations of the model are based on the assumption that food production amounts on an average (for agricultural land, for all of Asia) to four tons per ha. Now the assumption is tentatively raised to an average of six tons per ha. With this raised assumption,

The results indicated that basic needs could be satisfied to the desired levels. Per capita food consumption reaches 3,000 calories in 1994, and six years later the required consumption of protein is also achieved. [pp. 93–94]

In spite of this considerable improvement, food is still a problem for the region. In the mid-2030s the remaining land has all been used although adequate food supplies are maintained until the end of the run. . . . In the last years of the run, however, the capacity to produce food is stretched to its limits, and *it is inevitable that some years after 2060 Asia will not be able to feed its inhabitants adequately.*

To solve the food problem in the long term, the region could adopt other measures. It could try to increase agricultural yields even further and produce food from nonconventional sources. These measures could be implemented *with an effective family planning policy.* . . . There is sufficient time available before the crisis for an effective policy in both directions to be adopted. [p. 94, emphasis added]

At this point the reader, if he doesn't happen to be an expert, is hardly in a position to judge the adequacy of this change in the assumption of the model from four to six tons average yield of grain per ha, Asiawide. It may be useful to cite in this context two well-known experts, both of whom are quite optimistic in their outlook on the future of mankind.

The first is Professor Fritz Baade, from the Institut fuer Welt-wirtschaft in Kiel. In *Der Wettlauf zum Jahre 2000* (The Race to the Year 2000), Baade (1960/1967) calculates for Japan—which has the highest yields per ha of all the countries in Asia—with four tons per ha (his calculations for Japan remain unchanged in his second, revised edition of 1967). For China he assumes only about half as much, and for India, Indonesia, and Burma, about one-fourth of the yields of rice per ha as those in Japan (1967, p. 42).

Professor Colin Clark, one of the most outspoken critics of the whole Club of Rome approach, in *The Myth of Overpopulation* (1973), sees no reason to worry about any of the impending catastrophes about which Meadows et al. warn. Clark assumes an average of 4.4 tons per ha "achieved on very productive farms in Europe; these, however, are well above the average for the USA" (German edition, p. 39).

This would seem to raise serious doubts about whether the recomputation of the food production for Asia within the Bariloche model based on an average yield of six tons of grain per ha, instead of the first computation based on four tons per ha, can be justified as a serious—even if somewhat optimistic—scientific estimate for the current and the next few decades. Or one may question whether this creates the impression of a mere play with figures in order to circumvent an otherwise inevitable, rather pessimistic conclusion.

For a better understanding of the magnitude of the figures under discussion concerning the food situation in Asia, as presented by the Bariloche model, I shall cite some figures from *Mankind at the Turning Point*, the so-called Second Club of Rome Report (Mesarovic and Pestel, 1974). These figures presumably must, for better or for worse, have been known to the authors of the Bariloche model long before their own report appeared in print in 1976.

Mesarovic and Pestel also go through altogether five different scenarios for South Asia. (The Bariloche model deals with only four regions, one of which is "Asia," while *Mankind at the Turning Point* deals with ten regions, one of which is South Asia.)

> The purpose of the first or standard scenario is to provide a clue to the persistence of the food deficiency problem during the next fifty years. [That is the computational period of their model, from 1975 to 2025—

P.N.] The scenario assumes, that the historical pattern of development based on a somewhat optimistic view of the past and present situation will continue. . . . We again assume that an equilibrium fertility level will be attained in about fifty years. We also assume, quite optimistically, that the average use of fertilizer per hectare in the entire region [South Asia] will surpass the present North American level toward the end of the fifty-year period. At that time South Asia alone will consume more fertilizer than the whole world consumed in 1960. . . . Still proceeding optimistically, we assume that all remaining arable land in South Asia is quickly brought under cultivation and that all technological inputs, such as irrigation . . . will be available as needed. . . . The difference between the food needs of the region and the food production of the region dictates the quantity of food that must be imported and it is assumed to have been made available by other regions. [Mesarovic and Pestel, 1974, p. 121]

After pointing out that the deficiency of protein is already the worst aspect of the food problem in the South Asia region, Mesarovic and Pestel continue:

Our computer analysis, pregnant with optimism, shows clearly that the food crisis in South Asia will worsen. In spite of all the advancements assumed, the availability of fertilizer and land assumed, the protein deficit will continuously increase; by the year 2025 it will be up to 50 million tons annually. [Note that "one million tons of protein" is not a quantity to be shipped, but merely a computing unit, just as "100 grams of protein per person per day" is not a quantity to be consumed separately but also merely a computing unit implied in the consumption of food.—P.N.] Such deficits could never be closed by imports, South Asia would have to spend one-third of its total economic output, and three times what it earns from exports. But even if South Asia had that kind of money, the physical problems of handing those quantities of food would be incredible. In one year the region would then have to import 500 million tons of grain—*twice as much as the total tonnage of all goods now being shipped overseas from the United States.* And that is assuming that that quantity of grain would be grown for export elsewhere—500 million tons, after all, is larger than the total grain production of the entire Developed World. Moreover, these quantities would have to be delivered every year, in ever increasing amounts, without end. In sum, it would be impossible. [p. 122]

At this point, the German edition of *Mankind at the Turning Point,* referring to the same 500 million tons required annually, continues with the following passage, which is not contained in the American edition:

> This quantity would be twice as much as the total tonnage of all goods that are presently being shipped from the United States to overseas countries. If one considers that the grain would have to be transported from the Middle West of North America to the harbors over an average of 2,000 km, then this would require a transportation effort of 1,000 billion ton-kilometers in order to move these huge quantities of grain by rail from the fields to the harbors for shipping overseas. This transportation effort corresponds to about the total annual transportation of all goods within the United States. And it must not be overlooked that these masses of grain would have to be shipped to South Asia year after year, not only in the year 2025, but beyond that without end and in ever-increasing quantities, if no other development should occur. [Mesarovic and Pestel, German ed., 1974, p. 115]

A better understanding of the orders of magnitude of these tonnages of grain and of grain deficits for South Asia as computed by Mesarovic and Pestel may be gained from the following production and export figures presented by Lester Brown (World Watch Institute) in "The World Food Prospect" (Brown, 1975, p. 1054), and in *The Twenty-Ninth Day* (Brown, 1978, p. 135):

In 1971–72, the United States, Canada, and Australia, the three chief exporters of grain, produced together

$$232 + 37 + 14 = 283 \text{ million tons of grain,}$$

of which they exported together,

$$42 + 18 + 11 = 71 \text{ million tons.}$$

Poor harvests both in the export and in the import countries occurred in 1974–75. The consequence was necessary increases in both imports and also exports, the latter accomplished mostly out of existing reserves. In that year of poor harvests, the three grain-exporting countries produced together

$$199 + 30 + 17 = 246 \text{ million tons,}$$

and exported together

$$60 + 30 + 17 = 107 \text{ million tons.}$$

It should be noted that Canada and Australia in particular exported as much as they produced, so that in these two countries, the equivalent of the total home consumption was the amount by which reserves were reduced.

With a total world consumption of about 1,200 million tons, world reserves had melted down to about 100 million tons. With a world population of 3,800 million people, this amounted to not more than thirty-one days worth of world grain reserves. (In 1961, world reserves amounted to 163 million tons in storage, plus the equivalent of 68 million tons in the "American soil bank"—areas that, with the help of premiums paid to the farmers as price support, had been taken out of production but could be reactivated within twelve to eighteen months. Those 163 + 68 = 231 million tons amounted, with a world population at that time of 3,000 million people, to about 105 days worth of world grain reserves.) Thus, apparently in 1974–75, that year of poor harvests—and they were by no means extraordinarily poor ones, just "ordinarily poor" ones, the kind that recur with some regularity every now and then—the world barely passed by a major catastrophe.

Meanwhile, a few better harvest years have improved the situation again and in various developing countries new storage facilities have been added to facilitate the tiding over during emergencies.

Still, in view of the drastic depletion of world reserves within that one year of poor harvests, and in view of the fact that this all took place with a total annual world consumption of some 1,200 million tons, of which altogether in the three main exporting countries only some 250 to 300 million tons were produced and only some 70 to 100 million tons were exported, if one accepts the Mesarovic and Pestel computations of a grain deficit of 500 million tons by the year 2025 for South Asia alone (and that within the most optimistic of their five different scenarios—"pregnant with optimism," as they put it), one will understand their judgment that it would be impossible to cover this deficit with imports from outside, regardless of who would pay for it, and how, even if the grain could be grown in the exporting countries.

(To all of which comes the impossibility, should these huge quantities of grain really get shipped from the North American Midwest to the harbors, of then unloading them in the harbors of India, Pakistan, or Bangladesh, which are totally underequipped for such quantities, and then transporting them to the interior.)

The computations of food (grain) requirements and possible deficits in the two models are based on the following figures and assumptions concerning population size and annual population growth:

For the South Asia region for 1975, Mesarovic and Pestel list 1,300 million people and an annual rate of increase of 2.5 percent. Under their "scenario no. 1," which is their most optimistic scenario, they assume that under a successful population policy within the next fifty years (i.e., until 2025), fertility will have been brought down to replacement level. In that case, they assume for this region by 2025 3,800 million people (about three times the figure for 1975) and an annual rate of increase of 1 percent.

The Bariloche model presents figures for all of Asia with alternative computations, one assuming an average grain production of four tons, the other an average of six tons per ha in twenty-year intervals from 1960 to 2040 and 2060, respectively, in two tables (Herrera et al., 1976, tables 10 and 11, p. 94). In order to make these figures comparable with those of Mesarovic and Pestel, their 1980 and 2020 figures have been proportionally adjusted, the former back from 1980 to 1975, the latter forward from 2020 to 2025, to cover the same fifty-year period.

Both tables begin with a population (for all of Asia) of 2,526 million in 1975, with an annual rate of increase of 2.5 percent (the same rate Mesarovic and Pestel list for that year for South Asia). Then, assuming an annual yield of four tons of grain per ha, they come for the year 2025 to 7,225 million people (three times the 1975 figure) and an annual growth rate of 1.47 percent (compared with 2.5 percent for 1975).

In their second table, assuming an annual yield of six tons per ha, they assume that, due to the better standard of living that goes with this higher yield, the annual increase of population has gone down to 1.07 percent and total population for Asia has risen to only 5,557 million— that is, to 2.3 times as much as in 1975 (compared with three times as much under the assumption of a yield of four tons per ha).

Thus, where the Bariloche model uses an average grain yield of four tons per ha, which is still in line, although perhaps somewhat on the optimistic side, with the estimates of Baade and of Clark (who are themselves by no means pessimists concerning the future outlook of mankind), it comes to population figures and developments for all of Asia that more or less parallel the corresponding computations of Mesarovic and Pestel for the region of South Asia: approximately a three-fold increase of total population between 1975 and 2025, with 1 percent to 1.5 percent annual growth toward the end of that period.

Things begin to change quite drastically with their (as it seems to me quite arbitrary) assumption of an average yield of six tons per ha for all of Asia, which would be one and a half times or more than current yields in the most advanced agricultures of Western Europe and North America.

Still, the point of discussion is not the more or less optimistic assumption about grain yields but the manner in which this assumption is built into the Bariloche model, where higher grain yields are immediately translated into an overall improvement of standards of living, which are in turn immediately translated into a systematic lowering of the annual rate of increase of the population and thus into a desirable slowing down of the increase of regional populations. We ought to keep in mind that Asia alone already contains close to 60 percent of the world's population, and there are still other developing regions, especially in Africa and in part in South America, with similarly growing populations and similarly increasing deficits of grain (and other food) production. All of these areas clamor to be satisfied either out of increased production within their home region or with imports from the traditional export regions, especially from the United States, Canada, and Australia.

This, finally, is the crux of the matter: What is a necessary conclusion, if one starts out with the essentially Malthusian assumption that continued rapid growth of the world's population (and also of its per-capita consumption of irreplaceable materials) must eventually lead to an exhaustion of the total maximal food and other supplies (the only point of debate being when is "eventually"?), when this assumption occurs within a model as blatantly anti-Malthusian as the Bariloche model? This must be considered an intolerable contradiction that completely denies the meaningfulness of the model.

Let me at this point talk briefly about the development of population growth in Western Europe during the latter part of the eighteenth century and then much of the nineteenth century—that is, from the beginning of the Industrial Revolution. Birth and death rates were at that time in near balance; there were annually about forty births and thirty-seven deaths per 1,000 population for an annual population increase of about 3 per 1,000 or 0.3 percent (about one-seventh as much as the current annual increase of the world's population of about 2 percent and less than one-tenth of the 3.5 percent and more in some countries, especially in Africa. In particular, high infant and child mortality was part of the high death rate—and an indirect cause for the continued high birth rate, because steady procreation was necessary to have at least some children survive into adulthood.

Slowly, as living conditions, medical care, and general hygiene improved (especially with canalization and safer drinking water in the cities), people began to realize that children, once born, had a good chance to survive, so that continued procreation was no longer necessary. At the same time, continued procreation now also meant a greater burden on the parents. But it took some two to three generations until this led to a widespread social adaptation to families with fewer children. Thus, birth rates stayed high for a long time while death rates declined, and as a consequence growth rates grew from some 3 per 1,000 around 1780 to about 10 per 1,000 by 1870 (with a maximum of about 11 or 12 per 1,000 in England and the industrialized parts of Germany). Only then did birth rates slowly begin to decline and growth rates for the next 100 years stayed around 8 per 1,000 per year for most of the industrialized countries.

American demographers who called attention to this phenomenon during the 1930s called it the "demographic transition," which denotes a process leading from a fairly steady relation of high birth and high death rates with low growth rates in between back to a fairly steady relation of much lower birth and death rates with lower growth rates in between again. But between the beginning and end of this development was a period of "transition" during which death rates declined fast, while birth rates stayed high, so that for quite a number of decades, covering about two generations, growth rates kept increasing until they at first declined somewhat and eventually stabilized at about 0.8 percent per year (for most industrialized countries).

In most of the colonial world of the nineteenth and early twentieth centuries—now largely the "developing countries"—the same phenomenon set in much later, around 1870. But with the rapid introduction of methods of mass medicine and hygiene, especially after World War II, the decline of birth rates came much more rapidly, while the social adaptation to this—the recognition that children, once born, now tended much more often to survive to adulthood—took almost as long as it took in Europe. Thus, the annual growth rates, which in Europe hardly ever exceeded 10 to 12 per 1,000, grew generally to about 25 and in many countries to 35 per 1,000 per year, with Kenya currently having the highest annual growth rate of 40 per 1,000.

What the authors of the Bariloche model did now was first to assume improvements in the general living conditions (food, housing, schooling, etc.) and then to translate these into corresponding automatic reductions in birth and growth rates. But since it is patently easier to build houses and schools than it is to convince people that the time has come to cut down on procreation, this automatism in the model, which apparently did not take into consideration how long it actually takes for societies (especially "primitive" ones) to adapt socially accepted norms concerning the number of children appropriate to changed survival conditions of the children (as well as of the adults with the eradication of major killer diseases such as malaria, cholera, small pox, etc.), it was inevitable that the Bariloche model should contain this contradiction: as the authors themselves wrote, their model showed a high average life expectancy for a time, for which the food sector no longer provided the wherewithal to survive that long. The computer listed people as no longer able to be fed while they still had that long life expectancy before them.

As one way out of this contradiction, Herrera et al. computed how long it would take for all mankind to achieve the minimum of standard of living that the model assumed in the beginning (3,000 calories and 100 grams of protein per day, decent housing, and twelve years of schooling) if the "have" countries supported the "have-not" countries in the following manner: at first, over a ten-year period, they would contribute in the first year 0.2 percent, in the next 0.4 percent, then 0.6 percent, and so on, of their gross national product until, after ten years, the annual contributions reached 2 percent of their GNP. Then, the contributions would stay at that level until the above-described minimum standard was reached, whereupon they would gradually decline at the same rate again: from 2 percent to 1.8 percent to 1.6 percent, and so on, until at the end of ten years the contributions would stop. While this is an interesting suggestion, it is not part of my discussion of a serious contradiction with the Bariloche model.

In conclusion, let me briefly restate the main thesis of *The Limits to Growth* by Meadows et al., the main points of attack on it by critics from the political Left and from developing countries, and how all of this turns out in the end in the Bariloche model, which comes from the political Left ("What is proposed is a shift toward a society that is essentially socialist"—Herrera et al., 1976, p. 8), and from a developing country (Argentina).

Meadows et al. (1972) essentially warned that if the world population continued to grow at an annual increase of about 2 percent and the consumption per capita of nonreplaceable resources continued to grow at 1.5 percent annually, as has been the case during the last few decades, this would have to lead to general catastrophe within 100 to 120 years.

This could be avoided, however, if both the growth of world population and the increase in per-capita consumption of nonreplaceable resources could be brought to a halt within thirty to sixty years. Meadows et al. added that, even so, the developing countries were by no means condemned to eternal poverty but could within those thirty to sixty years achieve an overall standard of living about half as high as current standards in the Western countries. Let me emphasize that this would still sound for many of these countries like a utopia that is way beyond what currently seems to be within their reach.

Still, this was attacked as a kind of plot of the economically dominant West and the former colonial masters, a kind of imperialistic stratagem to preserve their position and rule, which was being threatened by the increasing industrialization of their former colonies and other poor countries whose growth in population threatened to overwhelm the former ruling powers by sheer numbers. And the theoretical basis of it, being essentially Malthusian, was attacked as a pseudoscientific smokescreen to cover the evil intent.

And now we have the Bariloche model, which bravely sets out to attack and to disprove all this—and in the end winds up with the same gloomy conclusion that rapid population increase, if not stemmed in time, must lead mankind to the limits of its supplies of food and material resources, and that, at least as far as Asia (comprising almost 60 percent of mankind) is concerned, even sooner than the "100 to 120 years" Meadows et al. predicted because, to repeat that fateful passage once more:

> The rate of population growth is reduced very slowly, and the population [of Asia] increases fivefold in 80 years, reaching 7,840 million in 2040. Life expectancy at birth improves, but is always below levels in other regions. . . . *The runs were stopped at the year 2040 because after that date the indicators (particularly life expectancy) cease to have any meaning.* Although the calories provided by the food sector drop below

the minimum required for survival, life expectancy remains relatively high owing to the effects of education and housing. . . .

The problem of Asia arises in the food sector. By 2010 all available land is being cultivated. Thereafter, economic effort in the sector is devoted to increasing livestock and fisheries. This, however, is not enough to feed the growing population adequately, and consumption drops rapidly to below the minimum needed for survival. [Herrera et al., 1976, emphasis added]

This agrees exactly with Mesarovic and Pestel in *Mankind at the Turning Point,* published two years earlier, computing that enormous food deficit of 500 million tons of grain for South Asia by 2025 if rapid population growth is not brought to a halt long before then.

Recall at this point a second passage from Herrera et al. cited above (p. 94) in which they suggest that, because food remains a major problem for the region (i.e., for Asia), it might try to increase agricultural yields and produce food from nonconventional sources:

These measures could *be implemented with an effective family planning policy.* . . . there is sufficient time available before the crisis for an effective policy in both directions to be adopted. [Emphasis added] (p. 94)

Ironic though it may sound, for the 60 percent of mankind who live in the Asia region, this is practically the same suggestion Meadows et al. offered for all of mankind (to bring the steady increase of the world's population to a halt within the next thirty to sixty years), yet the latter were raked over the coals by numerous authors from the political Left and from Third World countries (and Herrera et al. are both!), calling them imperialists and racists and accusing them of suggesting genocide for the Third World to stave off the threat that the West might be overtaken by the overwhelming power of numbers of the growing populations in the poorer countries. (I still recall the formulation of a Third World representative at an international population conference in Washington: "We are going to outbreed you!")

Again, what must be a more or less natural conclusion for Malthusians like Meadows et al. is, when reached by decided anti-Malthusians like the authors of the Bariloche model as the computational outcome of their model, not a mere concession to the other side but a contradiction in terms that in fact vitiates the meaning of their model.

References

Baade, Fritz. *Der Wettlauf zum Jahre 2000—Paradies oder Selbstvernichtung* (The Race to the Year 2000—Paradise or Self-destruction). Non-stop, Oldenburg, Buecherei, Gerhard Stalling Verlag, 1960 [2d ed. 1967].

Brown, Lester. "The World Food Prospect." In *Science,* December 12, 1975, pp. 1053–59.

—————. 1978. *The Twenty-Ninth Day.* W. W. Norton, New York 1978.

Clark, Colin. *The Myth of Overpopulation.* Melbourne: Advocate Press, 1973. [German ed.: "Der Mythos von der Ueberbevoelkeung." Adamas Verlag, 1975.]

Herrera, Amilcar O., et al. *Catastrophe or New Society? A Latin-American World Model.* Ottawa, Canada: International Development Research Center (IDRC), 1976.

Meadows, Donella H.; Dennis L. Meadows; et al. *The Limits to Growth. A Report to the Club of Rome's Project on the Predicament of Mankind.* New York: Universe Books, 1972.

Mesarovic, Mihajlo, and Eduard Pestel. *Mankind at the Turning Point.* New York: New American Library, 1974. A Potomac Associates Book. [German ed.: *Menschheit am Wendepunkt.* Stuttgart: Deutsche Verlagsanstalt, 1974.]

Chapter 7

The Price and Availability of Oil and the Food Situation in the Third World

In recent years several developing countries, especially China and India, have gone over to the large-scale application of artificial fertilizer in order to increase the yield of agricultural production. Some, especially China, have begun to develop their own artificial fertilizer industries in order to become as independent as possible from the rather expensive imports of either the fertilizer itself or the by-products of the oil industry from which much artificial fertilizer is being made.

How much the addition of artificial fertilizer can increase the yield per acre depends, of course, on the quality of the soil, the kind of grain or what else is to be planted, the specific kind of fertilizer to be applied, and several other conditions. As a very rough estimate, it is often assumed that on the average one ton of artificial fertilizer will bring eight additional tons of grain. This 1:8 relation is meant not as a basis for estimating how much additional grain or other crops to expect when applying the fertilizer to a particular field, but only as an overall average when artificial fertilizer is to be introduced for larger regions where little or none has been used before.

From a lecture at the University of Munich, Spring 1986, "Bevoelkerungsprobleme der Dritten Welt und die Weltmodelle."

In regions where indeed much of it has already been applied, the yield relation can rapidly drop to 1:5 (five additional tons of grain for one additional ton of fertilizer) and even as low as 1:3.

Since much artificial fertilizer is produced from the side and waste products of the oil industry, this is the point where the food problem touches on the problems of the availability and the price of oil. Any serious rise in the price of oil also increases the price of artificial fertilizer or of the by-products of the oil industry from which it is being made. Thus, any serious increase in the price of oil threatens indirectly but fairly immediately the food supply of Third World countries that are always hard pressed for the cash to pay for those imports.

But the consequences go even further. As a prime example, when OPEC in 1973—in the famous "first oil shock"—suddenly quadrupled the price of oil, Morocco, one of the biggest exporters of phosphate, immediately followed suit with a slightly greater price rise for the latter: from $14 to $63 per ton. And ever since, when the price of oil rose, Morocco followed suit with the price of phosphate.

The main consequence of a price rise in oil is, of course, a rise in the price of gasoline, which drives not only cars but whole industries in both industrialized and developing countries—including water pumps and the machinery for large-scale irrigation of fields. This in turn concerns not only Third World countries but also the industries, including the highly mechanized agriculture in countries like the United States, Canada, Australia, and New Zealand, the main producers of surplus grain for export to the rest of the world. On these exports depend not only most of the industrialized countries of Europe, but to a steadily increasing extent countries like Egypt and India, among others—especially in times of poor harvests as a consequence of drought or flood. This growing dependence of Third World countries on the availability of surplus grain and other food products from countries with highly mechanized agriculture is particularly felt where there are as yet no major storage facilities to tie the countries over crisis periods. Especially where agriculture is still operated on such a primitive level that it yields barely more than a subsistence for the peasants, any serious increase in oil prices, if it leads to an increase in the price of imported food, constitutes a double threat for the food situation in these countries. They themselves may not have enough cash to pay for the increased cost of imports, and in the food exporting countries, rising production costs may make it not sufficiently profitable to keep on producing food for export.

The same problem, although generally on a smaller and therefore less immediately threatening scale, holds for the Soviet Union and its satellites: since the satellites import most of their oil and natural gas from the Soviet Union, and since the latter too raises its prices more or less in line with rises in world market prices in oil, any rise of the latter also affects the satellites of the Soviet Union.

All of this may give a first indication of the close interrelation between the increase of population, the food supply, and the production and the price of oil. And, in line with our topic here, it is this kind of interlocking relationship between these and many other factors that gave rise to the development of world models.

At the same time, this also gives a first indication of the limits of what can possibly be accomplished with the help of world models. Because the latter cannot take into account in any systematic numerical fashion the possible changes in these and other factors and their interplay, which have to be expected in case of major political changes or in case of war, not only for the nations immediately involved but also for those whose supplies are threatened even if they themselves are not involved in war. The same holds concerning major political or economic decisions such as the earlier-mentioned sudden increase in OPEC oil prices or China's sudden decision to adopt its "only one child per family" policy. While it may always be possible in principle to anticipate such changes or decisions, there is hardly any way of translating such anticipation into the hard numbers and equations required for a computer model.

As to oil, the most basic question, on which the experts' assumptions differ most widely, is this: How far into the future can we expect with reasonable certainty oil and natural gas to be available as the main sources of energy? One of the most widespread assumptions among reputable experts—although heavily disputed by other, equally reputable experts—is that world reserves of oil and natural gas will last for another thirty years or so. This does not, of course, mean that one day around the year 2010 or 2015 the last drop of oil or gas will come out of the last pipeline, but that after about thirty years oil and natural gas will constitute only a much smaller part of total energy used in this world than they do today, regardless of what may replace them—nuclear energy, or solar energy, or a return to coal, or the large-scale development of biomass, or any combination of any or all of these—or possibly even some newly discovered deposits of oil that are today wholly unanticipated.

Concerning the latter possibility, there is a beautiful and utterly simply argument by E. Arab-Ogly, professor at the Russian Academy of Sciences (1975): it can be considered as highly unlikely, that of a material as widespread over the globe as oil, more than two-thirds should occur in just one spot, the Persian Gulf and Saudi Arabia (p. 247). I can hardly imagine a more immediately plausible argument. But what responsible statesman or economic leader could dare, trusting the relatively irrefutable strength of this argument, now to call off the planned or in-progress development of nuclear or other forms of energy in his country? Certainly Arab-Ogly's own countrymen, who have to make the appropriate decisions for the Soviet Union, have not dared to do so, or they would not continue to pursue the rapid development of nuclear energy to the degree to which they are doing so.

Arab-Ogly, in this book, which is primarily a critique of *The Limits to Growth* (Meadows et al., 1972) and of Western futurology as a whole, points out that the discussion about the potential exhaustion of the world's oil reserves has been going on for a long time already and that it has repeatedly led and continues to lead to rather grotesque results because such anticipations of depletion have again and again been made obsolete by the discovery of new deposits:

In the 1920s, total oil reserves were estimated at 8,000 million tons. At the then prevailing rate of annual consumption of 270 million tons, that would have lasted for about thirty years, or until about 1950. But at the end of these thirty years in 1950, with annual consumption having in the meantime doubled to about 500 million tons, total deposits were estimated at 13,000 million tons, which should have lasted for another twenty-five years. But toward the end of this period, in 1974, with consumption having meanwhile risen to five times as much— namely, to 2,500 million tons per year—the remaining deposits were estimated at another 80,000 million tons (i.e., six times the 1950 estimate of still remaining reserves). Assuming that annual consumption remains constant at 2,500 million tons, this should again last another thirty-two years, until about the year 2007. "The more oil gets taken out of the ground," Arab-Ogly adds, "the higher grow the estimates of what still remains in it—and thus, the longer also grows the period for which the world's requirements for oil still appear as assured." (All of the foregoing following Arab-Ogly, 1975, p. 246–47.)

So far, so good.

Now comes the counterargument: Philip Abelson, the editor of *Sci-*

ence, points out in *Energy for Tomorrow* (1975) that in 1975 annual world consumption of oil amounted to 15 billion barrels (that approximately corresponds to the 2,500 million tons of annual consumption cited by Arab-Ogly). But, according to Abelson, at that time discoveries of new deposits amounted on the average to about 8 billion barrels. Should that difference between annual consumption and annual discoveries of new deposits continue for a prolonged period of time, then it is a matter of simple arithmetic to compute the not too distant time when all deposits would be exhausted.

King Hubbert, one of the United States' foremost oil experts, warned in the mid-1950s that American oil production would reach its peak in the early or mid-1970s and would decline thereafter (Hubbert, 1969). The oil industry furiously disputed that claim—but his prognosis proved correct even before the founding of OPEC.

Arab-Ogly's figures for 1975 (2,500 million tons annual consumption), which according to then current estimates (heavily disputed by him) should allow for another thirty-two years, more or less agree with figures cited in Meadows et al.'s *The Limits to Growth* and in Mesarovic and Pestel's *Mankind at the Turning Point* (1974). But they go one step further: should annual oil consumption continue to increase each year by 4–5 percent, as was the case during the last few decades, then the deposits would last not thirty-two but only twenty-two years (Meadows, 1972, p. 66). It seems now that, as a consequence of the dramatic price increase through OPEC, annual consumption in the industrialized countries is not rising as fast as it used to, even in spite of continuing increases in population and industrialization. Thus, one may assume that the estimate of how long the oil deposits will last may fall somewhere between the two figures cited above—that is, somewhere between twenty-two and thirty-two years.

Since both sides in this discussion start with the same publicly known figures about annual production and consumption, and in addition know the published estimates made by the various experts concerning the size of still remaining reserves, what conclusions one will draw about future prospects seems patently a matter of either optimistic or pessimistic interpretation of both the figures themselves and the estimates: whether oil as a main source of energy is threatened with exhaustion within a few decades or whether there is enough left that we do not need to worry for a long time to come. I myself do not consider it my task or topic to pursue this play of optimism versus pessimism in the interpretation of figures and estimates any further. However, we ought not overlook the role that political ideology, in addition to personal optimism or pessimism, also seems to play in how various authors judge the future prospects.

The following figures may help to elucidate the magnitude of this problem: World consumption of oil amounted in 1930 to 5.5 million barrels, in 1950 to 12.5 million, in 1970 to 44 million, and in 1975 to 57 million barrels per day. This represents a tenfold increase in forty-five years. During the same time the world's population doubled from about 2,000 million in 1930 to about 4,000 million in 1975. This means a *fivefold* increase of the per-capita consumption worldwide in *forty years*—actually, much more than that in the industrialized and in those Third World countries where industrialization is just beginning on a larger scale, and correspondingly less in the less developed countries. Moreover, a little closer to our own days, from 1950 to 1975 annual oil consumption the world over increased 4 1/2-fold, while population increased only by about 60 percent, or an almost *three-fold* increase of the per-capita consumption worldwide in only *twenty-five years*.

Into this discussion of how long we may expect oil to last as the main source of energy fits a presentation by Abelson (1975) showing how the main source of energy in the United States changed in the course of 120 years, from 1850 to 1970, from wood to coal to oil, and finally to oil plus natural gas. (He takes the data, presented in an impressive graphic, from Linden, 1974.): Around 1850, the main source of primary energy in the United States was wood: 73 percent of all primary energy came from it. Eighteen percent came from water power (though this was still before the large-scale use of hydroelectricity), with coal running a poor third, supplying only 9 percent of all primary energy.

Only fifty years later, around 1900, coal had already replaced wood as the main source of primary energy, with 75 percent, and only 10 percent still coming from wood. The direct use of water power hardly counted any more. Oil and natural gas were beginning to be a significant source, constituting 10 percent of all primary energy (only forty years after the first successful oil drill in Titusville, Pennsylvania, in 1859). Hydroelectricity, also just developing, supplied 5 percent of all primary energy.

Another forty years later, by 1940, just before the United States' entry into World War II, coal had already lost much of its importance as a source of primary energy, supplying only 37 percent of it while more than half of it (54 percent) now came from oil and natural gas and 6 percent came from hydroelectricity.

By 1970 coal had lost even more of its share: it was down to supplying only 18 percent of all primary energy, while oil and natural gas together provided 76 percent—as much, as a percentage, as coal seventy years before and wood another fifty years back. The use of nuclear energy, supplying thus far only 1 percent of all primary energy, was barely registered as a source.

Thus—and this may be relevant for a longer-term perspective—it took fifty to seventy years for one predominating source of primary energy to be replaced by another—first wood by coal, then coal by oil and natural gas. To repeat: 1870, 73 percent from wood; 1900, 75 percent from coal; 1970, 74 percent from oil and natural gas.

Let me repeat also that all of this refers only to the United States. It stands to reason, however, that the process must have been about the same in most industrial countries, even if the exact figures might vary.

As a sideline, let me note that hydroelectricity, though never a negligible contributor to total primary energy consumption since its first use around the turn of the century, has never up to the present, in spite of the gigantic increase in total consumption, amounted to more than about 5–6 percent of total primary energy. This is in spite of the fact that especially during the 1930s and 1940s some of the world's then greatest dams were built in the United States (Hoover Dam, Bonneville Dam, Grand Coulee Dam, and the whole series of dams of the TVA [Tennessee Valley Authority]. This is worth remembering by those engaged in the current discussion about the use or the danger of nuclear energy who might think that its development could easily be avoided through the utilization of as yet untapped water power for more hydroelectricity.

It is of course not easy to anticipate what is going to happen next concerning the primary sources of energy. It is an undeniable fact that just now, while the United States with its growing consumption of oil is becoming increasingly dependent on imports from other countries, other claimants too are demanding more and more oil from the few places that have enough to be able to export it. In addition to the similarly growing demands for oil by other industrial countries come those of numerous developing countries both for the development of their own industries and for artificial fertilizer and other by-products.

Thus increases the demand for additional production from already known deposits and for finding and developing new deposits of oil and natural gas, as well as for the further development of other sources of energy. It may be relevant therefore to point out this difference: during the preceding 120 or so years, one source of energy was being replaced by another, generally for the sake of higher efficiency and better economy, whereas now (despite the ever so convincing arguments of those who think there is still enough oil for a long time to come) the frantic search for new sources of energy, especially nuclear energy, is driven by the fear of those who think that soon there will not be enough oil and natural gas to meet the ever-increasing demands. And should the deposits really come near exhaustion, then what?

This brings us now, particularly in light of the existence of OPEC, to the necessity of developing resources independent of this oil-producing cartel, regardless of whether this means searching for and developing new deposits of oil and/or natural gas outside of OPEC's reach or developing alternative forms of energy (not to speak of the less wasteful and more efficient use of whatever oil and gas may still exist). All of this is of course a question not only of the physical and technical possibilities in the development of new or alternative sources of energy, but also of political conflict and political decisions, including the politicization of the question in view of the potential dangers of nuclear energy. This political aspect too, however, I consider outside my immediate topic, except that I would point out that the more the potential dangers and damages in connection with nuclear energy become a subject of political discussion, the more requirements for safety and for environmental protection will be imposed on the development of nuclear reactors, which then means, aside from everything else, that if it can go on at all, it also becomes increasingly expensive.

It is this latter point that may lead to the postponement of the full development of nuclear energy even where it might already be technically possible, until such time when a more seriously visible threat of exhaustion of the oil deposits than is currently only claimed by some, but by far not by all experts might eventually force the issue. Here, too, I approach the realm of pure conjecture which I had better leave for another discussion.

In this context in particular one begins to ponder the question (which may eventually become quite acute) whether the utilization of solar energy can be developed fast enough and on a large enough scale to obviate the need for the large-scale development of nuclear energy. That the development of energy out of biomass should be accomplished on a large enough scale to become a serious competitor with other major sources of energy within a generation or so, especially to fill a potential gap between the decreasing availability of oil and gas and the not yet sufficient solar energy, still seems unlikely. But, of course, this too is mere speculation.

At the beginning of this chapter I pointed out the interconnection between the price of oil and the price of artificial fertilizer and thus the indirect relation between the price of oil set by the OPEC countries and the amount of food available in countries that need oil for their agriculture and for artificial fertilizer. In this context it may be useful to point out certain price relations that the nonspecialist is seldom aware of, but that are very important and have been very stable over decades, until they did get upset with the sudden change in OPEC oil prices.

As a good lead example, let us look at a set of figures presented by Lester Brown (1981): From 1950 to 1973 (i.e., up to the first oil shock), one barrel of oil (about 159 liters) cost about as much as one bushel of wheat (about 36 liters): this is a fairly stable relation of 1:1—one barrel of oil for one bushel of wheat. After the oil shock of 1973, the relation changed within only a few years to 1:2, then 1:3, until by 1977 it was already 1:4 and by 1980 1:6. In 1972 one bushel of wheat and one barrel of oil each cost about $1.90. By 1980 the price of one bushel of wheat had gone up to $5.00 and the price of one barrel of oil was up to about $30.00. Thus wheat had gone up to two and a half times and oil to fifteen times its pre-oil-shock price. The fact that the United States, which exports wheat but imports oil, thus has to export much more of the one in order to continue paying for the other has been discussed often enough (Brown, 1981, p. 67).

Less often discussed and particularly less well known among nonspecialists is what havoc this same change in the price relation between needed imports of oil and what little export goods they may have, plays with the economy of developing countries, especially when it comes to paying the increased prices for artificial fertilizer or for the side products of the oil industry which they have to import in order to make artificial fertilizer, which they urgently need to produce more food for their rapidly growing populations. The vaunted "Green Revolution"— that is, the transition to the newly developed higher-yielding strains of rice and wheat and the like—required much more artificial fertilizer and much more irrigation, meaning more machinery to operate the irrigation, more oil to operate that machinery. Since the increased yields of that "Green Revolution" barely kept pace with the increased food requirements of the steadily growing population (remember: 2 percent or more annual population increase), any diminished ability of these countries (e.g., India) to pay for the import of oil and artificial fertilizer means an immediate reduction of the standard of living and, looming not far behind the horizon, outright famine.

References

Abelson, Philip H. *Energy for Tomorrow*. Seattle: University of Washington Press, 1975.

Arab-Ogly, E. *In the Forecaster's Maze*. Moscow: Progress Publishers, 1975.

Brown, Lester. *Building a Sustainable Society*. New York: W.W. Norton, 1981.

Hubbert, M. King. "Energy Resources." In Preston Cloud (ed.), *Resources and Man*. San Francisco: Freeman, 1969.

Linden, Henry R. *Energy Self-Sufficiency: A Look at the Future*. Chicago: 1974. (Cited by Abelson.)

Meadows, Donella H.; Dennis L. Meadows; et al. *The Limits to Growth, A Report to the Club of Rome's Project on the Predicament of Mankind*. New York: Universe Books, A Potomac Associates Book, 1972.

Mesarovic, Mihajlo, and Eduard Pestel. *Mankind at the Turning Point. The Second Report to the Club of Rome*. New York: E.P. Dutton, 1974.

Chapter 8

Chinese Population Policy from 1949 to 1984

When I came to China in May 1981 (not with any special study group, but with an ordinary commercial guided tour), I was greatly surprised to learn that the former policy of "two children per family is enough," espoused since 1971, had only recently been replaced by the much more restrictive policy of "only one child per family." It seems that in spite of its dramatic impact upon the lives of the people of China and eventually the whole world, the Western news media had thus far not found this newsworthy enough to make a big splash. Not only I but practically everyone else on that tour was still soundly ignorant of this change. When I gave my first paper about today's topic about a year ago, I still made a big effort to cite Chinese sources, the higher up, the better, for fear that otherwise I might not be believed when talking about this new policy and some of its side issues.

Meanwhile all of this has changed and the "one child per family" policy of China has become something of a household word. All we now need is some analysis of the reasons that led up to it, a description of how it works today, and some discussion of its prospects for tomorrow. This in essence will be the content of this presentation.

Paper given at the Columbia University Seminar on "Content and Methods of the Social Sciences," April 11, 1984. Published (in German): *Journal fuer Social Forschung, 25*, 1 (1985), pp. 39–56.

You may recall that about a year ago a doctoral student of anthropology by the name of Steven Mosher was thrown out of Stanford University and denied his degree for some alleged transgressions and improper conduct while doing research on his doctoral thesis in a village in China. While not enough about the case has been presented to allow an outsider to form a considered judgment, it seems—at least from a three-page article in *Science* in May 1983—that although the case itself had been simmering for quite a while, what finally brought it to a boil was an article by Mosher in May 1981 in a popular weekly in Taiwan in which, according to *Science,* Mosher had been "detailing third-trimester abortions in a Chinese village. . . . The article, which criticized China's family program, included photographs of Chinese women undergoing the abortions; their faces were not masked. The article incensed the Chinese" (*Science*, 1983, p. 692).

That at long last seemed newsworthy enough for the Western press to report with a sense of outrage over these abortions in such a late stage of pregnancy. And this outrage in turn, following the report in *Science,* incensed the government of mainland China which decried the report as being either a complete falsehood or a deliberate exaggeration of some isolated action of overzealous local officials in order to give a bad name to the whole program—reminiscent of the exaggerated reports of forced sterilizations in India some years ago which eventually contributed to Indira Gandhi's defeat in the next election.

Meanwhile the Chinese government must apparently have changed its mind about how much publicity to give to such incidents, because with its permission a British television team last year produced a documentary about the family planning program in the city of Chanzhou, which currently serves as a model city for successful population control. The documentary shows the arrival and reception of a delegation of family planning officers from another city who have come to see how it is being done.

This documentary, aired in the United States on public television on February 14, 1984, indeed brought details about exactly those late-pregnancy abortions, the detailing of which by Mosher two years before had so incensed the Chinese authorities. The film shows close-ups (certainly unmasked) of a woman, six months pregnant, lying on an operating table undergoing an abortion, and includes a close-up of a syringe filled with yellow fluid being injected into her womb to kill the fetus and bring about an abortion within twenty-four hours, all of it carefully detailed by the narrator. In an interview that woman tells (in Chinese, with English subtitles) that she had been determined to have her child but then the family planning officer had come and tried to persuade her to have an abortion; at first she had resisted, after which the officer brought along the other officers of the community, and, as she still resisted, higher and higher ones. They came every day and talked to her—and none of her friends stood up for her. At long last, seeing that this would go on day in and day out for many months, eventually she gave in to have the abortion. On the same television documentary, an interview with the family planning officer who had persuaded her confirms every word of the story.

This documentary also presents an interview with another family planning officer who tells of a woman seven months pregnant, who had hidden in her mother's house twenty miles away, whom the family planning officer had herself brought back and persuaded to have an abortion.

Then the chief family planning officer of the city of Chanzhou tells yet another story of a woman who had hidden her pregnancy for quite some time until she could hide it no more and then was persuaded to have an abortion, for which she was brought to the hospital. But the night before the operation she escaped and fled to Shanghai. The good people of Shanghai, however, had cooperated in finding her so that she could be brought back to Chanzhou for the abortion.

This reminds me of a story some years ago in the *New York Times*. An American journalist visiting a jail in China had wondered why there was no wall, no fence, nothing. Weren't they afraid that the prisoners would run away? The answer was "No—why should they? Where would they go?"

At any rate, here the family planning officer continues on television: "We were all busy finding her. Such things happen."

And thus the city of Chanzhou kept its record clean as a model city with one hundred percent compliance with the family planning program, and received yet another annual award for this at a big ceremony, also shown on television, in which a group of little children sang a wonderful little song (quoted from a transcript provided by WGBH in Boston):

Mummy had only me. We don't want brothers and sisters.
Everyone is happy. The whole house rejoices. Laa, La, la. [Transcript, p. 16]

Until fairly recently not enough was known about the size of the population of China, and particularly not about its annual increase, to allow for a systematic population policy. Demographers estimated that it may have been about 410 million in 1840 and might have grown to over half a billion, perhaps as high as 540 million by 1949 when the Communists came to power.

With the cheerful optimism of the victorious revolutionary and innovator, Mao Zedong, at the time when they did seize power, proclaimed on September 16, 1949, that from now on hunger and mass starvation, which had only been the consequences of feudalism and of capitalist exploitation, were a thing of the past, and that a country with the vast agricultural lands and with all the other resources of China need have no fear of population growth. Like the mercantilists in seventeenth- and eighteenth-century Europe, who had seen the wealth of a country in its productive capacity and with that in the size of its working population that produced its wealth, Mao declared that "people are the most precious thing in the world" and that the more people, the more production, and with that a faster building of socialism. "Revolution plus production" would surely suffice to create enough work and enough food for all. Said Mao: "The absurd theory that increase in food cannot catch up with the increases in population, put forth by such Western bourgeois economists as Malthus and company had been refuted by Marxists in theory, but also had been overthrown in practice in the post-revolutionary Soviet Union and in liberated China" (quoted in Aird, 1981).

That was in 1949. With the first population census of 1953–54 came the first sobering up. It turned out that China had about 583 million people, perhaps some 30 to 40 million more than expected, and an annual growth rate of about 2 percent, or 11 to 12 million people per year. That certainly gave pause to be concerned about how these rapidly growing masses of people were to be fed a few decades hence.

Thus, in 1954, a high-level government committee was set up to study the question and, following its suggestions, in 1956 Prime Minister Zhou Enlai formally set in motion the first wave of propaganda for birth control. Before it got into full swing, however, it was interrupted in 1958 by Mao's "Great Leap Forward," which was introduced with the anticipation that economic developments would soon overtake population growth—there was again nothing to fear from growing numbers. Those who had advocated a restrictive population policy, especially Ma Yinchu, then president of the University of Beijing, were again attacked as Malthusians and removed from their posts. All debate about possible demographic dangers was successfully stifled.

But the "Great Leap Forward" did not bring the hoped-for improvements. Optimism turned again at least to doubt, if not outright pessimism, reinforced by three years of drought that cut down drastically on agricultural production. Thus, in 1962 another campaign for birth control got under way, again formally opened by Prime Minister Zhou Enlai who emphasized that "if we control population development . . . our country will become wealthy and powerful more quickly"—only to get stopped again in its tracks before it had a chance to really get going. This time it was the Cultural Revolution of 1966–68 and its aftermath, for which "birth control" was a decadent bourgeois concept that did not belong in Communist China.

It was not before 1971 that Zhou Enlai formally opened the next campaign, this time no longer simply calling for birth control but pronouncing quite definitely: "one child is ideal; two are enough; three are too many." Under the slogan "later-longer-fewer" people were expected to marry later, to space their children more widely—at least four years between them in the city, three years in the country—and to have fewer of them—preferably not more than two in the city and three in the country.

Pressure toward compliance was at first comparatively mild, taking the form primarily of propaganda and simple persuasion. But when, after a few years, voluntary compliance proved disappointingly low, more serious pressure was applied in the form of incentives for compliance and disincentives for noncompliance. Most of these are still in use. I shall come back to them below.

Yet by the later 1970s it became quite clear that even full compliance with this two-children policy would not suffice, for the simple reason that by the early 1980s and then still into the early 1990s those greater cohorts of children born during the Great Leap and during the Cultural Revolution and its aftermath, when all population control had come to a standstill, would be coming of marring age. There would be about 25 million of them each year, meaning approximately 12 million marriages. If most of these were to have two children each, this would mean such an upsurge in the annual number of births that it would threaten the new post-Mao program of the "four modernizations" in agriculture, industry, defense, and science which was designed with the hope that it would double the per-capita Gross National Product within the next two decades and then double it once more within the third and fourth decade. In the long run this sudden baby boom would produce a serious threat to the total food supply because even a steadily improving agriculture could not be expected to keep pace with it.

It became quite clear that in order for agriculture to be able to cope with the growing population, fertility would have to be reduced to well below the replacement level. This meant that a very large number of families would have to be restricted to not more than one child.

Under this fairly straight economic pressure, and contrary to all earlier ideological pronouncements against Malthusianism as a kind of primeval bourgeois sin, China's "one-child policy" was born.

When, immediately after my return from China I pointed out to Mr. Tuan, China specialist at the East–West Population Institute in Honolulu, that this was Malthusianism pure and simple, he explained to me that in the eyes of the Chinese policy makers this was no contradiction: They consider Malthus wrong on theoretical grounds and they restrict population growth because otherwise they would not have enough to eat. In one of his papers he spelled that out more fully:

> Chinese authorities maintain that a different social system poses a different population theory. And overpopulation is only the avoidable result of a system of private ownership. So it is not applicable to socialist China. What is important to note is that the Chinese position was not necessarily opposed to contraception. It is only opposed to the point of view that population per se is the root cause of poverty. [Tuan, 1979, p. 251]

After this brief excursion into the theory or nontheory of Malthusianism and anti-Malthusianism, let me return to the cold facts of the present-day world.

The new policy was set in motion with paragraph 53 of the new constitution of 1978, which simply states:

> The state advocates and encourages birth planning.

It also set the minimum age at marriage for women at twenty and for men at twenty-two, but added that "late marriage and late procreation are to be encouraged."

In view of this latter provision the provinces set their own minimum ages much higher. Thus, Guangdong (Canton) made it twenty-three for women and twenty-six for men in the city and twenty-five in the country. Beijing made it twenty-five for women and twenty-eight for men.

When a proposed plan for implementation was circulated to the provincial governments for suggestions, they took this more or less as a guideline for working out their own rules, which now vary considerably from province to province.

When in the summer of 1980 the whole matter was brought before the National People's Congress, serious questions were posed, primarily from rural delegates who wondered whether the rural communes would later be able to feed the many old people who would not have sons to support them. And from the military, who wondered whether this might not lead to a weakening of the army, particularly whether families would not tend to resist having their young men go into service when that meant giving up their only sons. At that point, rather than risking complications with the National People's Congress over the question whether or how much of this should become law, it was put forth in the form of a recommended program of the Party that in an open letter asked both its own and the members of the Young Communist Youth League to take the lead in setting their own example and exhorting others to follow it.

In what follows I shall primarily rely on the ordinance for Guangdong province of February 1980 in the translation of Mr. Tuan and on the regulations for Shanxi province of June 1982 as published in *Population and Development Review* in September 1983. (The latter, having been introduced about two and a half years later, are already much stiffer than the former.) Thus, the Shanxi regulations state that "Except in special circumstances or real difficulties [both are technical terms, carefully described in subsequent paragraphs] rural commune members are allowed one child per couple." This constitutes a hardening of the rules which, either in the words of the law or in actual practice had still been less stringently handled in rural communities before. Likewise, the Shanxi regulations provide specifically that "Under no circumstances is the birth of a third child allowed," with absolutely grim provisions in case such third births should still occur.

Generally the following holds:

1.   Couples who pledge to have not more than one child receive the "one-child honors certificate" that carries certain privileges.
2.   If a second child is born, the certificate is withdrawn and all

privileges received on it so far must be paid back; thus, the Shanxi regulations provide stiff penalties already for parents of a second child, which was not yet the case in the earlier Guangdong ordinance.

3.   If a third child is born, various penalties are imposed—again much more severe ones in the later Shanxi regulations.

First, here are the *incentives* in detail:

For holders of the one-child honors certificate, all health services in connection with the birth of the child are free; so are all health services for the child until it is fourteen years old. The Shanxi regulations provide in addition that "when only children are sick, they shall be given priority in registration, examination and hospitalization." The mother receives a two-month maternity leave at full pay, which is otherwise only granted to workers in government industries, and an extra two weeks if she has herself sterilized at the birth of the child. The Shanxi regulations provide an extra fifteen days leave for both parents if they have married "late" (meaning three years past the legal minimum age for marriage), and a 100-day maternity leave for the mother if she has deferred having her first child until she is at least twenty-four years old. The child can attend kindergarten and school for free, and it is entitled to preferential treatment when applying for college or university or for a job in a government enterprise. Until the child is fourteen years old, the parents receive a monthly stipend of five yuan or, in agricultural communes, the equivalent in work points (for an ordinary worker that amounts in the course of one year to about one month's wage or a wage boost of 8.5 percent). The parents have priority for living space in the city or for building materials and the land for a house in rural communities, and claim to the same amount of living space or land as have families with two children. The parents receive for the only child about one and a half to two times the ordinary ration of grain for one child. The parents receive a 5 percent higher pension than they would otherwise. Should the child die or be otherwise unable to support its parents, then agricultural communities are asked to provide for holders of the one-child certificate the "five guarantees" of "food, housing, clothing, health care, and burial," whereby the Shanxi regulations state specifically that "It shall be ensured that their living standards are not lower than the average living standards of the local commune members." If the child is seriously crippled, so that it could not later on support itself and yet later on be unable to support its parents when they are old, the parents can apply for permission to have another child with the same privileges as applied to the first one—provided the child's deficiency is not hereditary in nature.

The Shanxi regulations, after defining in detail what "special circumstances" and "real difficulties" mean (for examples, the first child is deformed; one party of a remarried couple has a child from a previous marriage and the other does not; both parties of a couple are returned overseas Chinese; after marriage the husband settles in with the family of an only daughter; only one of three brothers or more is fertile; and so on), provide that in these cases "people . . . may apply for a second child. After confirmation by discussion of the masses [meaning discussion by the local work team or community organization or rural work unit—P.N.] their application will be referred to the neighborhood office or the people's commune for examination, approval and planned arrangements."

But, as mentioned above, this is the place where it states: "Under no circumstances is the birth of a third child allowed."

And now for the *disincentives*:

If a second child is born—which is only permitted when the first child is at least four years old—then the honors certificate is withdrawn and all benefits received on it so far must be paid back. If a third child is born, parents suffer a cut of 5 percent in their monthly wage or work points until the child is fourteen years old. These were provisions of the earlier Guangdong ordinance of 1980.

Here are some of the provisions of the newer (1982) Shanxi regulations:

> The following restrictions shall be applied to married couples who still do not practice planned parenthood after being educated several times:
>
> 1. With regard to those who are pregnant with the second child, the units or communes and brigades to which they belong should persuade them to take timely remedial measures [i.e., to have an abortion—P.N.]. When the persuasion is ignored, a 20 percent deduction of the combined annual basic pay of a married couple shall be applied to cadres and staff and workers; . . . or other corresponding measures . . . to rural commune members. If remedial measures are taken, the deducted money will be paid back.
> 2. On the unapproved birth of a second child . . . till he is seven

years old, both parties . . . shall have 15 percent of their monthly pay deducted and they shall be deprived of the medical, material, and other benefits granted to reasonable births. Both . . . shall be deprived of one chance for future wage adjustments. . . .

[Similar provisions are made for rural communes about deduction of work points or "they shall be allowed less productive plots or assigned higher output quotas, one of their private plots shall be called back. . . . In addition 10 percent of their total annual income shall be deducted in the two years following the child's birth. . . . " Whereby all of these provisions also hold, if a child is adopted—P.N.]

3.   Those who are pregnant with the third child should take timely remedial measures. If they refuse . . . both . . . shall have 30 percent of their total annual basic pay deducted; . . . once remedial measures are taken, the deducted money will be paid back.

4.   On those who give birth to a third child . . . they shall be demoted by one grade . . . 10 percent of their monthly wages shall be deducted . . . till he is fourteen years old; they shall be deprived of one future chance for wage adjustments and of all medical, material, and other benefits granted to reasonable births; their maternity leave shall be granted without pay.

[Similar provisions are made for rural communes including " . . . they shall be allotted less productive plots and assigned higher output quotas; their private plots shall be called back; or their proportion of produce to be retained by the collective shall be increased. In addition, 20 percent of their total income shall be deducted in the three years after the child is born or adopted. . . ."—P.N.)]

5.   After several efforts of persuasion cadres, staff members and workers who still stubbornly refuse to give birth according to plans and whose offenses are serious and are very bad influences shall be given severe disciplinary or administrative punishments in addition to economic sanctions. . . .

[*Regulations of the Shanxi Provincial People's Government on Planned Parenthood*, 1983]

Some of the restrictions quoted above refer already to the so-called responsibility system that was introduced in 1979; under this system, in rural communes single families or small groups of families together are given responsibility for a given plot of land from which they have to deliver an agreed-upon amount of produce to the commune. Anything beyond that they can keep for themselves or sell in the open market for their own profit. By all accounts this system seems to have led to a considerable increase in agricultural productivity. Of late it is often described as a major step toward dismantling again the system of complete communal ownership of the land and returning toward at least a semblance of private ownership, even though the commune retains title to the land and can take it back (for example, as a disciplinary measure to enforce birth control).

Be that as it may, couples unwilling to comply with the planned family program are not allowed to apply for the necessary "responsibility contract" in the first place, and if they already have one, their plot of land will be "called back."

Further, the Shanxi regulations provide that for

> those who give birth to two or more children without approval, in urban areas no additional housing will be granted and in rural areas no additional land for house construction or additional private plots will be granted. Those who have difficulty in livelihood because of unapproved births . . . shall not be given subsidies. A married couple giving birth to more than two children . . . without approval shall not be recruited for five years. If they are contract workers . . . they shall be dismissed.

One of the many other provisions is that only unmarried people can apply for admission to college or university. Should students get married while studying at the university, they would have to give up their studies permanently.

Until fairly recently, the minorities (other than the majority Han people) and the border people, who between them make up about 6 percent or 60 million of the total 1,000 million population, have been exempted from these rules. That is still written into the Shanxi regulations. Of late, however, plans seem to be under way to include them, at least those who live in the cities, also under these rules.

The Shanxi regulations do not spell out what "severe disciplinary or administrative punishments in addition to economic sanctions" are to be meted out in cases of "stubborn refusal to give birth according to plans," just as our travel guide in China only said "they have means to persuade her" without any further elaboration, and as the doctor in charge of the family planning program in the City of Chenzhou answered during the television interview, "if someone is determined to have a second baby, there is some special rule to deal with it"—also without further elaboration. Some people in the West claim, on the basis of supposedly Chinese sources, that those who stubbornly refuse to comply are being sent off to "reeducation camps" or "labor camps." I do not know of any official confirmation or, for that matter, any official denial of this.

And now for the practice of the system:

First of all, all means necessary for birth control, such as IUDs, pills, condoms, and other contraceptive materials, but also all necessary medical services such as the fitting of IUDs, regular checkups to see whether they are still in place, sterilization, vasectomy, abortion, and so on, are free and carried out on demand. Abortion, however, is not recommended as a general means of birth control but only as a necessary remedy when other means happen to fail. As I mentioned earlier, women who agree to have themselves sterilized at the birth of the child get an extra two weeks of maternity leave; in some places they get more.

Birth control pills are available at the place of work or are delivered to the home. The family planning unit at the place of work, factory, or commune keeps a card file of the menstruation periods of all women within its labor force with details about pills given or IUDs inserted.

A special "visitor's pill" is given to women whose husbands are back only temporarily from a prolonged absence for work or for military service elsewhere. A pill for men is in the experimental stage.

The family planning system is closely linked to the general health system, which makes great efforts to secure the health of those "only children." More doctors have been sent to the countryside than ever before. Many of the "barefoot doctors" are trained in the fitting of IUDs and other services connected with birth control.

The system is organized hierarchically from top to bottom, from the highest State Council Birth Planning Leading Group headed by a vice premier of the People's Republic of China, through committees at every intermediate level, down to the last working group within a factory or an agricultural commune. At every level the Party and its various organizations are represented within these committees, with the secretary of the Party on each level serving as its chairman.

The top committee at the central government works out the general guidelines; the highest committees within the provinces work out the appropriate birth quotas for their major subdivisions, which in turn work out quotas for those beneath them until the last working group at the bottom—for example, a group of twenty to forty families within an agricultural commune—knows exactly how many births it is permitted within any given year. The actual decisions, which individual couples within each group will be given permission to try for a child within a given year, are then made at meetings of the eligible couples within that group. Only those who are given permission may try for a child that year.

Couples who intend to marry must inform the committee at least a year in advance. At that time, or at the latest at the time of marriage, they must indicate in which particular year they intend to have their child. That will be registered in the file and will, where possible, be considered at the time when the individual birth quotas are being distributed. Those who have married late or who have delayed having a child will get priority.

If a woman gets pregnant without permission, she will either ask on her own for an abortion or she will be persuaded to have one. Group pressure is used to enforce compliance. The most serious pressure of course comes from those women who are themselves in line to have a child because for every woman who might insist on having a child out of turn, another loses her permit to have one, since the group as a whole is responsible for keeping within its assigned quota.

Group pressure is also used in other ways. Thus, under the new responsibility system, agricultural communes receive up to 20 to 30 percent of their income in the form of bonuses for overfulfilling their prescribed production quotas. But the whole community loses its bonuses if it does not at the same time keep within its assigned quota of births.

Party secretaries and other officials connected with the family planning program also receive part of their pay in the form of bonuses for the good performance of their respective groups. They lose their bonuses if their groups do not stay within their assigned birth quotas—a system reminiscent of similar arrangements in India at the time of forced sterilizations, when government officials connected with family planning were first reprimanded, then blocked in advancement, and finally lost their jobs if they did not produce the assigned numbers of certified sterilizations.

Yet another measure for assuring group pressure I read about recently: that in some places the monthly stipend of five yuan or the equivalent in work points for all holders of the one-child honors certificate will be suspended for a time from one to twelve months if any one of them goes back on the one-child pledge.

It was only after I had learned all of these details, long after I returned from China, that I began to understand the deeper meaning of a conversation I once had with our Chinese travel guide. One day I had asked him: "What happens if a woman simply wants to have her child?" Answer: "She will be talked to." "All right, so she is stubborn about it—then what happens?" Answer: "She will be criticized." That is the technical term for being confronted by her whole group, her working group in a factory, or the working team in a commune. "Now suppose she is so stubborn that she withstands all that pressure—then what happens?" Answer: "They have means to persuade her." On this he did not elaborate, and I did not ask for an elaboration. But I had one more question: "All right, we won't get anywhere this way. How many women do get children that they are not supposed to get?" At this he gave me a strange look, wondering how I could be so dense as not to understand what he was trying to tell me: "I can't imagine anybody not following the advice of the government."

This, of course, is essentially what the doctor in charge of family planning in the city of Chanzhou answered on television to practically the same question from the narrator (quoting from the WGBH transcript):

> Q: . . . what would the factory do with a woman who refused to have an abortion?
>
> Dr. Chen: In five years we've not had a second birth. . . . We've definitely never had anyone who objects fiercely to the plan. Because I haven't met this situation, I've no idea how I would deal with it, if I did meet it. If someone is determined to have a second baby, there is some special rule to deal with it. . . . But we've never had this! . . . We would persuade her to accept abortion. [Transcript, p. 9]

The narrator too did not insist on learning what that "special rule" was.

The program's success in terms of compliance is truly phenomenal: in 1979, the first year of the new one-child policy, 5 million couples took out the one-child honors certificate. By June 1981 there were already 11 million holders of the certificate. By February 1983 their number had risen to 16 million and that was already about two-thirds of all families eligible, a total of some 25 million.

True enough, there also seem to be some difficulties, some resistance here and there, occasionally reflected in statements by some high government or Party officials. Here is one from Mr. Quian Xinshong, head of the Birth Planning Commission of the Central Government, as printed in the *Beijing Review* of February 1983 (translated from the German edition):

> On the other hand, crimes that do occur in some places of female babies being drowned and their mothers mistreated, are to be condemned most seriously. Such crimes will be punished severely according to the law.

In the same issue of the *Beijing Review* a correspondent writes from Shandong province:

> Although the province conducts annually several courses for the instruction of cadres in the matter of birth control, there are yet some cadres that do not carry out careful indoctrination at the base but give only administrative orders and take economic measures, so that parts of the peasantry are dissatisfied with birth control.

Now for an overview of the food situation.

Total world production of all sorts of grain, including wheat, rye, rice, and millet, currently amounts to about 1,500 million tons per year. Of these, some 90 percent are consumed within the regions where they are produced. Only some 10 percent, or 150 million tons, enter interregional world trade. This does not include trade between neighbors within the same region or any grain imports compensated for by grain exports, but only net trade from region to region. That has to be kept in mind when we talk later on about imports of wheat into and exports of rice out of China.

Of these 150 million tons in 1980, 131 million came from North America, mostly from the United States; the remaining 19 million tons came almost exclusively from Australia and New Zealand. South American exports played no appreciable role in this.

Let me mention at this point that for much of what follows I rely largely on A. Doak Barnett's *China's Economy in Global Perspective* (1981) and on his earlier book, *China and the World Food System* (1979), which was included in an updated form in the former. Barnett, who is with the Brookings Institution in Washington, DC, has assembled and carefully analyzed an incredible amount of information from various official and unofficial sources in China, at the FAO (Food and Agricultural Organization of the United Nations), the U.S. Department of Agriculture, and many others, much of it from exactly the same point of view from which I am myself trying to present the total situation.

In 1980, China produced some 225 million tons of grain. (Under a different system of counting the figure is sometimes given as 300 million tons, but then it includes potatoes and soybeans, which are not included in the world figures cited above. Barnett very carefully unravels this mixup of figures.)

Between 1961 and 1977 China imported a total of 85 million tons, mainly wheat, and exported a total of 17 million tons, mainly rice, for a net import of 68 million tons in 17 years or an average of 4 million tons per year, a figure that varies from year to year between a minimum of one million tons net imports in 1976 and a maximum of 6 million tons net imports in 1977, which was a year of particularly poor harvests. (In the latter year this amounted to 6.8 million tons of imports and only 0.7 million tons of exports. In 1973, also a year of very bad harvests, imports went as high as 7.6 million tons, and exports to 2.1 million tons, for a net import of 5.5 million tons. Chinese economists stress that they export the more expensive rice to be able to pay for the less expensive but more voluminous imports of wheat without too much pressure on their balance of foreign exchange, which they need for other purposes.)

What is relevant for our discussion is not the individual figures but the fact that China's net imports of grain amount in an average year to not more than about 2 percent, and even in a maximum year of particularly bad harvests to not more than about 3 percent of its own total production. Thus, even if in a crisis situation with particularly poor harvests imports may become momentarily quite important, they do and can in fact play only a minor role in China's total food supply. That becomes even more clear when we go back to the overall world figures cited above. Should China, for whatever reasons—be it an increase in population, or an attempt to raise the standard of living, or some sudden catastrophe of nature—want to increase its imports in any given year to about 10 percent of its own total production, that would currently mean net imports of about 23 to 25 million tons. This in turn would amount to about one-sixth of all the grain that enters interregional world trade within any one year. But that big a share of world trade could simply not be made available for China alone, even if this were not a question of money. There simply are too many other claimants on the world's grain who also need it to cover their own deficits.

Thus, and this is the importance of these figures, it must be understood that to the extent that the population of China may be expected to grow within the next few decades, the food necessary to feed the additional multitudes must essentially be grown on China's own soil. Thus, all discussion about whether or not it may be necessary to limit its population growth must in the last analysis hinge on the assumptions one can reasonably make about possible increases in the productive capacity of China's agriculture—whether that takes the form of increasing its land under cultivation or of increasing yields per acre, or, more likely, a combination of both. To the extent that possibe increases in total agricultural production appear limited, say, over a given period of a few decades hence, to that degree the possibilities for a growth in population also appear limited. This may sound both ironic and tragic in view of the persecution of the so-called Malthusians some twenty years earlier, who had warned that China would be unable to sustain a continued population growth of 2 percent per year because her agriculture would not be able to keep pace. This, divested of all the political and social interpretations that they had given it, and of all the moral exhortations they had added as well, is essentially the old position of Malthus and his followers: that, were mankind to continue multiplying in its traditional manner, then it would, unless prevented from so doing, eventually—and that not in any far away future but within a fairly limited amount of time—outrun its own food supply. The only difference is that Malthus assumed that in that case "Nature"—whatever that may mean—would interfere with her "positive checks" of war, pestilence, and hunger, while in today's China it is the government that interfered, at first with its policy of two children per family and, when that proved insufficient to stave off the possibility of future starvation, with a policy of only one child per family, and all the necessary measures to enforce this policy, however grim they may have to be.

Now let me go back to a few figures for international comparison: Between 1954 and 1973 the population of the *industrialized countries* grew by 22 percent, their grain production by 65 percent, and thus their per-capita production by 35 percent; in the *noncommunist developing countries* population grew during the same time by 61 percent, grain production by 75 percent, and thus per-capita production by 9 percent;

in *China* during the same time population grew by 50 percent, grain production by 60 percent, and per-capita production by 7 percent.

For *China alone* figures are available for 1949, the year of the Communist rise to power, through 1975. During that time population grew by 70 percent, from 537 to 914 million, grain production by an admirable 150 percent, from 108 to 270 million tons, for an astonishing increase in per-capita production of 47 percent, from 440 to 650 pounds per year. It must be kept in mind, however, that the base year used in this comparison, 1949, was the last year of a prolonged period of civil war that adversely affected agricultural production. The 7 percent increase in per-capita production between 1954 and 1973 probably gives a more realistic picture of the prospects for possible improvements during the next few decades.

During that same time, 1954 to 1973, the area under cultivation increased by about one-third, from 102 to 135 million ha and yields per ha almost doubled, from 2,300 to 4,440 pounds, certainly a most impressive achievement of the new regime.

If we now apply the 1949 yield per ha to the cultivated land of 1975, we come to a theoretical 144 million tons or an increase of 36 million tons over the 1949 total production. This difference could reasonably be assigned to the increase in acreage. The remaining increase of 126 million tons would then be assigned to the increase in yield per ha. That would in part simply be due to the more intensive tilling of the soil after internal peace had been restored, but the bulk of it would presumably be due to the improvement of agricultural technology which was also one of the impressive accomplishments of the Communist regime. That would include, for example, the construction of well over a million tube wells, the installation of countless electric water pumps for irrigation (and the power stations and power lines for the necessary electricity), the construction of dams, and the improvement of the total infrastructure, including roads and transportation as well as better organization of agricultural production and distribution. In particular, it would be due to the revolution in the use of artificial fertilizer.

Of the latter only 10,000 tons had been used in 1950. By 1957 it was already 400,000 tons. But then came the big step: 6.7 million tons in 1975, 9 million tons in 1978, and still more to come. In 1978, 1.5 million tons were still imported but with the importation of altogether thirteen huge fertilizer factories, begun in 1972, the country would soon be independent in this respect.

In a somewhat rough computation, one counts on eight tons of additional yield for one ton of fertilizer. That figure is very rough indeed; it depends on several factors, such as the kind of soil, the particular kind of produce—say, wheat or rice—the particular kind of fertilizer being applied, and, finally, whether or how much fertilizer has been used on the same soil before. If there has been much of it, the yield factor may go down to six or five additional tons of yield, or even lower, for one additional ton of fertilizer.

Still, a relation of eight to one is often used in making rough overall computations for large regions in developing countries.

Now Barnett (1981) cites Deng Xiaoping as having stated that China would need about 12 to 14 million tons of fertilizer per year. That would be 3 to 5 million tons more than in 1978. With a yield factor of eight to one, that would mean, if it were all applied to the production of grain, an additional 24 to 40 million tons of grain per year. Now let us assume a similar increase in the use of organic (animal and human) fertilizer, and that it also increases the grain yield at the same eight to one ratio. Then all of this together would amount to an additional 50 to 80 million tons of grain per year. That in turn would, at the per-capita consumption of 1978, amount to food for an additional 165 to 265 million people. Adding these to the 964 million population of China in 1978, and assuming that all other food requirements, besides grain, could be taken care of, this would add up to food for a total of 1,130 to 1,230 million people. If Deng, while using this figure of a required 12 to 14 million tons of fertilizer per year, meant that this was all that China could be expected to produce during the foreseeable future—say, up to the year 2000—then these 1,130 to 1,230 million people would be about the maximum number of people that China could be expected to feed up to the year 2000 at present per-capita consumption rates. This corresponds quite closely to the maximum of 1,200 million people by the year 2000 that is the declared aim of the current policy of one child per family: 1,200 million people and zero growth by the year 2000. The figure of about 1,300 million, which would have to be expected if the previous policy of "two children per family is enough" had been continued, would already lie well beyond this number.

While the Chinese government and its planners must of course have had much more detailed and reliable figures at their disposal than this one figure of Deng's about the requirements for artificial fertilizer, their argumentation and their computations must, in principle, have been of the same type as those above: so and so much arable land available now with so and so much addition to be expected within the next few decades; so and so much average yield per acre now with so and so much improvement to be anticipated during the same time; such and such standard of living, as far as food is concerned, to be maintained—all of this together results in so and so many millions of people that can be fed under these assumptions.

If, then, the Chinese government concludes that for the next few decades this figure cannot be larger than about 1,200 million by the year 2000, and cannot be appreciably increased during the immediately following decades—presumably with some safety margin built into it—it becomes a comparatively simple task for demographers to compute the fertility rate necessary to keep population growth within these limits. Their answer is well known: the general fertility rate would have to be kept well under the replacement level—which would be about 2.1 to 2.2 children per family; in fact, it would have to be brought down for quite some time to about 1.7. In other words, for quite some time to come a very large proportion of all families would have to be required to have only one child.

If either we or even some of the Chinese people do not relish some of the methods that the Chinese government considers necessary to bring fertility down to this level, that belongs in an entirely different realm of discourse.

Lest there by any misunderstanding: all of this is not meant to say that China could never feed more than 1,200 million people. It is only meant to say that with such arable land and such agricultural technology as China now has, and such increase of the one and improvement of the other as may safely be anticipated over the next twenty to thirty years, China can feed at present rates of consumption per capita a population of some 1,200 million with some, but not too much safety margin built in for major catastrophes of nature or otherwise. Nothing is said about future potentialities of perhaps entirely new discoveries in agriculture or ways to irrigate huge tracts of arid or even of desert land or about any other future developments that may allow again for more population growth. What the Chinese government did was in essence to assign as best as they could numerical values to a risk that is certainly there but whose numerical values cannot really be ascertained because they hinge on

too many as yet undetermined and probably altogether quite undeter-
minable factors.

Some people may (and in fact do) argue that with just as much
justification, other, perhaps more optimistic assumptions about the future development of agriculture could have been made, leading to a
more optimistic outlook for the food and therefore for the general
population situation, and thus to less stringent means to enforce compliance with an utterly restrictive population policy. True enough. But
the Chinese government and its people are just now paying the price
for excessively optimistic assumptions made in the past, which were
then argued at least as forcefully as they might be argued now. And I
am sure that should all those startling new discoveries and developments in agriculture and irrigation and the like come to pass, which
optimists now cite in support of their position—and whose possibility
can certainly not be denied on any theoretical grounds—the Chinese
government, already uncomfortable with the joyless acquiescence of
many of its people with the stern measures that it has found it necessary to impose, would gladly give them up again and cheerfully pro-
pound an entirely new anti-Malthusian theory, once more condemning
as an error all that has gone before and starting on an entirely new
pronatalist track.

Meanwhile, however, it is almost pitiful to read their breast-beating
about their own anti-Malthusian errors in the not too distant past. Let
me cite just one single such statement by a person high enough in the
Chinese government that it can stand for many others that could be
cited as well. This one comes from Madame Chen Muhua, vice premier of the People's Republic of China and director of the Birth Planning Group of the Council of State:

> There are some who feel that population control, by implicitly emphasizing
> man as mouth (consumer) and not as hand (producer), tends to neglect the
> creative role of man as hand. . . . It is one-sided to stress the one at the ex-
> pense of the other, and vice versa. In our previous critique of the Malthusian
> theory of population, we one-sidedly stressed man's role as producer, even
> going so far as to assert that the more people the better, and that the more
> producers, the quicker, the better and the more economical would be so-
> cialist construction. In doing so we neglected the other side, namely, that
> man, having a mouth, is also a consumer. . . . Where the level of produc-
> tion is relatively low, the aspect of man as consumer tends to be pre-
> dominant; of the total material goods he produces, he consumes the bulk

to support himself and his family, leaving little surplus for society. This is the condition characteristic of our country at the present time.

It takes more than ten years, or even twenty years, for a newborn baby to mature into a producer capable of creating wealth for society. . . . Therefore, without detailed analysis, it is unrealistic to say that the larger the population, the more producers. . . . As Marxism tells us, the so-called producers of material goods are those who have certain productive experience and skills, and can use tools and machinery to produce material goods.

Then, without using his name, but citing in fact the famous speech of Mao's, the writer continues:

Some say that ours is a country with vast land areas and abundant resources . . . and that a large population is not something to be afraid of. . . . This argument is erroneous. . . . Controlling excessive population growth via a well-run planned-birth program will vastly reduce the population pressure on employment, facilitate the accumulation of capital on the part of the state and the collective and improve the people's standard of living. [Chen Muhua, 1979, pp. 76–77]

If at first it may sound a little surprising that this somewhat mechanistic picture of man as an object in the process of production, which proper planning has to make sure contributes more to overall production than it itself consumes, is ascribed to Marxism, then we need to be reminded that this indeed goes back to a passage in a letter from Engels to Kautsky on February 1, 1881, often quoted by Chinese and other writers on the political Left:

The abstract possibility that the number of people may get so big that it must be limited, does indeed exist. But if one day communist society should find itself forced to regulate the production of men in the same manner as it already has regulated the production of things before, then it will be it [communist society—P.N.] and it alone, that is going to carry this out without any difficulty. [Engels, 1955, p. 13]

Some authors—and, incidentally, also the narrator of the television documentary mentioned earlier—claim that the Chinese government intends to enforce the present one-child policy until the total population not only reaches its intended maximum of 1,200 million by the year 2000, but goes back to well below the present 1,000 million—some talk about 700 million—in order to raise the standard of living. I have my doubts about this, because within no more than about twenty-five years India will have a population of about 1,000 million. I find it difficult to believe that the Chinese government would deliberately want to force its own total population down lower than that of India.

Be this as it may, this all sounds quite ironic when we remember the storm that broke loose over Dennis Meadows and his coauthors of *The Limits to Growth* and their sponsor, the Club of Rome, when they warned in 1972 that if mankind were to continue to increase its own numbers by 2 percent per year and its per-capita consumption of irreplaceable goods by 1.5 percent per year, a general catastrophe would result within 100 to 120 years. They also advised that such a catastrophe could be avoided if both population and industrial growth were brought to a halt within thirty to sixty years—that is, between the years 2000 and 2030.

This was immediately attacked, especially from the political Left and from countries of the Third World, as nothing but an imperialistic plot by the industrialized countries of the West who saw their hegemony threatened by the growing populations and the advancing industrialization of the developing countries. The representatives of the People's Republic of China at the United Nations World Population Conference in Bucharest in 1974 were among the foremost to inveigh against this notion—at a time when their own attempt to restrict their population growth with their "two children per family" policy had already been in operation for three years.

Now, only seven years after the publication of *The Limits to Growth,* we have the government of the People's Republic of China proclaiming to its own people and for all the world to hear that population growth for this one-quarter of the world's population has to come to an abrupt halt, not gradually within thirty to sixty years, but in one fell swoop within all of twenty years. And they have not only proclaimed this as a doctrine but are enforcing it with methods so stringent and so invasive in the most intimate sphere of human life, procreation and birth, that nobody would have believed such policies possible before they had actually been applied in Communist China.

In conclusion, let me raise a few questions, to none of which I pretend to have an answer. First, an economic one: Will this dramatic restriction of births lead two or three decades hence to a shortage of labor, especially agricultural labor? Or can it safely be assumed that agricultural technology will have been improved so much by that time that the missing human hands will no longer be needed to produce all the food necessary for 1,200 million people?

Then a question referring more to the social structure: What will be the consequences for a society in which traditionally the oldest son was and to a large extent still is not only economically but even more so socially responsible for the carrying on of the family—its name, its tradition, its role in society—when one-half of all families will not even have a son at all because their only child will be a daughter?

Here is a related question. It seems that one form of resistance to the new one-child policy is an increasing frequency of female infanticide or, as I heard it once formulated more mildly, a conspicuously greater susceptibility of girl babies to all sorts of illnesses. What does this mean not only socially and psychologically within the family, but as one way in which people learn to resist the demands of the government when these seem to become intolerable and too much in conflict with the last remnants of traditional values?

Or, in a more psychological direction, which in the end, however, also leads to a social one: What will it mean when within just a few years practically all newborns will be "only children" without brothers or sisters, with practically no cousins or other relatives of their own age and, a couple of decades hence, with no more uncles and aunts, and the like? What will it be like when every single child becomes more literally an absolutely irreplaceable jewel on which all the concern of its parents and the remaining grandparents is lavished? True enough, it is claimed that the new methods of cooperative education will counteract this psychological factor of a feeling of stardom being practically born or at least bred into every single child, but will that really be enough? And what will all of this mean to the family as an institution and to a society in which for centuries the larger family has always been a mainstay and one of its most stabilizing factors.

The next question is economic again in two ways: First, what will happen when at least one-half of the whole generation that is now being born and raised becomes old and has no sons to support it, so that the community, especially in the countryside, will have to take care of them? It is easy enough right now to show with pride to the visitor the communal institutions provided for such cases, while these are still the exceptions. What will happen when they are the rule?

Second, in the same vein, but even closer in time to the present: with two-thirds of all eligible couples already having obtained the one-child honors certificate, what does it mean to get a bonus for taking it out? If everybody has the same bonus—what happens to the glamour of the bonus as an incentive to strive for it? What special honor, aside from the bonus, is still attached to having been a faithful pledger to the one-child program, when everybody else has made the same pledge? Where, then, is the difference between whatever voluntarism may at one time have been behind the pledge and the sheer obedience to orders from on high? To what extent might this wearing thin of the glamor of the pledge and the de facto disappearance of the bonus system eventually produce mass resistance even beyond the already existing psychological dissatisfaction?

Finally, more or less in line with the political end of the preceding question: Currently the one-child program is presumably still spearheaded by the younger generation of Party and Communist Youth League members who were asked at the beginning of the new policy to "take the lead." What will happen some ten to fifteen years from now when these people, who will then be some forty years old and with the enthusiasm of youth behind them, come to realize that if they do not have a second child soon, they will not be able to for sheer biological reasons? Will that create any kind of midlife panic among them, leading to disobedience against a Party program? And if that should happen at all on a larger scale, beyond only individual cases here and there—might that perhaps lead to something more?

As I said at the beginning, I am not raising these questions with a pretense of having any answers to them. I only raise them at this point because experience tells me that if I do not raise them myself, then some of you will; and then you will get annoyed at me because I have no answers. So I'd rather raise them myself and sit back and see whether you can do any better than I.

Bibliography

Chinese sources

Dixin, Yu. *The Chinese Way of Modernization and Prospects for China's Economy. Lecture at East–West Center, Honolulu, 10* (December 10, 1980). Honolulu: East–West-Center, 1981.

Muhua, Chen. "Birth Planning in China." *Family Planning Perspectives*, 11, 6 (1979).

Xiaobing, Yang. "Geburtenkontrolle in der Provinz Shandong (Birth Control in Shangdong Province)." *Beijing Review*, 15 (February 1983).

Xinshong, Qian. "Die Kontrolle des Bevoelkerungswachstum (Controlling the Increase of Population)." *Beijing Review*, 15 (February 1983).

Yueli, Cui. "China's Policy of Public Health." *Lecture at East–West-Center, Honolulu 10* (December 1980).

Ziyang, Zhao. "Rede zum sechsten Fuenfjahresplan" (Speech on Occasion of the Sixth Five-year Plan) (1981–85) and "Rede vor dem Sechsten Nationalkongress (Speech at the Sixth National Congress)," 6 June 1983. *Population and Development Review, 9*, 1 (March 1983); *9*, 3 (September 1983).

American Sources

Aird, John S. "Recent Demographic Data from China: Problems and Prospects." Mimeo. Washington, DC: U.S. Bureau of the Census, 1981.

Bannister, Judith. "What Is China's True Fertility Level?" Paper given at meetings of Population Association of America, Washington, DC, 1978.

Barnett, A. Doak. *China's Economy in Global Perspective.* Washington, D.C.: Brookings Institution, 1981.

Chen, Pi-Chao. "China's Birth Planning Program." In Lapham and Bulawao (eds.), *Research on the Population of China.* Washington, DC: National Academy Press, 1981.

Population Reports. "Population and Birth Planning in the People's Republic of China." Series J, 25 (January–February 1982). Baltimore: Johns Hopkins University, 1982.

Science. The Mysterious Expulsion of Steven Mosher, Science, 220, pp. 6921–94.

Tang, M. Anthony, and Bruce Stone. 1980. "Food Production in the People's Republic of China." Research Report no. 15. International Food Policy Research Institute, Washington, DC, May 1980.

———. "Changing Population Policy Approaches in China." *Intercom.* Washington, DC: Population Reference Bureau, October 1981.

Television transcript of Program NOVA #1103, China's Only Child originally aired on PBS February 14, 1984; WGBH Transcripts, Boston, MA.

Tien, H. Yuan. "Demography in China: From Zero to Now." *Population Index, 47,* 4 (Winter 1981).

Tuan, Chi-Hsien. "China's Population and Organized Transition of Fertility. In Chao and Kobayashi (eds.), *Fertility Transition of the East Asian Populations.* Honolulu: University of Hawaii Press, 1979.

Chinese Laws and Ordinances

"China's New Marriage Law" (of 1980). *Population and Development Review, 7*, 2 (June 1981).

"Guandong Province Planned Birth Ordinance" (of February 13, 1980). *Uebersetzung von Chi-Hsien Tuan.* East-West-Center, Honolulu (mimeo).

"Regulations of the Shanxi Provincial People's Government on Planned Parenthood" (June 29, 1982). *Population and Development Review, 9*, 3 (September 1983).

Other Sources

Engels, Friedrich. *Briefwechsel mit Karl Kautsky.* Vienna: Braumueller, 1955.

World Population Data Sheet. Washington, DC: Population Reference Bureau, 1983 and 1984.

Chapter 9

Population Policies in Japan, China, and India: A Comparison of Problems and of Measures Taken

Until a few decades ago, at least up to the time of World War II, the traditional view in most countries was that, even though governments conducted censuses and collected demographic data, it was not their task to concern themselves directly with the growth of population. In times of growing nationalism or when populations seemed to decrease, governments tended to support larger families. In ordinary times it seemed enough if they upheld traditional values that tended to consider large families socially desirable, economically useful, especially in agricultural societies, and from a religious point of view a blessing. All that governments usually did in this respect was prohibit or at least severely restrict the spread of knowledge and the distribution of the means for birth control and forbid abortion.

Matters changed after the war. In most Western countries population growth rates, after a brief upswing and baby boom primarily to make up for war-delayed marriages and other adaptations, soon re-

Paper presented at the Dialogue Congress Western Europe—USA—Japan, Alpbach, Tyrol, July 7–13, 1984.

verted to prewar levels of about 1 percent increase per year, which meant that populations would double in about seventy years. Liberalized attitudes toward birth control and abortion, where they did occur, were less a result of a desire to inhibit growth of population than of new ideas about individual rights and decision making.

In most developing countries the situation was different. Annual growth rates, already on the increase before the war, rose to 2 percent per year in most and to much more in some countries. An annual increase of 2 percent or more means a doubling of population in thirty-five years or less. An annual increase of 3.5 percent means a doubling in twenty years. Mexico, with an annual increase of 3.3 percent for some decades, which only in recent years has come down to 2.6 percent, is a case in point. Its population almost quadrupled in only four decades—from 20 million in 1940 to 70 million in 1970 and almost 80 million in 1984.

With such rapidly increasing numbers the question eventually had to arise: If this trend should continue for another few decades, is it safe to assume that there will always be enough food to feed the growing multitudes? And if not, what if anything could be done about it? To begin with, both experts and laymen were and still are not all of one mind about the situation: some question whether there is any danger at all, while others question how imminent it might be. Discussion was heavily stirred up with the 1972 publication of *The Limits to Growth* by Dennis Meadows et al., the first of the so-called Club of Rome Reports on the Predicament of Mankind.

Whether they liked it or not, governments too, regardless of whether or not they agreed with the basic idea of a threatening danger of shortages of food and other supplies, had to take up the question and, where it appeared urgent, had to try to deal with it. The first attempt was generally to increase the food supply, mostly to develop agriculture but to some extent also to develop industry and the production of raw materials for export to pay for additional grain and other food imports. But eventually governments also began—in some cases very reluctantly, in others with more alacrity—taking measures toward limiting the rate at which population grew.

These efforts of course varied greatly from country to country, depending on the state of agriculture and industry, religious and social traditions, and finally the extent to which, under their respective political and ideological forms of government and social organization, governments felt free to interfere with such an intimate sphere of human life as procreation and birth. In what follows, I shall briefly compare the situation in this respect in Japan, China, and India, and the measures their governments are taking to deal with it.

My first point of comparison will be the possibilities for increasing food production within each of these countries. These are most limited within Japan, where practically every piece of land that could be cultivated is already under cultivation. The tilling of the soil, by hand, animal, and mechanical means, is already so well developed that yields per acre cannot be expected to be improved materially very soon. While there will always be some improvements, at times even spectacular ones, still, those responsible for governmental policies and decisions concerning the next twenty to thirty years cannot count on the latter with any degree of certainty. They can only reckon with such improvements as can be expected on the basis of what they can see before them. The same holds for decision makers in China and in India.

China offers better prospects for increasing her agricultural production. It is currently improving land and has still more land available that could be improved through irrigation either with newly constructed canals or with deep wells with electrically driven pumps. The tilling of the soil, although on the average more advanced than in India, still leaves scope for improvement.

China currently has slightly over 1,000 million people, and although their diet could be improved, none of them are starving. Government plans call for improving the standard of living, including improvements in the consumption of food. Chinese agronomists seem to think that with such improvements in overall food production as can be expected over the next twenty to thirty years, and such improvements in average diet as are planned, China will be able to feed about 1,200 million people by the year 2000 and in the decades thereafter with the products of its own agriculture.

The prospects for potential improvements during the next thirty years seem much better for India because, although most of its arable land also is already under cultivation, more semiarid tracts could be made fertile, not through any farout utopian schemes that would "make the desert bloom," but with canals and similar means of the kind that India has begun building in the recent past. In addition, much of India's agriculture is operated on such a primitive level that many farmers hardly produce more than they themselves require for their own needs. Sizeable improvements in yields per acre can still be expected from relatively limited investments in better tools, minor mechanization, the wider application of artificial fertilizer, and the wider spread of the newer high-yielding varieties of rice and wheat. While the latter did not relieve the general food problem by as much as was expected of them when they were heralded in the late 1960s as the "Green Revolution," improvements were certainly considerable. China too has had success using these new varieties.

My second point of comparison concerns the possibility for sustaining a growing population with increased imports from the outside. Total world production of grain currently amounts to 1,500 to 1,600 million tons, about 90 percent of which is consumed within the regions where it is produced. Only about 10 percent, or 150 to 160 million tons, enters interregional trade (this does not include trade between adjoining countries within the same region).

Of the three countries only Japan, with its much smaller population of 120 million, is basically in a position to provide a major share of its grain requirements for food and feed through foreign imports. For China, with more than 1,000 million, and India, with nearly 750 million people, under current conditions of worldwide agricultural production and distribution that is totally out of the question.

A few figures will simplify comparison at this point: Japan currently consumes about 36 million tons of grain each year for food and feed. China consumes about 230 million tons, and India about 150 million tons. This comes to an average of about 300 kg per capita per year in Japan, 230 kg in China, and 200 kg in India. The great difference between Japan and the other two countries primarily reflects a much larger consumption of meat and dairy products, and with that a much larger use of grains for animal feed. The difference between China and India is more a reflection of a difference in the average amount of food available for their people: it needs to be emphasized that distribution is much more equitable in China—none of the people have to starve, while in India large masses of people live continuously on the brink of starvation.

If, for any reason whatsoever—particularly in order to sustain a growing population—each of these three countries intended to cover another 10 percent of their total grain requirements with imports, that would mean for Japan an additional import of 3.6 million tons, for

China 23 million tons, and for India 15 million tons. The extra 3.6 million tons Japan would require would certainly be available on the world market and Japan could most likely afford to pay for them. For China and India, under current worldwide conditions of agricultural production and international trade, this would be impossible, both because that much grain is simply not available for international trade now or within the near future and because, even if it were available, presumably neither China nor India could afford to pay for such huge quantities without totally disrupting their own economies.

Over the last twenty years China has generally exported 1 to 2 million tons of rice and imported 2 to 6 million tons of wheat, for an average net import of 4 million tons of grain per year, with a maximum of some 6 million tons in years of extremely bad harvests. India, too, has imported up to 4 or 5 million tons in one year in years of extremely bad harvests due to weak monsoons, but has done so under greatest difficulties for its economy in terms of foreign exchange. Therefore, as soon as the worst was over, India immediately had to revert to self-sufficiency.

Many writers have suggested, and the figures above can be recomputed to show, that an equal worldwide distribution of all of the 1,500 to 1,600 million tons of grain produced in the world each year would mean about 330 kg per capita, which would be well enough for all. This would, true enough, require a complete restructuring of the conditions under which grain is being produced, distributed, and consumed the world over and such a general restructuring could only be brought about through some worldwide revolutions. These, however, although perhaps fervently hoped and striven for by revolutionaries in many countries for a future day, cannot very well be taken for granted by current governments making decisions about economic plans and population policies for the next twenty to thirty years. Should such big revolutions indeed come to pass, it will be up to such future governments to change all plans and policies—as happened in Russia in 1917 and in China in 1949.

For the time being, at any rate, the principal difference between Japan and the other two countries regarding food supplies is that Japan could basically feed a growing population for quite some time to come by increasing its imports of grain for food and feed. Its most serious concern would be the consequent ever-growing dependency on these imports, which would leave Japan even more vulnerable to the vagaries of world conditions in production and trade in agriculture and allied products as well as in general world trade in industrial products which it would need to pay for the growing grain imports. By 1955, Japan imported about 20 percent of its total caloric requirements for food and feed; this amount was still manageable in the sense that, had Japan been cut off from it or any major part of it—whether through bad harvests abroad or bad economic conditions or even war—it could still have gotten by. Of course, this would have meant cutting down the total food intake and again omitting meat, which had only fairly recently been introduced on a larger scale, from the diet. But currently (1984), about 50 percent or more of Japan's total caloric requirements are being imported. It seems difficult to imagine how Japan could do without a major part of that, for whatever reason. War, in particular, even if fought in some distant places without Japan's direct involvement, if it involved countries that produce and deliver grain for Japan, would constitute an almost unimaginable threat to the country's survival. Japan's attempt to reduce population growth is largely an effort to reduce this dangerous dependency on foreign food supplies. That it is practically running out of space on which to settle its people is a second major consideration, which at least for the time being is not yet quite so pressing.

In China and India, the limiting condition is not, as in Japan, the danger of overdependence on foreign food supplies but that, lacking any realistic possibility to feed a growing population with imported grain, they are both tied to the limits of their own agriculture. Any sizeable increase in their populations must be fed from a corresponding increase in their own agricultural production. To the extent that this is limited, at least for the foreseeable future, the potential growth of their populations must be limited.

The Chinese government has, undoubtedly on the advice of its own agronomists and other experts, decided and proclaimed to its own people and thereby also to the world that 1,200 million is the maximum that China can safely be expected to be able to feed by the year 2000 and within the decades immediately thereafter (presumably, some safety margin is built into the computations). With this limit before them, five years ago in 1979 they changed their policy of "two children per family is enough" to the much more restrictive policy of "only one child per family."

Although the Indian government has not proclaimed to its people a similar more or less fixed limit for population growth, it certainly would not be difficult to compute one on the basis of officially published data about actual and potential land use and current and expected agricultural productivity. One may safely assume that the Indian government, even without any such proclamation, has the necessary computations at hand and that it is guided by them in such measures as they are actually applying or trying to apply in their attempt to slow down the growth of the country's population.

My final point of comparison concerns the ups and downs of population policies in the three countries during the last few decades. My indication of the overall policies and the differences between them will, of necessity, be brief.

Here are, to begin with, the current (1984) birth, death, and growth rates: Japan's current birth rate is 13 per 1,000 population, China's is 21, and India's is 34. The death rates are 6 for Japan, 8 for China, and 14 for India. These represent annual growth rates of 0.7 percent for Japan (this is about the same as for the United States and only two-thirds of that of Russia); 1.3 percent for China, and 2 percent for India. Thus, Japan currently adds 840,000 people each year to its 120 million, China adds about 13 million to its slightly over 1,000 million, and India adds about 15 million to its nearly 750 million.

Within each country, population policies have changed a couple of times from pronatalist to antinatalist and vice versa. Beginning in 1920, the Japanese government for almost two decades maintained a tolerant attitude toward birth control. During that time the birth rate in Japan declined systematically from 36 per 1,000 in 1920 to 26 in 1938. Then a more nationalistic government forbade all further propaganda and the distribution of the means of birth control. Within three years, from 1938 to 1941, the birth rate was back up to 34 per 1,000. Then, as in other warring nations, the birth rate fell considerably during the war but climbed up again immediately after the war to its prewar level of 34 and 35, with a baby boom in the wake of war-delayed marriages and other factors. Then came a rapid decline that within only ten years, from 1947 to 1957, cut the birth rate in half, to 18 per 1,000.

The most remarkable aspect of this decline—probably due in large part to the rapid urbanization and industrialization of the country during that time—was that it took place without any active government interference: the government offered no incentives or disincentives, economic or otherwise, as was the case later in China and in India. All that government contributed was:

1.   To let it be know that government approved of birth control;
2.   To let mass media and private organizations discuss and make propaganda for birth control as they pleased;
3.   Not to obstruct the distribution of the means of birth control;
4.   To help with establishing training facilities for personnel concerned with family planning; and
5.   To ease the law on abortion.

The latter, however, was not meant as a measure toward bringing down the birth rate but as a means to protect the health and lives of many women threatened by a sudden upsurge of illegal abortions and the unsanitary and unsafe conditions under which these are usually performed.

For a better understanding one may consider that the sudden return of millions of soldiers after World War II brought with it not only a sudden increase in the number of marriages and the reestablishing of family relations, but also a sudden increase in the number of unwanted pregnancies. These in turn led, under the prevailing, very strict anti-abortion laws, to a dramatic increase in the number of illegal abortions—with the mentioned increased threat to health and lives of the women.

It was because of the latter that the government eventually found it necessary to ease up on the restrictions and to make it easier to obtain abortions legally. The first Eugenic Law of 1948 still required the consent of two doctors and closely circumscribed the conditions under which this consent could be given. But when the number of abortions reported under these slightly milder provisions went beyond one million within one year, with perhaps still another half million illegal ones, the provisions were liberalized once more. Now the approval of only one doctor is sufficient, and economic reasons are permitted. That made at long last abortion under sanitary and medically safe conditions available to most women who wanted and needed it.

Eventually, after that first big wave of unwanted pregnancies that had come with the return of the millions of soldiers had subsided, the number of abortions dropped back again to about one half of what it had been at its maximum.

Into this period of changes came 1966, the "Year of the Fiery Horse." According to an old folk belief, women born in that year—which according to the zodiacal calendar recurs once every sixty years—make bad wives. During that one year the birth rate dropped by a full 26 percent, from 19 to 14 per 1,000, though it reverted promptly the following year to slightly above its previous level, to 20 per 1,000. Most demographers took this as proof (if proof was still needed) that, if people wanted to, they could reduce the birth rate much further—because here many couples had apparently simply decided not to take a chance during that year. Other interpretations of this unusual drop, however, were more sanguine: twenty-two years before, it was pointed out, in 1944, a deep drop in the birth rate may have contributed toward a smaller cohort of women of childbearing age in 1966.

When the Communists came to power in China in 1949, they at first pursued a strong pronatalist policy, following Chairman Mao's dictum that a country with the vast resources of China need have no fear of population growth, that more people meant more production and that meant a faster building of socialism. When the first census of 1953, however, showed that China had apparently more people (some 583 rather than the expected 540 million) and a faster growth rate (some 2 percent, or about 11 million per year) than had been anticipated, the government launched its first campaign for birth control. Before it got into full swing, however, it was halted by the optimism of the "Great Leap Forward" of 1958. A succession of three years of poor harvests brought the campaign back in 1961, only to get stopped once more by the Cultural Revolution of 1966 and its aftermath. It was not until 1971 that the government, concerned by problems of agricultural and other production, embarked upon its next campaign of birth control under the slogan, "Two children per family is enough." This brought the birth rate down from 34 per 1,000 in 1970 to 18 in 1979—the same numerical result within the same short span of only ten years that had been seen twenty-five years before in Japan. But with this major difference: in China this was achieved with an enormous amount of direct government interference, with regulations, monetary and other incentives and disincentives, and organized group pressure on recalcitrants.

Even though this brought the annual growth rate down within those ten years from 2 percent to 1.3 percent, that was still not enough, particularly in view of the fact that beginning with the early 1980s, the greater cohorts of children born in the wake of the Great Leap of 1958 and the Cultural Revolution of 1966, when all governmental activities to control population growth had been suspended, were about to come of marrying age. There would be 25 million of them every year, creating yet another baby boom that threatened to upset the already precarious balance between population and food supply.

It was at this point that the government instituted its new policy of "only one child per family," designed to bring population growth to a complete standstill by the year 2000, with a population of about 1,200 million.

Now whole working teams in urban factories and in agricultural communes were assigned the exact number of babies to be born in any given year, with the members themselves deciding which particular couples were to be given a permit for trying for a baby in any given year. The group took over the distribution of pills, securing the insertion of IUDs, the supplying of condoms, and so on, but also checking that members were actually using them and keeping track of their women's menstrual periods, and other forms of control. With the whole group responsible for staying within its assigned quota, every woman who has a child out of turn means that another has to give up her permit for having one; this, of course, tremendously increases the pressure of the group on recalcitrant members. A woman who got pregnant out of turn would face great pressure to have an abortion, even in a fairly advanced stage of pregnancy, and to have herself sterilized. With this policy came a whole set of incentives for those who took out the so-called one-child honors certificate and severe penalties for those who refused to comply, including cuts in wages and in chances for promotion, or assignment of worse plots of land and increased quotas of produce to be delivered from them to the commune.

It is easy enough to question whether all of this will lead to a shortage of labor (especially agricultural) in fifteen to twenty years, or to problems in forty years supporting the many people growing old who have no children to support them. One might also wonder what will become of the family as a functioning unit, or of the whole social fabric of a society where large families had always been a stabilizing factor. Questions, questions, questions! It may still be too early to answer some of them but it is also possible that if and when, at a later date, the answers should come in and some of these measures turn out to have been mistaken, it may then be too late to do anything about it.

India too has been through some ups and downs of population policies. After World War II the government, although not exactly pronatalist, did little or nothing for a long time to stem the rising tide of population growth. It was not until the late 1960s that government began to exert greater efforts in that direction, establishing more clinics and dispensaries to give advice and provide the means of birth control. One of the more important of these efforts was the offer of a small monetary incentive meant primarily to cover a few days' loss of wages for voluntary sterilization, especially of men. During the late 1960s and early 1970s, 1.5 to 2 million sterilizations were recorded each year.

When all of this proved too little and too late, the government decided in 1977 upon really forceful action. The official 1981–82 *Year Book* of the *Family Welfare Program in India* lists some 1.4 million sterilizations for 1974–75, some 2.7 million for 1975–76, and suddenly for 1976–77 some 8.3 million, though the number drops back just as suddenly the following year, 1977–78, to under 1 million and then only slowly increases to between 2 and 3 million by 1981–82.

This sudden rise and fall reflects more than anything else what happened at that time: the government suddenly decided that simple persuasion was not enough, and began to apply a dramatic amount of pressure, primarily by requiring families with two or more children to have one of the parents sterilized if they applied for government jobs, government loans, or any number of permits to operate various kinds of businesses, but also for free schooling or government housing, or other state-controlled benefits. In addition, it imposed a system of sterilization quotas threatening all personnel at first only in family planning organizations, but eventually also in many other government agencies with reprimands, cuts in salaries, and finally dismissal from their jobs, depending on the degree of nonfulfillment of their assigned quotas. This produced enormous pressure on all government officials, high or low, to pressure or convince those under their jurisdiction to have themselves sterilized. We will never know how many people were sterilized in those years against their will, how many actively resisted, and how many were at least forced to submit under threat of imminent economic sanctions. But we do have Prime Minister Indira Gandhi's word on October 27, 1976, in open Parliament, after some people had been killed in some North Indian villages while protesting and resisting forced sterilizations, that she regretted such excesses as might have occurred here and there, but that nevertheless, in the interest of the nation, the program as such would have to be continued (Borders, 1976). It certainly defies the outside reader's credulity that even a major part of that officially registered jump from 0.9 to 1.4 to 2.7 to 8.3 million sterilizations within only three years could have been truly voluntary, within any serious meaning of the word. The payoff came when Mrs. Gandhi lost the next election. All experts agree that these forced sterilizations must have been a major factor in her defeat. Indeed, for the year 1977–78, fewer than one million sterilizations were officially recorded, with the numbers rising again only slowly to at first 1.5, then 1.8, 2.7, and finally 2.8 million by 1981–82.

We are unlikely soon to know the long-term effects of these forced sterilizations in another direction: for years to come they gave everything having to do with family planning a bad name in India. Some people—we don't know how many—for some time shunned even ordinary hospitals and dispensaries, the insertion of IUDs, and even injections against wholly unrelated diseases for fear of getting sterilized in the process. It will be difficult to find out how much this may have contributed toward an increase in the cohorts of children born during that time, children who will come of marrying age toward the turn of the century. One can only keep in mind the lessons of increased cohorts in China as a consequence of the halts in its campaigns for birth control in 1958 and in 1966 in the wake of the Great Leap Forward and the Cultural Revolution. There may yet loom an extra problem in this for the future governments of India.

In conclusion, it would seem that, at least as far as sheer numbers are concerned, the way that Japan, in comparison with India and China, chose to reduce its rate of population growth, relying essentially on genuine persuasion by private organizations and mass media and not hindering the distribution of the means of birth control when people wanted them, together with loosening restrictions on abortion, was and promises for the future to be the most successful one. It certainly appears less fraught with social, psychological, and, particularly in the case of India, political complications and friction. One could well imagine that once the pill, which is still not permitted in Japan, presumably for health reasons, is also legalized, the annual growth rate there may yet go down below the current 0.7

percent, as it did in a number of West European countries, where it went down to 0.3 percent and even 0.2 percent, even zero, and in some cases even below zero, meaning a slight decrease in population—all without any governmental action. On the contrary, some governments are again beginning to support larger families where people want them for fear that otherwise their populations might decline.

I have not touched on a major factor in all of this—namely, the enormous degree of urbanization that began sooner in Japan than in the other two countries and that undoubtedly provided an earlier spur to people's practice of birth control on their own as soon as they knew how to do it and as soon as they had the necessary means at their disposal. But I am afraid that would have to be the subject of another paper.

Bibliography

Japan

Linhart, Sapp. "Demographischer Ueberblick (Demographic Overview)." In *Die Japanische Gesellschadt*. (Japanese Society Notes) Skripten, Institut fuer Japanologie, Universitaet Wien, 1975.

Muramatsu, Minoru. "Japan." *Encyclopedia*, pp. 385–90.

Muramatsu, Minoru, and Tameyoshi Katagtri, eds. *Basic Readings in Population and Family Planning in Japan*. Tokyo: Japanese Organization for International Cooperation in Family Planning (JOICFP), 1981.

Sanderson, Fred H. *Japan's Food Prospects and Policies*. Washington, DC: The Brookings Institution, 1978.

Smith, Thomas C. *Nakahara. Family Planning and Population in a Japanese Village, 1717–1830*. Stanford, CA: Stanford University Press, 1977.

China

Aird, John S. *Recent Demographic Data from China: Problems and Prospects*. Mimeo. Washington, DC: Foreign Demographic Analysis Division, Bureau of the Census, 1978.

Barnett, A. Doak. *China's Economy in Global Perspective*. Washington, DC: The Brookings Institution, 1981.

Chen, Pi-Chiao. "China's Birth Planning Program." In Lapham and Bulatao, eds., *Research on the Population of China*. Washington, DC: National Academy Press, 1981.

Muhua, Chen. "Birth Planning in China." *Family Planning Perspectives, 11*, 6 (1979).

Tien, H. Yuan. "Demography in China: From Zero to Now." *Population Index, 47*
4 (Winter 1981), 683–710.
Tuan, Chi-Hsien. "China's Population and Organized Transition of Fertility." In
Lee-Jay Cho and Kazumaska Kobayashi (eds.), *Fertility Transition of the East
Asian Population*. Honolulu: University of Hawaii Press, 1979, pp. 247–85.
Population and Birth Planning in the People's Republic of China. *Population
Reports* (January–February 1982), Baltimore: Johns Hopkins University.
Provincial Regulations for Planned Parenthood. For *Shanxi Province* (1982).
Transl., *Population and Development Review 9*, 3 (September 1983), 553–61.
————. For *Guangdong Province* (1980). Transl. Chi-Hsien Tuan. Honolulu:
East–West Center.

India

Borders, William. "Mrs. Gandhi Confirms Some Died in Protests over Steriliza-
tion Drive." *New York Times,* October 28, 1976.
Cassen, R.H. *India: Population Economy, Society*. London: Macmillan, 1978.
[Rpt.: 1980].
Government of India, Ministry of Health and Family Welfare. *Family Welfare
Program in India. Year Book. 1981–82* New Delhi: Government of India
Press. 1983.
————. *Statement on National Health Policy*. New Delhi: Government of India
Press, 1982.
Government of India, Ministry of Information and Broadcasting. *New 20-Point
Programme: Family Planning—A People's Programme. Background to the
News, 27*, 3 (February 1982).
Gulhati, Kaval. "Compulsory Sterilization: The Change in India's Population
Policy." *Science, 195* (March 25, 1977), 1300–1305.
Gulhati, Ravi. "India's Population Policy: History and Future." World Bank Staff
Working Paper no. 265, Washington, DC, 1977.

Other

Meadows, Donella H.; Dennis L. Meadows; et al. *The Limits to Growth. A Report
to the Club of Rome's Project on the Predicament of Mankind*. New York:
Universe Books, A Potomac Associates Book, 1972.

Chapter 10

The Great Migrations of the Nineteenth and Twentieth Century

Introduction

The big migrations of the nineteenth and twentieth century may be looked upon primarily as a social or as an economic or as a political phenomenon, or as a combination of all three, with each of the major waves of migration having another of these three characteristics as its most conspicuous element.

While most of this is obvious enough not to require further elaboration, the magnitude of the various waves is usually less well known to anyone who does not have a special interest in the subject. Most of us know only that it was many, even millions. I shall try here primarily to give an overview of this, touching only cursorily upon the causes behind the various waves of migration.

Carr-Saunders, in his standard work *World Population* (1936), estimates that throughout the seventeenth century hardly more than three-quarters of a million people crossed the Atlantic to what is now the United States and Canada—some 250,000 from England, 200,000 from Germany, and another 200,000 from Holland and France

Paper presented on May 9, 1991, to the Columbia University Seminar on "Content and Methods of the Social Sciences," augmented with materials from a similar paper given at the University of Munich.

(Woytinsky and Woytinsky, 1953, p. 69). Hardly more than another two million came during the eighteenth century and up to the time of Napoleon.

The first real mass migration was that of the "Potato Irish" in the middle of the nineteenth century: between 1846 and 1849, a widespread blight destroyed most of Ireland's potato crop, the main food supply of an already dreadfully impoverished people who had practically no other reserves to fall back on. Tens of thousands perished in the worst famine to strike a European country in a long time. As a consequence, fully one-quarter of the population of Ireland, some 2 out of 8 million, emigrated, mostly to the United States.

Migrations as such of course are about as old as man himself. But in such ancient migrations as the "Great" or "Teutonic" migrations in the fourth to sixth centuries, which eventually brought an end to the Roman Empire, it was always whole tribes or whole peoples that moved together, a few thousand or some tens of thousands at a time. Throughout the nineteenth century and deep into the twentieth, it was generally individuals or individual families or at the most small local groups who made their own decisions. Even when large numbers of people left the same country more or less at the same time and even in the same direction, out of the same motives of poverty or oppression, it was essentially individual people who made the decision to move. This characteristic changed only with the big mass flights and expulsions of national or religious minorities after World Wars I and II, which I shall discuss separately.

Since figures about the most recent developments, especially with the opening of the borders between East and West in Europe, are not yet available, I shall for the most part limit myself to the time up to about 1975 to 1980, bringing in later figures only occasionally.

The Growth of the World's Population:
Differential Rates of Growth in More
and in Less Developed Countries

As far as demographers and historians can tell, the rapid growth of the world's population during the last few decades must be an altogether unique phenomenon in the history of mankind. The reasons for it, and particularly the reasons why it has occurred at a very unequal speed in various countries—fastest in the world's poorest and slowest in the world's richest regions—are not far to seek: the rapid spread of modern methods of general health care and hygiene throughout the world, especially through the countries of the Third World, with the wide-ranging elimination of malaria, cholera, typhoid, and other communicable diseases, and drastic reductions in infant and child mortality and a widespread raising of general living standards. To all of this has to be added the fact that traditional, socially sanctioned notions of the "right" number of children per family did and still do not adapt themselves fast enough—even though these notions were developed in times when half or more of all children born ordinarily died before the age of five, necessitating a continuous supply of new births to at least keep the size of the population stable.

Let me begin with a few overall figures: In 1650 the world's population was about 545 million; within 200 years it had grown to about twice that much—to some 1,250 million by 1850, at an annual rate of growth of initially about 0.3 percent, but already somewhat higher toward the end of that period. The world population then doubled again in only 100 years to 2,500 million by 1950, at an annual rate of growth of about 1 percent. After World War II came the real "population explosion," with growth rates worldwide of up to 2 percent each year, which doubled the world population within only thirty-seven years to 5,000 million by 1987. Currently (in 1991), there are 5,400 million people on this earth, with an annual growth rate of about 1.7 percent and an annual increase of about 93 million. The population is expected to reach 6,300 million by the year 2000, 8,200 million by 2020, and still to keep growing, although at a slightly decelerated pace.

The annual rate of growth is 0.5 percent in the more developed countries; in China, with its policy of "only one child per family" instituted in 1979, it is 1.4 percent (down from 2.1 percent). In all other developing countries together it is 2.4 percent, barely down from 2.6 percent some twenty years ago. For the 1,200 million in the more developed countries, this means an annual increase of 6 million; for the 1,150 million of China, it means an increase of 16 million annually, and for all the other less developed countries together, with 3,100 million people, still 56 percent of all mankind, it means an annual increase of 72 million.

Annual growth is well above 3 percent in some of the poorest countries of Africa and Central America. The highest rate currently is recorded for Kenya where it is 3.8 percent. If this rate were to remain constant, the current population of Kenya of 25 million would double within eighteen and a half and quadruple within thirty-seven years. One may well ask: How is Kenya going to feed 50 million people eighteen and a half years from now and 100 million thirty-seven years from now, by the year 2027?

It is always easy to pooh-pooh such computations as sheer numerology having no bearing on reality. Some even try to show them up as completely absurd by extending the computations through a few more consecutive doubling periods until the numbers immediately become astronomical and impossible, and then assert that such overwhelming figures are proof that even the first one or two doublings are distant from reality.

So, I think I'd better explain what reality really is like with these kinds of figures.

"Doubling time," that is, the length of time that it would take a population to double its size (its numbers) if its current annual rate of increase remained constant, is computed by dividing the number 70 by the annual rate of increase in percent. For example, a population with an annual rate of increase of 2 percent would reach twice its size within $70 \div 2.0 = 35$ years. (This is the formula for computing the time within which a given capital would double at constant interest [so and so many percent per year] compounded annually.)

In 1952 Kenya, then still a British colony, had 5.7 million people, and an annual growth rate of about 4.0 percent. To that rate corresponds a doubling time of $70 \div 4.0 = 17.5$ years so that, should that rate remain constant, this would mean that the population of Kenya could be expected to reach after 17.5 years $2 \times 5.7 = 11.4$ million; and, should that annual rate of increase of 4.0 percent still continue, twice as much again, that would make it $2 \times 11.4 = 22.8$ million after $2 \times 17.5 = 35$ years, that is, by the year $1952 + 35 = 1987$. And indeed, Kenya had in 1987 22.4 million people—almost on the dot what a demographer could have projected in 1952 on the basis of the population of 5.7 million, the annual growth rate of 4.0 percent, and the mere computational assumption that this growth rate would remain constant during the next 35 years.

Some critics try to sidestep the issue by asking how the computations for a small population like that of Kenya, which began in the above computations in 1952 with only 5.7 million, would hold up for bigger populations.

Here are the corresponding figures for a much bigger country. In 1940, Mexico had a population of 20 million and an annual growth rate of 3.2 percent—considerably lower than Kenya's but still one of the higher rates even among developing countries. This annual rate of increase, if it were to remain constant, corresponds to a doubling time of $70 \div 3.2 = 22$ years. If the rate of increase were to remain constant, this would produce a population of $2 \times 20 = 40$ million by 1962 and $4 \times 20 = 80$ million by 1984. Continuing at the same rate of 3.2 percent for six more years—adding $6 \times 3.2 = 19$ percent of 80 million—adds up to another 15 million, and thus a total of 95 million by 1990. Indeed, in 1990, Mexico had 89 million people; if we add to this another 4 million who had emigrated to the United States, we reach a total of 93 million—again, almost as much as a demographer could have projected in 1940 based on nothing more than the 1940 annual rate of increase of 3.2 percent and the merely computational assumption that this rate would remain constant for the next fifty years.

To conclude this little excursion into demographic computations, I ought to point out that the figures for Mexico in 1940 (namely, 20 million) are of the same order of magnitude as those for Kenya today (namely, 25 million). It may therefore sound less absurd if we make a similar projection for Kenya, even if it leads us to that difficult question: How will Kenya be able to feed 100 million people forty years from now in the year 2031?

So much for demographic numerology.

Now for the relevance of all this for the problem at hand: that is, the impact of the differential annual rates of population increase between more and less developed countries on large-scale migration from countries with more to countries with less population pressure.

Before the mass flight and mass expulsions of people of different nationality, ethnicity, religion, or political persuasion after World Wars I and II, mass migration used to be interpreted primarily in terms of economically motivated "push and pull": in spite of all the other motives that also always made some people move, the most important forces used to be hunger and poverty acting as push, causing people to leave, and the prospects of better living conditions elsewhere acting as pull, usually across the sea, mostly across the Atlantic.

Up to about 1880, this meant that primarily large numbers of poorer people from what were then the richest countries of Europe (England, Germany, Scandinavia, etc.) migrated to the United States and Canada.

Then, beginning around 1880, the migrations were primarily of large masses of poorer people out of the poorer countries of Europe: Italy, Spain, Greece, Russia, Poland, and the eastern provinces of the Austro-Hungarian Monarchy, the greater part still to North America, but large numbers also to Central and South America.

Then came the interruption of World War I, and in the early 1920s limitations on immigration into the United States. This was followed by the Great Depression and finally World War II, which temporarily brought mass migration across the Atlantic almost to a halt.

It was only after the great dislocations of millions of people after World War II had been straightened out to some extent that mass migration resumed its former shape of primarily economically motivated push and pull, but with these important differences:

1.   Increasing mass migration, for the most part as supposedly temporary workers, from the poorer countries of southern and southeastern Europe into the richer countries farther north—especially Turks and Yugoslavs, but also large numbers from Italy, Spain, and elsewhere.
2.   Similar mass migration, also initially as supposedly temporary workers, across the Mediterranean, mostly from North Africa into France and Italy, some also into Spain, and some of them going farther north as well.
3.   Considerable migration out of Asia, from Korea, the Philippines, India, Southeast Asia, and elsewhere, primarily to the United States but also to Europe, especially England, and to Australia.
4.   Similar mass movements of workers with or without families into the oil countries along the Persian Gulf, coming mostly from Arab countries and from Pakistan and India (of course, during the Gulf War, large masses had to go back again, at least temporarily in flight or driven out).

The differential growth in populations and with that also in population pressure can readily be seen with a few general figures: Less than 100 years ago, in 1900, today's more developed countries had about 500 million people, and today's less developed countries had about 1,000 million, for a relation of 1:2. Fifty years later, by 1950, the numbers were 750 million and 1,750 million, respectively, making a ratio of 1:2.3. Twenty years later, by 1970, the numbers were 990 million and 2,600 million, respectively, for a ratio of 1:2.7. Currently the respective numbers are 1,200 million and 4,100 million, or 1:3.4. By 2020 they will be about 1,350 million and 6,900 million, or 1:5.

I still recall the neat formulation of a Third World representative at an international population conference I attended in 1975: "We are going to outbreed you." The implication is that, if the more developed countries do not agree to a more equitable sharing of the world's wealth, the others would eventually force the issue by the sheer superiority of their numbers. Although this is a gross oversimplification, because the two categories of countries do not act internationally as unified blocs but, on the contrary, deal with each other in very selective alliances and relations, it nevertheless highlights how differential population pressures between more and less developed countries are one of the most explosive issues of our time.

Consider the following figures: Between 1956 and 1960 a total of 2.9 million people immigrated to what used to be the domain of European migration: the United States, Canada, Australia, and New Zealand. Of these 2.9 million, 79 percent came from more and 21 percent from less developed countries. By 1976–80 the proportions were already almost reversed: of a total of 3.1 million immigrants into these four countries, only 29 percent came from more and 71 percent from less developed countries (computed from *World Population Trends, Population Development*, 1985, vol. 1, table 78, p. 209).

The Great Transatlantic Waves of Migration up to World War I

Migration figures up to about 1875–80 must of necessity be only estimates, because up to that time—that is, before the first more serious limitations on immigration were instituted—there had been no need to keep exact records. The first exclusions from immigration into the United States were legislated in 1875. These, however, pertained initially only to criminals, prostitutes, paupers, and the like. These were followed by the exclusion of would-be immigrants who, if older than seventeen, were illiterate even in their own language. In 1885 followed the exclusion of indentured labor; this affected people who paid for the transatlantic fare by obligating themselves to a long period (usually lasting quite a number of years) of work at little or no wage. (A special form of this was that some firm in Europe paid the fare for which the passenger contracted his future labor, and then the captain of the ship bought the contract and sold it in the port of arrival.) Since 1882 practically all Chinese immigration was forbidden (to prevent the immigration of labor satisfied with such low wages that they threatened the wage level of all the others). Exempt from this restriction were only more or less well-to-do businessmen, students, doctors, and a few others. This almost total Chinese exclusion (albeit violated through a not inconsiderable illegal Chinese immigration) stayed in force until China became the United States' ally in World War II.

Also, until the latter part of the nineteenth century, no exact figures were kept about the number of people emigrating from the United States (and even less so figures concerning the other immigration countries). The following overview results from an attempt to reconcile as best as possible what seemingly reasonable estimates by the best experts on the subject are available, especially in the two standard works of Carr-Saunders (1936) and Woytinsky and Woytinsky (1953).

From 1846 (the beginning of the big Irish migration) to 1932 about 60 million people migrated from Europe (Woytinsky and Woytinsky, 1953, p. 72; Carr-Saunders, 1936, p. 49). Slightly less than half of these, about 29 million, came from northern and western Europe— about 20 million from Great Britain and Ireland, 5 million from Germany, 3 million from Scandinavia, and another 1 million from the rest of western Europe. Slightly more than half, about 31 million, came from southern and eastern Europe—about 10 million from Italy, 5 million from Spain, 3 million from Portugal, 5 million from Austria-Hungary (many of these from the eastern provinces), about 3 million from Poland and Russia, and some 6 million from all other countries together.

Of these 60 million, about 40 million went to the United States, 6.5 million to Argentina, and 4.5 million to Brazil; 3.5 million went to Australia and New Zealand; over 1 million to South Africa, and about 4.5 million to British, French, and Dutch colonies in Africa and Asia.

Not more than about 5 million altogether migrated out of Asia, because the potential countries of immigration began quite early to exclude immigration from Asia, mostly, as mentioned above, especially in the United States, in order to keep out cheap labor that might threaten the domestic wage level. But xenophobia, of course, also played a decisive role.

Mass Migration into the United States

Immigration into the United States from 1820 to 1850 amounted to about 2.5 million people. During the next thirty years, from 1850 to 1880, total immigration tripled to 7.5 million, or about 250,000 people per year. Then came a sudden jump to about 500,000 per year until 1892, followed by a slight slackening off to some 400,000 per year during part of the 1890s, until it suddenly rose again to an average of about 1 million each year up to the time of World War I, with as many as 1.2 million immigrants in each of the years 1907, 1913, and 1914.

Simultaneously with this dramatic increase in numbers came a shift in regions of origin: from the former predominance of immigration primarily from northern and western Europe to a predominance of immigration from southern and eastern Europe. This shift in regions of origin brought with it more visible differences in languages and in social and cultural habits and traditions, as well as in traditional standards of living. It also led to increasing difficulties and conflict between "older" and "newer" immigrants and eventually to legislation limiting immigration altogether numerically, while at the same time favoring immigration from northern and western and discriminating against immigration from southern and eastern Europe.

Technically this discrimination was achieved through at first, in 1921, limiting total immigration to 3 percent annually of the total number of foreign-born in the United States according to the census of 1910. In 1924 this was reduced to 2 percent of the foreign-born in the United States according to the census of 1890. This effectively limited total immigration to 358,000 per year according to the legislation of 1920 and then to 164,000 per year according to the legislation of 1924, and was further reduced in 1927 to 154,000 immigrants per year.

Within these total annual limits each country was assigned a quota in accordance with the distribution of the foreign-born in the United States over their various countries of origin, according to the respective United States census—under the legislation of 1924 according to the census of 1910 and under that of 1927 according to the census of 1890. This shift back from the 1910 to the 1890 census increased the discrimination against immigration from southern and eastern Europe, by excluding from the count those large masses of immigrants from these regions around the turn of the century.

Of the total annual immigration of 154,000 allowed under the legislation of 1927, 66,000 were assigned to Great Britain and Northern Ireland, 18,000 to the Irish Free State, 26,000 to Germany, not quite 7,000 to all of Scandinavia, 6,000 to Poland, 6,500 to Italy, and about 24,000 to all other countries together, about 3,000 of them to Russia. Incidentally, the quota for Austria was exactly 1,413 (Carr-Saunders, 1936, pp. 191ff., 193).

At this point I might as well insert the further history of immigration and the corresponding legislation in the United States: The system of quotas by country of origin—considerably changed in practice through the many exceptions granted to refugees and others under racial, religious, and political persecution during and immediately after World War II—was replaced in 1965 by a new system that used various categories with different rankings of priority: the highest-priority ranking was assigned to immediate families of U.S. citizens and legal residents. The total number of immigrants permitted each year was raised at first to 540,000, and then in 1990 to 700,000 for each of the next four years, and 675,000 per year thereafter. Of these annual totals, in 1965 54,000 and in 1990 140,000 were reserved for immigrants with desirable skills.

To all of these can be added, beyond the established annual limit, up to 130,000 refugees per year under the Geneva Convention of 1951—namely, for those who can show a "well-founded fear of persecution" for political, ethnic, or religious reasons in their home countries.

This brings us to a total of about 54 million immigrants into the United States between 1820 and 1987, some 14 million of whom came after 1950.

Perhaps the most important and consequential part of the new regulations, both for the ethnic composition of immigration into the United States and for the total migration situation throughout the world, was the sudden admission of large numbers of immigrants from Asian countries. Whereas under the 1927 quota system not more than about 1,350 immigrants had been admitted annually out of all of Asia, beginning in 1965, there was a maximum of regular immigration visas provided for the western hemisphere of 170,000, and of 120,000 for the eastern hemisphere with a proviso for the latter that not more than 20,000 per year could come from any one individual country. These various limits were increased in due time, especially in view of the various exceptions made for refugees and victims of wars.

The shift in regions of origin between earlier and later periods is indicated in Table 10.1, which shows the period-to-period visibly growing share of "others," comprised in the beginning primarily of immigrants from southern and eastern Europe but in later periods of more and more immigrants from Latin America and Asia. The immigration from Latin America in particular grew from some 5 percent of the total immigration in 1900–30 to 40 percent between 1960 and 1974; similarly, immigration from Asia grew from only 2 percent of the total in 1900–30 to about 30 percent in 1970–74.

Altogether, immigration from Latin America amounted from the turn of the century through 1975 to 3.5 million, without counting the several million illegal immigrants from Mexico mentioned below. From Asia, immigration for the same seventy-five-year period amounted to 1.7 million. (Another 2.5 million came between 1975 and 1985.)

Immigration from Mexico presents a special problem. To a very large extent it involves illegal immigrants, some of whom come as temporary workers, but many of whom, whether they originally meant to be temporary or not, ultimately stay. Since any attempts on the part of the United States to increase its protection of the borders against illegal immigration and to send large numbers of illegal immigrants back home tends to foster serious diplomatic conflict with the neighbor in the south, Congress decided in 1985 on the well-known amnesty: those who reported themselves within a given date to the authorities as having lived in the United States since 1982 were acknowledged as legal residents. About 2.3 million people, mostly from Mexico, took advantage of this amnesty. Experts estimate that probably an equal number of illegal aliens did not report themselves, either because they had come into the country after 1982 or for other reasons. The problem of illegal immigration presumably persists in various forms.

Mass Expulsions, Flight, Exchange of National Minorities Connected with the Balkan Wars, World War I, and the Greco-Turkish War of 1922–23

It would take a Toynby, and considerably more time than I have at my disposal, to adequately present the historical bases and the interconnections between the various mass movements, mostly of people expelled or in flight during and after all the wars, big and small, that character-

Table 10.1

Immigration into the United States

Period	Total immigration (mill.)	From north and east Europe		Others	
		mill.	% of total	mill.	% of total
1820–60	5.1	4.8	95	0.3	5
1860–1900	14.1	9.6	68	4.5	32
1900–30	18.6	4.3	23	14.3	77
1930–60	4.1	1.7	41	2.4	59
1960–70	3.3	0.6	17	2.7	83
1820–1970	45.2	21.0	46	24.2	54

ized our own century and that may have bequeathed this kind of mass movement to mankind for centuries to come.

Certainly, several hundred thousand Huguenots were expelled from France in the sixteenth and seventeenth centuries, and the Protestants were expelled from Salzburg during the Counter-Reformation. Some 300,000 members or adherents of the nobility were expelled from France during the French Revolution, and history also witnessed the exiles from the defeated revolutions of 1848 and of various struggles for national independence. All of these, however, were expulsions of a country's own co-nationals.

The first large-scale expulsions in modern times of people because they belonged to an unwanted national minority came with the Franco-Prussian War of 1870–1871 when first, the French expelled some 80,000 Germans, and then some 170,000 French felt it better to leave or were forced out of Alsace-Lorraine.

But the first major prelude to the mass expulsion of national minorities in our own time came with the Balkan wars of 1912 and 1913, when first Serbia, Montenegro, Greece, and Bulgaria forced Turkey out of most of its European possessions and then the erstwhile allies battled with Bulgaria over the division of the newly won territories.

Then came the Greco-Turkish war of 1922–23, which was merely a delayed endplay, with the de facto division of Cyprus into a Greek and a Turkish part in our own time also but a greatly delayed aftermath.

We do not have room enough here to contemplate the significance of this event as the beginning of the dismantling of the former great

Ottoman Empire, which was in turn only the first in the process of the dissolution of the big conquering empires, including the colonial ones. The last of these, Russia's old tsarist empire, miraculously prolonged by the Bolsheviks for several decades beyond all the others, is dissolving before our own eyes.

Relevant in this context—that is, to our discussion of the great migrations in the wake of the two world wars and the mass expulsions of national minorities—is the fact, that both during and after the Balkan wars and the Greco-Turkish wars, huge masses of people were expelled from their habitats because they belonged to some national or ethnic minority or other. Moreover, these expulsions were solemnized in international treaties: after the Balkan wars in the Treaty of Bucharest of 1913, and after the Greco-Turkish war in the Treaty of Lausanne of 1923, which became in its turn an example and paradigm for similar treaties after World War I and World War II.

At this point I shall limit myself to the figures: after the Greco-Turkish war of 1923–23, during which the Turks forced the Greeks out of Asia Minor—memorable for the burning of Smyrna—about 1,400,000 Greeks were forced out of Turkey and in turn 400,000 Turks had to leave Greece. At least another 400,000 Turks, close to 300,000 Bulgarians, and yet another 400,000 Greeks and several tens of thousands of other, smaller minorities, during and after the Balkan wars, altogether about 3 million, were all driven out or forcibly exchanged because they now constituted national minorities, belonging, according to the new way of thinking, on the other side of the national border.

It was then with the settlements first after world War I and then, even more, after World War II, and after the dissolution of the big colonial empires that the expulsion of national minorities with subsequent solemnization through international treaties became a regular pattern for the settlement of international territorial disputes.

At the end of World War I, about 1.5 million Germans were forced or chose to leave (there still were choices to be made in those days) formerly German territories that, as the "Polish Corridor," became part of Poland and Alsace-Lorraine, which went back to France. Some smaller numbers left other, smaller ceded pieces of land. Some 400,000 Hungarians who had now become minorities in various countries went to Hungary; and so with other smaller contingents in various of the new countries, but most of it without the brutality that had accompanied those exchanges in the Balkans.

There was, however, quite a different kind of migration out of Russia: altogether, between 2 and 3 million (estimates vary) left or fled, about half of them because they were members of the "bourgeoisie" or belonged to the "intelligentsia" and opposed the new Bolshevik regime; this group also included members of the higher and lower nobility. The other half were members of the defeated armies of Wrangel, Koltschak, Denikin, Petljura, and others, who had tried to fight the Bolshevik revolution and its armies and had lost. Many of them eventually went to France; others dispersed throughout Europe, some—according to Friedtjof Nansen, then high commissioner for refugees at the League of Nations, about 60,000— went to China. Several hundred thousand Poles from the Polish provinces of Russia went to the new state of Poland rather than staying as an unwanted minority in Russia.

In another violent episode during World War I the Turks massacred by some estimates up to a million Armenians; about half a million Armenians made it into what became Soviet Armenia, while others migrated to many different countries; a sizable group lives even now as a highly unwanted minority in Syria.

Altogether it seems that about 10 million civilians ended up as emigrants as a direct consequence of World War I—about as many as had died as soldiers in that war on the fields of battle.

Mass Deportations and Expulsions Flight during and after World War II and with the End of the Colonial Empires

World War II in Europe

When it comes to estimating how many millions of civilians were forced to move from their homes during and after World War II, most people feel like members of those tribes, of whom anthropologists tell us that they can only count, "One, two, many. . . ." And so to estimate here: "One million, two millions, many millions . . ."—reminding one of Poincaré's saying: "Un mort, c'est une tragedie—une million morts, c'est une statistique."

Altogether about eight and a half million people were dragged by the Germans from all over Europe to Germany, or to German-occupied territories as slave labor to keep their war machinery going; another 4 million were moved with less force but nevertheless under considerable pressure as paid workers.

Between 10 and 20 million Russians fled inside of Russia before the onslaught of the German armies. To this number we must add some 2 million Volga Germans and a large number of Krim Tatars who were moved into Soviet Asia by the Russian government as presumably potential collaborators with the Germans.

Then, after the collapse of the Third Reich, it was the Germans' turn to flee or be expelled: some 9.5 million from east of the Oder-Neisse line, some 3.5 million from the Sudetenland, larger numbers from Hungary, Bulgaria, Rumania, Yugoslavia, and some even from Austria. Well over 8 million of these wound up in West and 4 million in East Germany, but then large masses of the inhabitants of East Germany in turn fled from the new communist regime into West Germany, a movement that went on, although eventually with diminished force, until the communists stopped it in 1961 by building the Berlin Wall and barbed wire entanglements and mine fields along their borders.

The literature on migration hardly touches on the fact that when its borders were redrawn, Poland not only got large new territories from Germany in the west, but also had to cede large territories to Russia in the east. That led to considerable migration of Poles. Probably upwards of 2 million Poles moved out of the territories ceded to Russia, preferring to live as immigrants in the reestablished Poland than as an unwanted minority vulnerable to persecution in Russia. At the same time, probably an equal number of Poles moved from inside the older territories of Poland into the territories from which the Germans had been expelled.

Had this been an isolated event and not simply part of the general reshuffling of millions when the former borders of Europe were redrawn, it would undoubtedly have ranked in the history books as one of the greatest migrations in modern times.

At this point, let me insert that although the mass deportations of millions from all over Europe to slave labor in Germany or German-occupied territories, and their subsequent return to their homelands or emigration to other countries are recounted here as part of the "migrations" of this century, the deportation of millions of Jews, of Gypsies, and of others to annihilation camps in Germany, Poland, and elsewhere, much as they belong in a book of "Horrors of the Twentieth

Century," are for obvious reasons not treated here as "migrations" within the meaning of this discussion.

Asia

Americans and Europeans are seldom aware that masses of people at similar orders of magnitude were moved or fled at the same time within or from various countries in Asia. Some 30 million Chinese fled before the Japanese into unoccupied areas of China. While after Japan's defeat, some 6 million Japanese were forced to go back to Japan—about 2 million each from China and from Manchuria, 1 million from Korea and 1 million from other territories; at the same time, well over 1 million foreigners left Japan. About 4 million people fled from communist North Korea into noncommunist South Korea, creating a problem similar to that of the Germans who were expelled or ran away from all over Europe into the two new Germanies.

Even bigger were the mutual expulsions between Hindus and Moslems with the partition of India and Pakistan, with about 7 to 8 million arriving in each case on the other side, for a total of some 15 to 16 million displaced people, while perhaps between 1 and 2 million were killed or perished in the transition. Some 2 million or so more were expelled or fled when the eastern part of Pakistan declared itself independent as the new country of Bangladesh.

Additional millions—the numbers are hard to establish—were uprooted in the struggles for independence and for power within and between the various countries of what used to be French Indochina: North and South Vietnam, Laos, and Cambodia.

Likewise, in the wake of the collapse of colonial power, millions of people were driven from their homes or fled before civil wars in the struggles for power in the newly independent countries of Africa, where different modern ideologies were combined with old tribal conflicts as slogans and bases for internecine warfare (see below).

The World Refugee Problem

Listed here are essentially people who had to leave their homelands to escape racial, or political, or ethnic, or other persecution or the threat of such, and who for the most part consider themselves, or who are considered by the countries where they currently live, as temporary or at least as not yet fully regularized immigrants. As my first point of departure I shall take the 1988 tabulation published in the World Refugee Survey by the United States Committee for Refugees, a private organization that regularly monitors the situation. Occasionally I shall add information from other sources.

The main category are some 14.5 million people who fit the definition of refugee and fall under the jurisdiction of the United Nations High Commission for Refugees (UNHCR), according to the Geneva Convention of 1951, as people who can show a "well-founded fear" of persecution for political, ethnic, religious, or other reasons, should they return or be returned to their home country.

Of these, there are 6 million Afghans—2.5 million in Iran, 3.5 million in Pakistan; 2.3 million Palestinians in states bordering on Israel, the majority of them living in various camps; 1 million Ethiopians, approximately two-thirds of whom are in the Sudan, with the other third in Somalia; over 1 million from Mozambique, about two-thirds of whom are in Malawi, with the rest in other neighboring countries.

There are between 300,000 and 500,000 each from Iran and Iraq (that was still before the Gulf War) and from Angola, Somalia, and Cambodia.

And there is a long list of countries with under 100,000 refugees each, too long even to be read here.

The next category are 3 to 4 million people in refugee*like* situations: this includes some 500,000 Palestinians living as of 1988 as workers in the oil fields of the Persian Gulf—by 1991 most of them had been driven out during the Gulf War and have become regular Geneva convention refugees again. There are 1 to 2 million in this category from the countries torn by civil war in Central America, one-third of them in neighboring countries, two-thirds in the United States, and yet another mass of perhaps 1 million in the border areas between the warring nations of Indochina; these people cannot be counted and cannot be helped by either the United Nations or private aid because of ongoing hostilities.

Next we have a category of altogether some 15 to 20 million people who have been *displaced* by civil war and similar actions *within their own countries*, and thus technically are not counted as refugees: 1.5 to 2 million in Mozambique, 1 million in Angola, several hundred thousand each in Chad, Uganda, and Sri Lanka, up to 1 million in Lebanon, as well as in the Philippines. This category also encompasses those who were forcibly resettled by their own governments: between 1 and 1.5 million in Ethiopia who were ostensibly moved from semiarid areas threatened by chronic drought into richer lands farther south, but seen in the West mostly as part of a government move to preclude further uprisings; up to 1 million Kurds who were forcibly resettled outside of Kurdistan by Iraq even before the Gulf War as a measure to weaken their striving for an autonomous Kurdish region; and, finally, some 3 million blacks in South Africa who have been forced into Bantustans, like Transkei and Lesotho, which have been given some pseudo-independence, thereby depriving the inhabitants, now technically citizens of a foreign country, of the right to return to their former homes in South Africa.

Altogether the survey identifies between 40 and 50 million people for 1988 (other, in part later, sources estimate the figure closer to 50 million) who, under one definition or another, may be considered refugees, outside or inside their own countries. This, with a world population of 5,400 million, means that about 1 in 110 people on this earth—man, woman, or child—has been uprooted from his or her home without yet being in a technical sense an emigrant or an immigrant. But in the countries that are actually immediately concerned, refugees amount in most cases to between 2 percent and 6 percent of the population, though there are cases of 15 percent to 20 percent, or even higher.

No longer counted as a separate refugee problem under the definition of the Geneva Convention are most of the Jews who went after the war to Israel or to the United States or some other countries, including Australia. The Jews who have begun of late to come out of the Soviet Union are also not counted. At first it was the British in particular who, as long as they held the League of Nations Mandate over Palestine, tried to have the Jews considered nationals of the countries whose citizenship they had held before, to avoid having to accord them a special claim for immigration.

Before the war there were about 400,000 Jews in Israel, some already born there, but most legal or illegal immigrants. Then within a short span of time some 1.5 to 2 million survivors of the Holocaust and of persecution in various countries came to Israel, including eventually also Jews from Arab countries. During the early 1970s some 60,000 to 70,000 came from the Soviet Union; for some years after that time there was almost no exit for them from Russia. but with the recent change in policy some 180,000 Russian Jews arrived in 1990, and up to 400,000 more were expected for 1991. Almost lost in these huge numbers are the 15,000 or so Jews recently airlifted out of Ethiopia and smaller contingents from elsewhere.

Guest Workers

"Guest workers" (Gastarbeiter) is a euphemistic neologism for a comparatively new category of foreign labor. Guest workers are usually much more permanent than the traditional seasonal workers, but at the same time for the most part neither they nor the host country intended for them to be permanent immigrants. Many however, staying on for years and years, eventually become, with or without legalization, just that: permanent immigrants.

In Central Europe the category developed essentially with the need for additional labor, mostly unskilled, in the reconstruction of countries devastated by the war, but then also in the development of new industries. This developed into a de facto mass migration of workers with or without their families out of countries with low wage levels and high population pressure into countries with higher wage levels and a need for labor mostly for heavy or otherwise undesirable work at low wages that the local labor force would not accept. For example, large masses of lowly paid unskilled labor work in the tourism industries of Austria, Germany, and Switzerland.

Essentially the same category of semipermanent foreign labor that in fact does stay for years—the greater the distances to be covered, the longer the stay and the rarer the visits home—either legally or illegally, developed with the large-scale operation of oil fields in the Persian Gulf. A similar movement, but with different problems and different occupations, developed in the United States, especially in agriculture in the states bordering on Mexico. But the same conditions also exist in various countries in Africa, as witnessed by periodic expulsions of masses of guest workers when the host country experiences economic difficulties. This was the case a few years ago when Nigeria expelled within a matter of weeks about half a million workers from Ghana, together with their families about one million people.

A 1985 United Nations publication lists 6.2 million guest workers in Europe alone: some 2.2 million in Germany, 1.5 million in France, over 1 million in England, half a million in Switzerland, and 1 million in other European countries. Of these, about 1.3 million came from Turkey and Yugoslavia, nearly 1 million from Italy, and nearly another million from Spain and Portugal, together with large contingents, as mentioned earlier, from across the Mediterranean as well as from various Asian countries. Together, as of 1985, the guest workers and their families amounted to 11 million people or some 3.5 percent of the inhabitants of the European Economic Community.

According to United Nations publications, in 1980 there were close to 3 million foreign workers in the oil countries of the Persian Gulf. Of these, about 1 million in Saudi Arabia, close to 600,000 in Kuwait, and similar numbers in the United Arab Emirates and in Libya. Some three-quarters of a million of these workers came from Egypt, some 400,000 were Palestinians, between 250,000 and 400,000 each came from Jordan, Pakistan, and India. Some 300,000 came from the Philippines, 100,000 from Korea, and smaller but still sizeable contingents from Thailand and from Sri Lanka.

Although the bulk of those who were in the war zone of the Gulf War had to go back to their countries—creating havoc there with the local economy—it may be anticipated that eventually they, or similar numbers in their place, will be called back to reconstruct the oil industry. From the point of view of world migration this might look like the de facto beginning of a long-range change in the size and composition of the populations of that region, which in its end effect may prove not dissimilar to what the big transatlantic migration from Europe meant for the population of North America.

The problems are not unlike those that attend the largely illegal immigration into the United States from Mexico and South America, which also began with regular seasonal workers coming across the border for the annual harvest and going back when that was finished. Eventually more and more of them stayed on for several years at a time, until the stay became as permanent as it could be made without being legal.

When the situation began to get out of hand and the United States attempted to stop further large-scale illegal immigration and to send back those already in the country, the government of Mexico protested furiously about discrimination against its own nationals. The United States then instituted the 1985 amnesty described above.

While I have limited my presentation to international migration from country to country and to some categories of refugees and displaced persons within their own countries, there have been and continue to be other huge waves of migration within the big continent-spanning territories of the United States, of Russia, and of China counting by many millions. For example, 10 million Russians moved before World War I, whether as regular settlers, as prisoners, or as political exiles, into Siberia, with large numbers following under the Communist regime. Similarly, even long after the U.S. occupation and settling of the West, still millions moved during and after World War II: blacks from the South to the big industrial cities in the North, and whites to the West Coast. For another example, millions of Chinese moved into Manchuria and other thinly populated, in part older, in part newer or recently occupied territories. But all this is beyond the scope of the present discussion.

Epilogue

With all the mass migrations and mass expulsions that have characterized our world during the last hundred and fifty, and especially during the last fifty years, mostly rooted in differential population pressures and in differences of available space and wealth the world over, anybody's question, "When will all of this end?" can hardly be considered as more than the outcry of an anguished soul over all the woe and horror that went with it.

It was with a world population of not yet 4,000 million people that the Population Division of the United Nations presented to the World Population Conference in Bucharest in 1974 an estimate that somewhere late in the twenty-first century the world's population might reach zero growth and stabilize at somewhere under 14 billion.

Even if this estimate were to come true, there would presumably still remain enormous differences in wealth and opportunities between have and have-not countries, with the latter clamoring for a bigger share of the world's wealth to feed their hungry multitudes or to be able to place them where there is still space and opportunity for them. Some of us may remember the German slogan "Volk ohne Raum" (People without space) used to justify the claiming of land in the East, and similar cries from Japan for space for its growing population. If, for example, India, whose population has grown since that 1974 conference from 600 million to 850 million, has not yet raised the same cry for more land for its people, it is certainly not for lack of need, but rather for lack of the necessary power to back up such a claim as well as lack of neighboring lands on which to lay any kind of a claim— India's neighbors, Pakistan and Bangladesh, are at least as overpopulated and in need of more land as India is.

It was in 1919 that Walter Rathnenau, German statesman, soon to be foreign minister of Germany (and soon thereafter to be assassinated by German Nationalists for trying to establish more peaceful relations with France and with Soviet Russia) wrote that it was an illusion to think that this had been the last of all big wars. On the contrary, he claimed that from now on, every generation was going to have its own world war—a prophecy that the next generation saw come true within only twenty years, and we have seen it almost come true on several occasions since, at times almost by a hair's breadth, as with the Cuban missile crisis. We have come equally close to Rathenau's prophecy with the many wars that have been fought the world over since the end of World War II, at several of which we could do nothing but hold our breath and ask: Is this again going to be the big one?

Thinking of all of these conflicts, and thinking of how every so often in the name of a clamor for more space for an overpopulated country or region millions are killed or driven out of their habitats all over the globe, and seeing how under all of this killing and destruction, what little amount of civilization and civility that mankind has been able to develop over the last few thousand years has been destroyed again, I am reminded of the end of a poem by the Swedish Nobel Laureate Hjalmar Gulberg:

Och Herren Gud skall experimentera
så, tills han skapad människan.
[And thus the Lord goes on experimenting
until at last He'll have created Man.]

Bibliography

Carr-Saunders, A.M. *World Population*. Oxford: Clarendon, 1936. [Rpt.: London: Frank Cass, 1964.]

"Fluechtlinge und Vertriebene" (Refugees and Expellees). In *Handwoerterbuch der Staatswissenschaften*, 1961, pp. 752–76.

Kirk, Dudley. "Major Migrations since World War II." In *Selected Studies of Migration since World War II*. New York: Milbank Memorial Fund, 1958, pp. 12–37.

Koehler, Fred K. "Europe's Homeless Millions." Headline Series, no. 54, Foreign Policy Association, New York, November 1945.

Massey, Douglas S. "Economic Development and International Migration in Comparative Perspective." Commission for the Study of International Migration and Cooperative Economic Development, Washington, DC, Working

Paper no. 1, February 1989. [Rpt.: *Population and Development Review*, *14*, 3 (September 1988), 383–413].

Population Reference Bureau. *World Population Data Sheet*. Washington, DC: various years.

Stahl, Charles R. *International Labor Migration. A Study of the ASEAN Countries*. New York: Center for Migration Studies, 1986.

World Refugee Statistics 1988 of the World Refugee Survey. Washington, DC: United States Committee for Refugees, 1989, pp. 32–36.

World Population Trends, Population Development, Interrelations and Population Policies. 1983 Monitoring Report, vol. 1: *Population Trends*. New York: United Nations, 1985.

World Population Trend and Policies. 1987 Monitoring Report. New York: United Nations, 1988.

Woytinsky, W.S., and E.S. Woytinsky. *World Population and Production*. New York: The Twentieth Century Fund, 1953.

Index

About the Author

Paul Neurath was born in 1911 in Vienna, Austria. He has studied law (Dr. jur., Vienna, 1937) and sociology and statistics (Ph.D., Columbia, 1951). He has taught sociology and statistics at City College (1943–46) and at Queens College (1946–77) in New York. Since his retirement he has been alternating between teaching as Guest Professor in Vienna, where he is also the director of the Paul F. Lazarsfeld Archiv, and as Adjunct Professor at Queens College. He has served as Fulbright Professor at Tata Institute of Social Science in Bombay (1955–57), at the University of Cologne (1959–60), and at the University of Vienna (1978–79). He was with the Ford Foundation and All-India Radio in Delhi, 1964–65. He is author of "Social Life in the German Concentration Camps Dachau and Buchenwald" (Ph.D. thesis, Columbia); "Radio Farm Forum in India" (1960); "School Television in Delhi" (1968); (two statistics books in German, 1966, 1974; editor (with Elisabeth Nemeth) of "Otto Neurath oder die Einheit vom Wissenschaft und Gesellschaft" (1994), and author of articles in books and journals on statistics, population problems, and related subjects. Currently he is working on problems on international migration and on a text in factor analysis for sociologists.